THEN THE WALLS CAME DOWN

All in all, if this book is more than a *Jail Journal*, it might be a symphony. For like music it is poignant and liberating; written out of the cloisters of imprisonment . . .

> Brian Keenan, The *Examiner*, 13.11.99

One of the most important books to emerge from the conflict in Northern Ireland . . . a vividly humane account of life in prison.

> *The Irish Times*, 21.10.99

The irony of post-ceasefire Northern Ireland is that the new thinking has come from those involved in the republican war. Danny Morrison's prison memoirs are an honest study of a man seeking fresh solutions to the stalemate the Provos found themselves in at the beginning of the Nineties.

> *The Observer*, 17.10.99

Morrison's book, while unapologetically hardline, is shot through with subtlety and feeling.

> *The Sunday Business Post*, 26.9.99

Like the best of novels . . . all human life is there, the world of the imagination and the realities of the unfolding political scene on the outside. . . invaluable as a rare look at prisoners as human beings.

> *Irish News*, 16.10.99

No bitterness, bigotry or bile . . . a far, far better read than John Mitchel.

> *Irish Independent*, 30.10.99

Remarkable as a human document. . . The flashes of humour and compassion bear comparison with those in Brendan Behan's *Borstal Boy*. A must-read for anyone interested in the North.

> *The Irish Times*, 13.11.99

Also by Danny Morrison

West Belfast
On the Back of the Swallow
The Wrong Man

First published in 1999 by
Mercier Press

Trade enquiries to CMD Distribution
55A Spruce Avenue
Stillorgan Industrial Park
Blackrock County Dublin
Tel: (01) 294 2556; Fax: (01) 294 2564
E.mail: cmd@columba.ie

© Danny Morrison 1999

ISBN 1 85635 277 3

10 9 8 7 6 5 4 3

A CIP record for this title is available
from the British Library

Cover design by Penhouse Design
Printed in Ireland by ColourBooks,
Baldoyle Industrial Estate, Dublin 13

To Edwin —
friend & comrade —
from Danny.

THEN THE WALLS CAME DOWN

A PRISON JOURNAL

Hope it doesn't bring
back 'bad' familiar
memories!

DANNY MORRISON

MERCIER PRESS

To Penelope

CONTENTS

GUIDE TO NAMES MENTIONED

1990

Ciaran – Morrison's brother, fifteen years his junior

Sandra – Morrison's wife, from whom he was separated

Kevin and Liam – Morrison's sons, aged fifteen and eleven in 1990

Uncle Seamus – brother of Morrison's mother, Susan

Da – Morrison's father, Danny

Lucy – wife of John 'Anto' Murray

Trisha Ziff – an English friend of Morrison's

Uncle Harry – Harry White, brother of Morrison's mother. Died in 1989

Teenager – Charles Love from Strabane, killed by an IRA bomb

OC – Officer Commanding, IRA military title

Martin McGuinness – a senior Irish republican

Geraldine – Morrison's sister, his senior by four years

Margaret – Morrison's sister, his senior by two years

Susie – Morrison's mother, Susan. Collapsed during a British Army raid on their street, Iveagh Parade, in October 1981. Suffered a brain haemorrhage and was invalided with loss of memory

Susan – Morrison's sister, his junior by four years

Tom – Tom Hartley, a Sinn Fein activist

Jim – Jim Gibney, a Sinn Fein activist

Loughgall – scene of an SAS ambush on an IRA active service unit which resulted in nine deaths

Mrs Brady – mother of Morrison's close friend, IRA Volunteer Kevin Brady, who, along with two others, was killed by loyalist paramility Michael Stone in Milltown Cemetery in March 1988

Catholic man – Eamon Quinn, killed by the Ulster Freedom Fighters

Mary Quinn – a friend of Morrison's

Chrissie – Chrissie McAuley, a Sinn Fein activist

Marie – Marie Morris, Morrison's niece

Zack Smith – Ciaran Smith, ex-prisoner. Husband of Jackie Burt

Paddy McGrory – P. J. McGrory, Morrison's solicitor. At the inquest in Gibraltar he represented the families of the three IRA Volunteers killed in Gibraltar by the SAS in March 1988

Sheila McVeigh – a friend of Morrison's

Sylvia Stevens – a London film-maker and friend of Morrison's

Aunty Eileen   Eileen McKee, sister of Morrison's mother

Siobhan – Siobhan O'Hanlon, a Sinn Fein activist and friend of Morrison's

Geraldine McAteer – a community activist and friend of Morrison's

Greg – Greg Morris, a soldier in the Green Howards Regiment. Married to Morrison's sister, Margaret

Aunty Cathleen and Charlie – Cathleen, sister of Morrison's mother. Her husband, Charlie Campbell

Aunty Eilish – Eilish White, married to Willie, brother of Morrison's mother

Eamonn McCann – a freelance journalist and political activist

Joelle – Joelle Gartner, wife of Tom Hartley. French teacher.

Pam Brighton – Head of Radio Drama at BBC, Belfast

David Beresford – author of *Ten Men Dead* (the story of the 1981 hunger strike) and South African correspondent for the *Guardian*

Barra – Barra McGrory, solicitor. Son of Paddy McGrory

Sandy – Alexander 'Sandy' Lynch, the informer in Morrison's case

Shorty – Brendan Short from Ballymurphy

Theresa Burt – a friend of Morrison's

Humphrey Atkins – Northern Ireland Secretary of State, 1979–81

Scéal – Irish for 'news'

PO – Principal Officer

UDA – Ulster Defense Association

UVF – Ulster Volunteer Force

Richard – Richard McAuley, Sinn Fein activist. Married to Chrissie McAuley

Seando – Seando Moore, ex-prisoner and Sinn Fein activist

Mrs Murphy – Nora Murphy, a middle-aged friend of Morrison's. Died in August 1986

Cleaky Clarke – Terence Clarke, sentenced in connection with the assault on the two army corporals who drove into Kevin Brady's funeral

Ex-RUC reservist – James Sefton, whose wife, Ellen, died later from her wounds

Brooke – Peter Brooke, Secretary of State for Northern Ireland in 1990

Derek Dunne – a left-wing, Dublin-based journalist

Gerry Fitt, Ian Paisley – Fitt, a nationalist politician, and Paisley, head of the Free Presbyterian Church (1968)

William Craig, John Taylor, Brian Faulkner – leading Ulster Unionists

Dave O'Connell – Former IRA leader and strategist. Split from Sinn Fein and helped found Republican Sinn Fein in 1986

Emmanuel Marley – nineteen-year-old son of IRA Volunteer Larry Marley, who helped plan the mass escape from H-Block 7 in 1983. Larry Marley was shot dead by loyalists in 1987.

Jimmy Quigley – eighteen-year-old IRA Volunteer and close friend of Morrison's who was shot dead by the British Army in 1972

Kidnapped RUC man – Detective Louis Robinson

Peter Taylor – award-winning British television journalist

Fionnuala O'Connor – journalist

Poilin – Poilin Ni Chiarain, journalist

IO – intelligence officer

David McKittrick – Ireland correspondent for the London *Independent*

Creaney – John Creaney, lawyer with the Director of Public Prosecutions

Bik – Brendan 'Bik' McFarlane, serving five life sentences. Former OC of the H-Blocks during the hunger strike. Escaped from prison in the mass escape, September 1983. Rearrested in Amsterdam, January 1986. Reimprisoned in the H-Blocks, January 1987

Paul Fox and Laura Crawford – killed in an explosion, December 1975

Rita O'Hare – Belfast republican living in Dublin. National Director of Publicity for Sinn Fein

1991

Ruairi – Ruairi Ó Bradaigh. Split from Sinn Fein in 1986. Founded and became President of Republican Sinn Fein

Brian – Brian Ordish. Divorced from Morrison's sister, Geraldine, 1981

Jack Ruby – assassinated Lee Harvey Oswald in Dallas, Texas, in the basement of a police station on his way to court. Oswald had been charged with assassinating President Kennedy.

Gill – Anthony Gillen

Mark Mahoney, Jim Harrington – two US lawyers who defended Morrison and Owen Carron MP when they were on trial in the United States in 1983 for illegally entering the country

Dessie Boal – Morrison's senior defence barrister

Mr Fenton – father of Joseph Fenton, an informer who was killed by the IRA in 1989. The Martins were charged with allowing the IRA to use their house for his imprisonment and interrogation.

Miriam Daly – Queens University lecturer. Member of Irish Republican Socialist Party. Assassinated in her Andersonstown home in 1980 by loyalists

Peter Duggan – a Downpatrick man who made allegations about Sandy Lynch

J. J. – John Joseph Bradley

UFF – Ulster Freedom Fighters

INLA – Irish National Liberation Organisation

Fitzy – Gerry Fitzgerald, a Belfast republican

Jackie McMullan – IRA lifer

Ella O'Dwyer – IRA lifer

Martina Anderson – IRA lifer

Hugh – Hugh Feeney. Former IRA lifer

Taoibh Amuigh – Irish for 'those outside', i.e. leadership of Republican Movement

Pennies – Morrison's code name during the hunger strikes

Paddy Devlin – politician and co-founder of the Social Democratic and Labour Party (SDLP)

24 November – An IRA bomb planted in the dining hall of C-Wing, Crumlin Road Jail, killed Robert Skey (UDA) and Colin Caldwell (UVF)

IPLO – Irish People's Liberation Organisation, small republican splinter group

1992

Hendron – Joe Hendron, SDLP representative in west Belfast. The UDA/UFF lobbied its supporters to vote tactically for Hendron in the April 1991 election, causing Gerry Adams to lose his seat

Jimmy Drumm – a veteran Belfast republican whose wife Maire, vice-president of Sinn Fein, was assassinated by loyalists while a hospital patient in 1976

UNO – National Opposition Union, the US-backed, anti-Sandinista coalition

Pat Finucane – Belfast solicitor. Shot dead at his Belfast home by loyalists in February 1989

Anne Cadwallader – an English-born journalist living in Belfast

STATEMENT OF OFFENCE
Belonging to a proscribed organisation, contrary to Section 21 of the Northern Ireland Emergency Provisions Act, 1978.

PARTICULARS OF OFFENCE
Daniel Gerard Morrison between the fourth day of January 1990 and the eighth day of January 1990 in the County Court Division of Belfast belonged to a proscribed organisation, namely the Irish Republican Army.

STATEMENT OF OFFENCE
False imprisonment, contrary to Common Law.

PARTICULARS OF OFFENCE
James Martin, Veronica Mary Martin and Liam James Martin, Daniel Caldwell, Gerard Hodgins, James O'Carroll, John Anthony Murray and Daniel Gerard Morrison, on a date unknown between the fourth day of January 1990 and the eighth day of January 1990 in the County Court Division of Belfast, assaulted Alexander Joseph Lynch and detained him against his will.

STATEMENT OF OFFENCE
Conspiracy to murder, contrary to Article 9 (1) of the Criminal Attempts and Conspiracy (Northern Ireland) Order 1983 and Common Law.

PARTICULARS OF OFFENCE

James Martin, Veronica Mary Martin, Daniel Caldwell, Gerard Hodgins, James O'Carroll, John Anthony Murray and Daniel Gerard Morrison, on a date unknown between the fourth day of January 1990 and the eighth day of January 1990, in the County Court Division of Belfast, conspired together and with others not before the Court to murder Alexander Joseph Lynch.

1990

Crumlin Road Prison
Friday 12 January
Hi love

In Castlereagh they took my clothes from me for forensics and gave me a boiler suit to wear. But on Monday night I got your parcel of clothes and it was like being in contact with you when I saw your handwriting on the brown bag. Throughout the questioning I remained silent, wouldn't give my date of birth. The usual. But on Tuesday morning two singing detectives came into the cell and serenaded me with 'Happy Birthday, Dear Danny', having sussed out it was my thirty-seventh.

I hope you have been okay and are not too shaken. Life turns around so quickly. Please keep your chin up because I am absolutely philosophical about myself and have fitted in here like a plug into a socket. You'll laugh at this but I'm a Red Book prisoner, the top security classification, which was introduced after the big escape from the H-Blocks in 1983. It means I'm not allowed to be taken to the visits or back with other prisoners and I am not allowed to share a cell with anyone. Anto Murray is also on a Red Book.

It is just after 7 pm, Friday evening, and we have come in from the canteen where we had association for about two hours, playing cards and table tennis. I am on the third landing, 'the Threes', of A-Wing. I am sitting on my bed writing this on a rickety table. I am drinking black coffee and eating a currant-square bun.

In the mornings the lights are switched on at seven. At about half eight we are either slopping out or breakfasting in the

canteen (depending on whether it's our turn or the loyalists').
At nights the lights are switched off at eleven but most are in
the sack before then. Weighed in with the prison doctor at 11
stones 4 pounds. I've begun training – doing sit-ups and press-
ups. The food is okay and the screws are not aggressive but there
is a lot of tension building up over the administration's policy
of refusing to separate us and the loyalists and give us our own
wings and landings. We self-segregate but this means that we
only get half our entitlements to the exercise yard, association
time and using the canteen, toilets and showers.

Our Ciaran saw Sandra about picking up Kevin and Liam.
He brought them on the visit, along with my uncle Seamus.
Although we are entitled to three visits a week I am quite
content with taking just two: Kevin and Liam during a weekday,
though it means them taking time off school, and you on
Saturdays when you're off work. I also hope that Sandra allows
the kids to go on spending their weekends at my da's.

I asked a prisoner if it was okay to use a second page for this
letter and he looked at me as if I had two heads. Many of the
men have a problem filling both sides of a page! Anyway, the
rules are one page only so I have to get permission from the
governor if I want to write longer letters.

Wednesday 17 January
I've been walking around the yard with this very funny fella from
Ardoyne called Butch Braniff who brightens up my day. His
brother, Anthony, was killed by the IRA in 1981 and his father,
David, was shot dead by loyalists last March as he was kneeling
on the living-room floor saying the Rosary. Butch was arrested
a week or two later and charged with possession of a rifle but
is confident that he will beat the charge. The loyalists charged
with killing his father are on the same wing here, so you can

imagine the tension and the stupidity of the authorities in trying to force us to integrate. He's trying his best to persuade me to become a vegetarian! I've a sixty-watt bulb in my cell which doesn't give out much light and isn't good on the eyes. I noticed that there were one or two cells with hundred-watt bulbs. I asked Butch how could I get a better light. He says: 'Dan, see the prison doctor. Because if you switch to a vegetarian diet you automatically get a more powerful bulb.' He said it with a straight face – before bursting into laughter! When we are playing table tennis and he scores a point he adds two on to his score! When his return shot misses my side of the table he shouts 'Yessss!' so convincingly that you wonder whether the ball was really out.

I've just finished Flaubert's *Madame Bovary*. Alan Russell, in his introduction, says: 'He devoted more care than any novelist, even any French novelist, had done before him to the actual writing of his sentences . . . "One week – two pages!"

'Such cries recur in his letters. The insistence he laid on rhythm can be judged from a remark he made when he was nearing the end of the book, that he had all the rest mapped out, he could *hear* the "fall of the phrases" for pages ahead, before he actually had the words.'

Thursday 18 January
I walked around the yard today with Big Eugene McKee – 'Griz' – from Andersonstown. He can be very funny. Griz and another fella were arrested in a small village, St Johnson in County Donegal, in July 1982. He and a number of others had taken over a large farmhouse where mortars were to be mounted on the back of a lorry, but the lorry on the farm wasn't appropriate so they had to take over another house and bring its occupants to the farmhouse. There was so much toing and froing that

neighbours saw what was going on and they had to be rounded up as well. It was at a weekend and some of the hostages had been expecting visitors so Griz had to go around pinning notes on their front doors saying, 'Back later'. The problem of feeding the multitude was solved when a mobile grocer called in and goods were purchased from his van.

As night-time approached the hostages were allowed to go to bed: 'Husbands strictly with their own wives,' said Griz! It was a big house, plenty of rooms and settees. Throughout the next day, Sunday, Griz kept them entertained, telling stories, and then explained to them that they would all get big compensation claims for being distressed. He thought they were all happy and smiling when they heard that. He told them to go to their doctors and say they were having nightmares and headaches, that they needed sedatives, that they had lost their appetites. They didn't have to take the tablets, he said, they could throw them in the fire. Unknown to Griz and his comrade the rest of the IRA unit had been caught a few miles away. The woman of the house shouted that there was a priest at the door and then they heard a loudspeaker announce, 'You are surrounded', etc.

The Branchmen, who knew all the IRA men well, slagged Griz and his mate. On his way down the road towards the squad car Griz said to the priest, 'Father, we've no cigarettes, could you give's a packet.'

The priest replied, 'Well, you know all about it now, ya cunt ya.'

Griz replied, 'Go on, you oul' cunt yourself!'

When the prisoners arrived in Letterkenny there were about 300 people out in the street cheering Griz and his mate who, of course, gave the *de rigueur* clenched-fist salute. At their trial, statements from the hostages – who were all neurotic and suffering from nervous debility on Griz's earlier instructions –

were given. But the young fella of the house took the witness stand and described the IRA men as 'perfect gentlemen', then turned to Griz and gave him a big wink! They were expecting fifteen years but by a stroke of luck they got three judges who hadn't sat in the Special Court before and they were given eight years. Griz was released in December 1988 and rearrested just one year later, in December 1989, along with Rinty McVeigh and Tom McAlister, etc., on a big explosives charge.

Sunday 21 January

Well, I was coming back from my visit with you on Friday and didn't even notice that I was in a party of other prisoners, when Butch, who was beside me, suddenly declared, 'You're off the Red Book! You must be off the Red Book!' When I got back the screws gave me a brown bag and told me to pack my things, I was being transferred to C-Wing. And so here I am on the Twos. In the next cell is a loyalist who has been charged with possessing RUC security files, including one with my personal details.

I'm sharing a cell with a young lad from Derry, Roy 'Finn' McCool. He is charged with possession of mortar bombs last October, one of which blew up in the tube and seriously injured a bomb-disposal expert who was trying to defuse it. Roy's been married about eighteen months. His wife is called Donna and they bought a house on the Buncrana Road. Outside he was a postman. In here he is a grandmaster at chess!

In this cell our window opens inwards and downwards from the bars by over 90 degrees, so we get lots of fresh air and light. We can see houses in Clifton Park Avenue and lights lit upstairs. We also have an unhindered view of Ligoniel and Cave Hill. There's no great room in the cell so I've done no exercises since Thursday night. Hope you got last week's letter on Saturday. It wasn't returned to me so presumably the screws found it, although the same thing happened to Anto. He spent three nights composing a letter to his wife Lucy. He ended up with about four paragraphs and all that it read was, 'How's Mary . . . How's Joseph . . . How's Mickey.' He said, 'There were that many "Hows" in it that I felt like a Red Indian!' And to crown it all she never even received it. Gerard Hodgins also told me before I left A-Wing that he was only inside a fortnight and already 'the vultures' were sweeping down on his property and that someone was trying to take his flat. I got a letter from Trisha Ziff, who now lives in Los Angeles. She said she read about my arrest in *Time* magazine and that I appeared in a column called 'Milestones' alongside a report on the English comedian Terry Thomas!

I saw the assistant governor, and because of the regulations he will not allow my hardback dictionary in. He says that if a soft back is put on it he can foresee no problem. I understand that Just Books in Winetavern Street will do the job. Could you, at your convenience, get that done?

Wednesday 24 January
Such a racket is going on now – the banging of doors, whistling and jeering! We were supposed to go to the yard for exercise between ten and a quarter past eleven but due to the overnight flurry of snow the yard was cancelled and we are locked up.

We could have gone to the canteen but were told it was being cleaned. But an orderly brought back word that the canteen was empty – thus the banging.

When I changed the radio station an old song was playing from a film you once recommended in 1982 and which I eagerly went to see in Dublin and reviewed.

Do you remember *Reds*, about the American journalist John

Reed, the legendary playboy who became the legendary revolutionary? Towards the end of the film, Louise Bryant is sitting in a rocking chair, bereaved, lost to the world, in sad reverie, singing a lullaby:

I'll be your sweetheart
If you will be mine.
All your life
I'll be your Valentine

Bluebells I've gathered,
Keep them and be true.
When I'm a man, my plan
Will be to marry you . . .

Do you remember that scene? Sad and beautiful. It seems no two people can have an equal relationship. Bryant lived in Reed's shadow. But listen to me – there is joy and happiness before us. After all, wasn't I born with a caul on my head? Haven't we been blessed and lucky so far. I am the eternal optimist, as you know. My uncle Harry was sentenced to death by hanging in 1946 but within three years was walking free! That is life. So don't be depressed and never despair.

Every night a prisoner directly above us delivers a homily at some length out his window in the voice of Norman Bates's mother in *Psycho*. Last night he broke his light bulb and tried to eat the glass. The screws decided he was trying to work his ticket so they gave him a new bulb. Tonight the screws couldn't see inside his cell when they opened the flap. They shone the torch in and our man was now slicing his wrists with his broken bulb. He's now been taken to a mental hospital.

Sunday 28 January

That was a terrible explosion in Derry during the Bloody Sunday march today and certainly subdued everyone in here. Roy is fairly upset, worrying about his wife and relatives. I'm not sure where the teenager who was killed is from, but in the case of someone belonging to a prisoner the prison chaplain would be in very quickly with the news.

Friday 2 February

I received two letters today. One from Gerry Hanratty, who is in prison in West Germany charged with possession of rifles and facing extradition to Ireland. He's in good spirits. He and his co-accused, Gerry McGeough, were arrested in August 1988 and first brought to Frankenthal Jail. He was so tired that he fell asleep immediately. When he woke up he thought he was in hell. He looked out into a bare yard. Opposite him were thousands of windows. Hundreds of transistor radios were blaring in Hebrew, Spanish, Turkish, Italian and German. He spoke to some Kurds and their accounts of imprisonment would make your hair stand on end. He's been moved since – into a 1,100-year-old monastery which has been converted into a top-security prison. He's isolated and on a twenty-three-hour lock-up. I wrote back and told him he had nothing to complain about: at least he's going to be incarcerated in a united Germany!

The other was from Martin Meehan in the H-Blocks. His daughter got married to a prisoner inside the jail last October. When she was born, in 1969, Martin was in jail for the first time. He wrote a little poem about their relationship over the past twenty years. He said: 'So I read it out at the end of the Mass and I looked across at her and saw the tears flow down her beautiful face.'

Thursday 8 February
Read a very moving interview with the Birmingham Six in the *Sunday Tribune*. One of the Six, Richard McIlkenny, was asked if he felt daunted at the publicity their release might bring – perhaps international fame. He said that he had begun learning Italian in prison and would like to take his wife to Italy. 'I'd like to go to Rome and meet the Pope, up on his balcony. And people will look up and say, "Who's that guy with Richard McIlkenny?"'

Friday 9 February
Well, Seanna Walsh, Ned Flynn and Bernard Fox were sentenced today for possessing mortars and it was pretty stiff.

Seanna himself was fairly uptight this morning and looked quite emotional when he was leaving us, even though he'll be glad to get to the Blocks, where conditions are much better. He had been the OC here. Ned didn't contest the case and got nineteen years. Seanna and Bernard fought the charges and for their effrontery were given twenty-two years each. Pat Sheehan is still on the boards – the punishment wing – in D-Wing on punishment from Tuesday. I don't know what's happening there. Sean Kelly, Pat Kane and Mickey Timmons from west Belfast landed on the wing tonight. They had been out on bail in connection with the killings of British Army Corporals Derek Wood and Robert Howes at Kevin Brady's funeral in March 1988, during that nightmarish time which began with the SAS killings in Gibraltar of Dan McCann, Mairead Farrell and Sean Savage.

I got the books, thank you. Among them, Brian Patten's *Love Poems*. I brought them into the canteen during recreation and there was a free-for-all.

'Don't forget, I bags that one after you.'

'Fuck off, I asked him first!'

'Look, I only need four lines.'

'So what! You can wait your turn.'

When it comes to love, comradeship goes out the window! Oh, the scramble for St Valentine's Day – the day when birds choose their mates for the year! I hope the wives and girlfriends never compare the poems their men have 'composed' for them.

Sunday 11 February

We saw a special news bulletin on TV late in the afternoon but were locked up for the main 6.30 programme. I had to control my emotions as I watched Nelson Mandela walk to freedom, taking to the streets of Cape Town for the first time since 1962. The canteen was hushed and what we saw was a tall, dignified but old man. What those bastards stole off him can never be replaced.

Friday 16 February

I've just heard that my old friend Brendan Green was buried last Monday. I must have missed the death notice in the *Irish News*. Every Christmas when I do my rounds I visit him and his brother Jimmy. Brendan, who just loved dancing the night away, took a stroke in December 1969, was paralysed, had to have a leg amputated and lost the power of speech. He was bedridden since then. Last year his sight began to go.

I remember the dark and cold winter afternoon after school in 1969 that Jimmy tried to get across to me the devastation that this represented to Brendan, their elderly mother, Jimmy himself and his brother Sean, who still lived at home. I remember thinking for two seconds, gee, that's awful, before trying to turn the conversation around to my suffering and the fact that I was sore from being in love with a girl who didn't love me: it was from this angst-ridden perspective that I viewed the entire world for about eighteen months, from August 1969.

I'll write Jimmy a letter of condolence early in the week. He'll be shattered. Jimmy has never enjoyed good health himself. He became agoraphobic when he was fifteen and has been house-bound for over fifty years. He has suffered down the years from insomnia, anaemia and regular gum bleeds. I measure my unbelievable good fortune against the fates of people like Jimmy.

It was through Jimmy and another friend, Robert, that I became interested in electronics. We used to have small pirate radio stations in our houses operating on the medium wave after midnight, when BBC Radio Ulster closed down for the day. We were from the Falls and Shankill, and we visited each other's homes, swapping valves, capacitors, resistors. We talked about 6AZs feeding into 807s, about carrier signals and oscillators, sometimes about books and music, but never about politics. One friend, Johnny Doak, from the loyalist Tigers Bay in north Belfast, was very embarrassed one night. Robert and I were visiting his house in July 1968 or 1969 when an Orange flute band was playing outside. Then Johnny's teenage daughter Eleanor arrived home – in her band uniform! On Friday and Saturday nights I would go on the air at about two in the morning after I came in from working as a waiter in the International Hotel. I called myself 'Harry' – we all used false names. It was illegal, and often the GPO would come out with tracking equipment trying to locate who was involved. Some of our group were students and lived over by Queen's University. The GPO's engineers declared in the *Sunday News* that they were going to close down one particular station, Radio Sunshine, which was run by Dave and Heather. Sunshine declared that it was not going to be intimidated and that it would be broadcasting as usual the following Sunday. Radio Sunshine went on the air and the GPO came out with their equipment, tracking the signal, and were getting 'hotter' and 'hotter' around University Road. They found the source okay, but they had red faces! A cheap transmitter with a cheap tape recorder attached to it was found inside a telephone kiosk, which had been cordoned off and had an 'Out of Order' sign on it. The power source was the overhead electric light socket!

Jimmy is a real character – a very kind person without any malice. He is a great storyteller and wit. Out in his small back garden in Iveagh Crescent on summer nights in the sixties a group of us from all ages and all walks would sit and discuss history and philosophy, music, books, films, astronomy, electronics, then the civil rights marches, then the Troubles, and then I disappeared from their company altogether, except for that one visit every Christmas. Jimmy's next-door neighbour – he's now dead – was the actor Albert Sharpe, who played the lead role in *Darbie O'Gill and the Little People*. Walt Disney called in to see Albert one day. Jimmy says that Albert was definitely in – hiding behind the wife, who was hiding behind the curtains – but wouldn't open the door. I can understand that. When we were bored we used to torture him and knock on his door and ask him had he seen any of 'the little people' recently. He used to tell us to fuck off. Anyway, the unflappable Jimmy says, 'Walt, come on in and I'll get you a cup of tea and a bit of bread.' Walt Disney came in and sat on the settee, eating sandwiches as Jimmy gave him some hints about directing!

Sunday 18 February

Mahler's last symphony, his Ninth, which he never heard, is on Radio 3 just now. Just over two years ago, when I moved in with my da for a while when I was between houses, I used to sit and listen continuously to this symphony and to 'The Great' by Schubert as I finished *West Belfast*. So this music – especially the

Mahler, which is a homage to life from someone facing imminent death – evokes February and March 1988 and my last conversations with Dan McCann and Kevin Brady, mixed shortly afterwards with the knowledge that they had been living their last days.

I called to see Dan's widow, Margaret, in her mother's house about six or seven weeks after his death. She was ill in bed but she brought out some memorabilia and showed me a letter/poem that Dan gave her the last time he was with her, on the day he left Belfast. It was very moving and presaged his death.

Monday 19 February
Lunchtime. Roy is under his blankets for his afternoon siesta. There is little activity out in the landings as everyone is locked up until two and I think most of the screws are away to lunch. A couple of orderlies can be heard kicking a ball in the yard but apart from that it is relatively quiet. There was a lot of excitement in the yard this morning when someone who had caught the ten o'clock news on Downtown Radio reported that Martin McGuinness had issued a statement asking the Brits what was on the negotiating table if there was peace. I never heard so much speculation! But by the time we came back to the wing the item had dropped right down the news, which seems to indicate that some journalist had been engaging in hype.

3.30 pm
I'm just back from Welfare. Somebody phoned the jail to say that our Kevin was taken to hospital on Saturday night. The welfare officer himself didn't take the call and that's all the detail he had. Fuck. Obviously I was a bit frantic, thinking the worse, and I asked him to try to get more information, which he is away to do.

Then about ten minutes later, I got a letter from you which

had been posted at 10.30 this morning and assumed that I was aware of what happened. I'm totally in the dark, although from what you say he appears to be okay.

7.30 pm

Well, I didn't receive any more word but having reread your letter a couple of times I feel a bit reassured that it's not too serious. I'll find out tomorrow, no doubt.

Tuesday 20 February

You can imagine my anger and frustration. I have now learnt that it was nothing to do with Saturday's football trouble. Kevin was coming out of St Agnes disco on Saturday night when the RUC jumped out of jeeps and beat him up. He has a blood clot on his testicle and is in the City Hospital.

Wednesday 21 February

Do you know that among the republican prisoners here in C-Wing I am the second oldest but for Paddy Murphy, a fifty-year-old from Ardoyne!

Received a nice letter from Timothy O'Grady. He said the launch in Dublin of his paperback *Motherland* was very successful. Remember, we had been invited to it but you were working the next day and I was busy getting charged with conspiracy to murder. He asked me if there was anything I needed, which was kind of him.

Thursday 22 February

The weather was really pleasant as Pat Sheehan, Jim O'Carroll, Danny Caldwell and myself walked the yard. You wouldn't think that Pat has been in since last April. He only had about eighteen months of freedom, having served ten years and been among the last men on hunger strike back in October 1981. We amused ourselves by gossiping. Just before the last lock-up was called –

there are three calls for lock-up but we only obey the call from
the republican OC – we totted up and reckoned we had back-
stabbed at least nine people.

Friday 23 February

'The House of the Rising Sun' by the Animals is on the radio.
It reminds me of our family holiday in 1964. My parents booked
a house for a week in the sleepy seaside village of Glenarm but
we would walk into the town of Carnlough, a few miles around
the coast. My uncle Seamus had a station wagon and drove us
from Belfast to Glenarm. We were all crammed in: three adults,
four kids (Ciaran wasn't yet born), suitcases, boxes of food, etc.
After a sit-down and a cup of tea Seamus took off for Belfast.
But our Geraldine, who was fifteen, dashed out the door after
his car as it was chugging down the street, tears streaming down
her face. When she was challenged, it emerged that she was in
love with Francie McDonald from Beechmount, whom she
mistook for her pop idol, Roy Orbison, and that she couldn't live
a week without him! My sister Margaret and I were pissing
ourselves with laughter but my mother, sensitive Susie, scowled
at us with a look that said 'Don't say a thing to your big sister.'
Nobody but our Geraldine could see the Roy Orbison resem-
blance, except that Francie, who did have a lovely smile and
brilliant eyes, used Brylcream and wore dark glasses once.

Anyway, Geraldine was told she couldn't go back to Belfast
and be on her own. I had a great time, swimming, fishing for
flatfish from Glenarm pier and forcing my mammy to fry them
in flour and butter no matter how small they were. Every time
we walked into Carnlough 'The House of the Rising Sun' was
blasting from speakers in the amusement arcade, and the sun
always seemed to beat down, and the boys sat outside chatting
up the girls, and I had a sense of something bubbling in them
which infected me.

When I think about it my uncle Seamus drove us everywhere. He took us on our holidays to Dublin, when we stayed in my uncle Harry's, and regularly drove us to Islanderry, a townland outside Donacloney in County Down, to the cottage where my granny White was born. He's a great accordion player and once had his own ceilidh band and he's brilliant to have at a party. He has the most infectious laugh in the world and everybody loves him. I once shot him. Accidentally.

It was only on New Year's Day this year, when you and I and Ciaran took my mammy for a walk through the park and we called in to see my uncle Seamus, that I realised that our Ciaran must have kept in close contact down the years because he was so familiar with all our cousins.

Anyway, one birthday, possibly his sixth or seventh, young Dan gets a bow and arrows as a present, which he uses to kill his two big sisters and the spoilt youngest at every opportunity. (Margaret and Geraldine also used to turn me into a dog and I would run around on all fours, barking at Susan until she climbed onto a chair, crying.) Uncle Seamus calls in for a visit and whilst he's eating his sandwiches Robin Hood takes aim with an arrow and pulls back the string.

'Danny! Don't be doing that,' warns Mom. 'It's dangerous and could hit your uncle Seamus.'

But I knew how far it was safe to pull back the string. 'No, it won't,' I said.

Shummmppp! Hit him right on the forehead. Initially I think he called me, *sotto voce*, all the wee bastards of the day. But if it hadn't been for his intercession my mother would have killed me.

Tuesday 27 February
That was a shock result in Nicaragua for the Sandinistas after all their sacrifices and suffering. The US not only embargoed

trade with the government in Managua in order to undermine it but also put $50 million into the coffers of the opposition party over a three-year period. If Gorbachev were to do the same with an opposition party his action would be condemned in the US as intolerable interference.

Wednesday 28 February
I got called early for my visit with Tom and Jim. Tom swaggered in, his usual self, requiring space and being loud, bewailing imprisonment and keeping me amused for fifty-five minutes. Jim was the chalk to Tom's cheese. Tom says they are totally confident I'm getting out. Then he told me the Movement has sold my car!

I was just thinking that at midnight, nine years ago tonight, Bobby Sands started his hunger strike. Thoughts of those seven months of continuous hunger striking still bring a lump to my throat and a weight of sadness to my heart. Well over half the prisoners in here were republican converts of that period or, later, of Loughgall and Gibraltar.

There are young lads in here, still in their teens, who are facing life sentences; they will *serve* life sentences unless our political problems are resolved. The British government is in the luxurious position of sitting the whole thing out; the cost to them appears to be tolerable.

Friday 2 March
Got the poetry book and *Dubliners* – how I love books! Roy and I had a laugh at a letter he received from a nun in Derry. At the end she wrote: 'I pray that you get the courage to serve your sentence and the insight to look into yourself and examine the reason why you are now in prison. You are in detention while the bosses who organise the crimes are free.'

Roy wrote her a courteous thank-you note and added a postscript: 'Danny Morrison, my cellmate, sends his regards'!

Monday 5 March
I believe that people with nicknames secretly despise them and prefer their proper names. Roy McCool here is dubbed Finn (legendary Irish hero), but when he is quoting conversations he had with his wife or mother he is always referred to by them as Roy. I must be the only one here who calls him by his Christian name. Pat Sheehan invents new nicknames for people at the dinner table every day. Seany Adams (Gerry's brother) he calls 'Head in the Clouds'. Young Gerard Magee from Antrim, who is charged with possessing explosives, he has christened 'Semtex'. A guy with stuck-out ears he has called 'Wing Nut'. Jim Donnelly from Ballymurphy, charged, along with my cousin Liam's girlfriend, Rosie McCorley, with planting an 'up-and-under' (booby-trap) using a magnet, he calls 'Limpet'! He calls Tom McAllister 'Ceefax' because he always knows what's been on the news.

My first nickname was 'Smiler', which I got in 1963 when we moved down to the Falls. It was given to me by Arthur McCallum, an avuncular neighbour from two doors down who I think had a crush on our Geraldine. Some people still call me that. But in December 1972 I was involved in a fight on the very first day I moved into Cage 2 from Cage 5, Long Kesh, with a fella called Hucker Moyna. Colm Meehan from Clonard broke it up and declared, 'We've another "Bangers"!' Apparently, some guy from north Belfast had just been released. His nickname was 'Bangers' because he was on edge all the time with his nerves (cockney: Bangor Reserves rhymes with nerves). I made the mistake of showing resentment and that was me saddled. Now that I'm older I'm once again being called Danny, but, increasingly, Dan.

I have written to Mrs Brady and thanked her for her regards via you. I must introduce you to her properly someday. She is a great woman and has had a fairly hard life of it, even before Kevin's death. Difficult as it is to believe, today is the second anniversary of Gibraltar. The weather this evening is like it was in Belfast on that Sunday night when the news started coming in – slightly cold and wet.

Friday 9 March
I don't know about where you are but last night was quite sultry here. The lights went out at eleven, as usual, and I listened to the radio a while longer as it helps me to sleep. I switched it off just as I was about to go over but then a screw did a check, putting the light on for a few seconds. Well, that was it. I couldn't get to sleep after that and had a great urge to get up and do some writing – which, of course, was impossible.

Ciaran told me that my butchers, Jim and John from Broadway, offered to buy me a book. That's good of them. One of the following: *Buddenbrooks* or *The Magic Mountain* by Thomas Mann, or *A Writer's Diary* by Virginia Woolf, or any novel by Joseph Conrad, except *Heart of Darkness,* which I've read.

Sunday 11 March
Reports are coming in on the radio of a shooting on the Kashmir Road. And I've been told that Clonard Martyrs Sinn Fein cumann are holding their commemoration in the district this morning. This is the first time: they usually hold it in the cemetery. Naturally, everybody is now dreading the worst. One of the lads here, Gerard McKenna, is from the Kashmir and his family would have been at the commemoration, so you can imagine how he's feeling until the news is more precise . . .

Later
The loyalists have just been up to their doors, banging, so I switched on the news and heard that a Catholic man was shot dead from a passing car on the Kashmir Road. The car was hijacked at the top of the Shankill.

Today's dinner is lying heavy in my stomach. I miss cooking and was particularly reminded of good food when I detected a whiff of garlic on the breath of a screw this morning.

Monday 12 March
It was a nice afternoon. I ran forty laps round the yard then had a shower at teatime. Some new remands came on the wing. I've gone down from being second-oldest to fourth! Three cheers for the Special Branch!

Tuesday 13 March
A reporter from Reuters, Paul Magendie, from Dublin, visited me today. He was supposed to have interviewed me in January, before my arrest. He said he wrote an 800-word article on *West Belfast* which was wired worldwide and sent a copy to Mercier Press, but I've yet to see it. He wanted to know was I writing any Behanesque novels at the moment. I said nope but filled him in on the segregation issue, which interested him. I asked him did he want some coffee but he had only punts with him so we had to do without.

Friday 16 March
In two weeks' time it's your birthday and I've nothing for you. Of course, you'll get a card. It may be gross – it's chosen by the tuck-shop screw.

I got lots of mail today: two St Patrick's Day cards (one from Mary Quinn and her daughter Leontia) and letters from you,

Margaret, Geraldine and Chrissie and one from friends in Draperstown – Patsy and Annis Groogan, who in 1986 named their daughter Danielle after me! Her birthday is the second of November, I think. Margaret sends her thanks for Marie's birthday card. Geraldine also sent me two books and was asking for you. Chrissie's letter was a real scream – written on the train journey from Dublin to Limerick. She should do a Dervla Murphy piece from around Ireland. She dropped her pen – accidentally, she says – under the table, whilst opposite her sat a dozing punk rocker. But it was really a ruse to check the nuts your man had!

Roy was asking me for a few lines of poetry to include in a letter to his wife. I spent the last ten minutes racking my brain and then came up with the words of a Labi Siffre song from 1971, 'Love Song for Someone' – another that I'll sing to you.

Sunday 18 March
A sober St Patrick's night was had by all here, although last night there was nothing but loud Irish music being blasted between here and B-Wing. I think everybody – regardless of what they're in here for – thoroughly enjoyed it. You know, when you listen to some of the lyrics of Irish songs it's no wonder we've a Paddy image:

I lathered him with me shillelagh
For he trod on the toe of me
Mush, mush, mush, tour-a-li-lady
Me mush, mush, mush tour-a-li-lay!

It's time to make one's bed. 'We have,' says you. 'I know,' says I.

Tuesday 20 March
My visitors arrived safe and sound and again the time flew by. What a haircut Zack Smith has! I thought Jackie looked a bit

pale, but given that Ciaran Senior (Zack) and Ciaran Junior are both hyper that's no surprise! Zack's nickname in here is 'Rubber Man' because his arms and head never stop wobbling.

I was telling them about Pat Sheehan's latest nickname. There's a young lad – Bio – who sits at our table in the canteen. I mentioned him in a letter last week – Gerard McKenna from the Kashmir. Bio is charged with having an AK-47 in a car stopped outside the Beehive Bar last September. Pat and he are always bantering. Bio has copied a habit of Pat's off to a 'T'. When Pat is exhaling cigarette smoke his head shakes a little bit from side to side, a bit like the model dog in the back windows of cars. Well, Bio christened him 'Shakey' (Pat's nickname is 'Sheeky') and he hates it! So, to annoy him, Bio has merely to draw on his cigarette and puff out with a shake of his head and the whole table erupts in laughter. Pat was told by Paddy McGrory that he could possibly be up for trial before Easter (it won't be a very long hearing), which means he could be away within the next six weeks. I certainly hope it's longer because he's brilliant company.

Got the apples and oranges. They were nice and fresh: a blaze of spray erupted from the orange peel when pressed. Thank you for looking after me.

Thursday 22 March

Roy is away to an art class for about forty minutes. Even though an hour might pass without a word being spoken and even though he is easygoing, simply constantly being in one another's presence without any privacy I imagine grates on him as much as it can on me. So it's quiet and peaceful now, nothing to disturb me for half an hour.

Soon the clocks will go forward, making the evenings brighter. The sun is already climbing in the sky and last night a few of the last rays struck our window, which overlooks the back of the jail. It'll get brighter (and more melancholy!) in the weeks to come.

I've just been ambushed. The emotional compactness of a memory springing itself on me. Two years ago. Light like this evening's. You making mashed potatoes and home-made coleslaw and frying big pork sausages for myself and Sheila McVeigh, who just happened to call in.

Saturday 24 March

I've just finished reading a book that Sylvia Stevens sent me, *In the Skin of a Lion* by Michael Ondaatje, a poet and novelist who lectures at York University in Toronto. Anyway, one particular sentence in the novel caught the mood of what I was trying to express to you yesterday about wishing I'd known you in your youth. The main character and his girl drive from Toronto out to the countryside, where she grew up and which she still pervades. Ondaatje writes: 'He loved the eroticism of her history, the knowledge of where she sat in schoolrooms, her favourite brand of pencil at the age of nine.'

Isn't that nice, and oh so true!

In 1957 I started primary school, St Teresa's on the Glen Road, Andersonstown. My sisters Geraldine and Margaret also went to this school, but in the fifties boys and girls were segregated, and I rarely saw them, even at break-time. We may have had different starting and getting-out times also.

After my mother's family moved to Andersonstown Park in the late thirties, my mother attended St Teresa's in a mixed class. Before her brain haemorrhage, if you got her going she'd talk about her schooldays and adolescence and her adventures with her best friend, 'Girlie' Brown. She also spoke of her mother's sufferings over the family twice being put out of their home,

Harry being an IRA activist, RUC raids on the house and Harry being sentenced to death.

On my first day at St Teresa's my classmates and our mothers all gathered in a classroom in the main building, where 'Bonzo' McGonigle, the principal, a short fat man with wavy hair, gave a speech. His deputy, Master Donnelly, on the other hand, was a long drip with a red nose who walked at an angle of 45 degrees. Whether or not all of this is totally accurate is moot. These impressions are in the inner rings of my infant memory. My first teacher was Miss Gilleece, a gentle spinster who wore too much powder on her face. She was warm and motherly and comforted those who cried on their first day when their mammies left.

Our classroom was a wooden hut, sheltered by the fir trees in the lane up to St Patrick's, where the 'Home Boys' were serving time. Every Saturday morning these youths, whom we were conditioned to fear, would be marched down the Glen Road to the Broadway picture house for the matinée, which they watched from the balcony.

In winter our classroom hut was freezing and reeked of fumes from the portable, paraffin-oil heater. We looked forward to our free milk and its half-inch collar of cream every morning. From across the yard in the main building you could hear one of the masters screaming at the more senior boys. Because of this menacing atmosphere, one reluctantly visited the toilets there, which gave off a glistening, pleasant smell of Jeyes fluid.

Our next teacher, Oliver Campbell, was a very tough former GAA hurler who took no prisoners, though Laurence Long sorted him out one day. On some Friday afternoons Oliver used to say that it would be a Bloody Monday if we hadn't our homeworks done over the weekend. So this Monday for some reason he bounced the wooden duster off Laurence's head from his table at the top of the class right to the back. Laurence picked it up and bounced it back off Oliver's head, spilling blood before running out of the classroom, our hero! My last teacher at primary school was John Sands, who had taught in England and was, I think, a school coeval of my mother. He returned home for God-knows-what reason and brought back too many glowing reports of the standards of his English pupils. He always took it easy with us on Friday afternoons, letting us paint or read. Sometimes he would ask a few of us to read aloud, which I enjoyed doing: novels by Mark Twain, Enid Blyton and Rosemary Sutcliff.

At secondary school some of the Christian Brothers and lay teachers were nasty, some were conscientious thugs and some, like our English teacher, Jimmy Brankin, were good people. I had great times and scary times. There is an irony about winsomely reflecting on the tortured aspects of your childhood because at the time you just wanted to escape at the speed of light into the future.

Tuesday 27 March
It's been in the news that the Northern Ireland Office is appointing a number of psychologists to advise prison staff because of a successful campaign of psychological warfare waged by republican prisoners that has been taking its toll on staff morale. After the stories appeared there was great banter in here. For example, there's a variant on the nice guy/tough guy scenario. A prisoner on the way to the wash-house is as nice as ninepence to the screw, cracking jokes, asking after his family. The screw smiles, relaxes, it's a wonderful world after all, overtime couldn't be better. Five minutes later, the prisoner comes out of the wash-house. The screw is still beaming. Prisoner says, 'What to fuck are you looking at? Are you looking filled in!' Both sides had great crack over that.

Friday 30 March

Hello again, precious. Had a visit with my aunty Eileen and my da this afternoon. She left me in a John Steinbeck novel and *Germinal*, which you also bought me in 1982.

I can't believe that Sean Kelly and his co-accused have been sentenced to life imprisonment! Wasn't that verdict a scandal! When Howes and Wood, the two army corporals, sped towards us I had just been relieved of carrying Kevin's coffin. We thought we were going to be killed. Sean and the others were nowhere near the two corporals when they were shot dead. I'm sure Sean and his family are shattered. There's no way he was expecting even ten years. The other verdict, on the UDR man who had parts for 1,000 Uzi submachine guns was, for different reasons, just as scandalous – fourteen years. The same judge gave Seanna Walsh and Bernard twenty-two years for having the parts for one mortar tube!

It's a funny old night; you wouldn't know what it was going to do outside. One moment the dead light from the overhead bulb, which is on all day, is unnoticeable and the next, when evening falls, it sharply lights up the cell. It's a seamless transition and always surprises.

Monday 2 April

That rioting in Strangeways Prison was serious business. As I write there are no confirmations of deaths but at one stage there were no denials. Speculation centred on rumours that an isolated wing containing sex offenders had been overrun and that those prisoners had been killed or mutilated. By sheer coincidence I had an idea for a story about a prisoner being held on sexual offences and have begun gathering notes. Could you do me a favour? It's quite likely that the *Guardian* and the *Independent* will do in-depth pieces on the riot; could you photocopy any features which appear and post them in to me?

There was a bit of trouble in here yesterday but I think it was an isolated incident. On the landing above there was a fight, and a prisoner who associates with us (as opposed to being a republican) got battered by the loyalists.

Jim O'Carroll told us a cracker in the yard. He was in a club one night when May McFetteridge, the drag comedian, came down from the stage and approached a big fat girl.

'Hey, love, did you have a bath before you came out?'

The girl said she had and May McFetteridge replied, 'Yeah, you must have fuckin' drank it!'

Wednesday 4 April

Just as I was finishing my letter last night the loyalists fused the lights. Then, at midnight, they banged their cell doors for a full hour. They are also on a go-slow and are refusing to talk to the screws. That lad who was beaten up on Sunday came back from the prison hospital today. He has two black eyes and had a tooth kicked out. Then John Cope, the Prisons Minister, said in an interview on BBC radio this morning that no prisoners had been injured recently and that that was a sure indication that the republicans and loyalists were in collusion and staging sham fights!

Siobhan brought Liam up and we had a good visit, bringing him into the conversation as much as possible and having a good laugh at some of his antics.

At long last I got around to writing to Martin Meehan. His son, also Martin, has been arrested and charged with opening fire on the RUC. He arrived in the canteen tonight.

Saturday 7 April

There are people in here, heavy-whacking it, trying to sleep, and from beyond the walls comes the shrill sound of an ice-cream van playing 'I'm Popeye the Sailor Man'. It comes around at the same time every night. There should be a by-law against it! Just when you get the prisoners tucked in for the night he wakens them and they start crying for 99s!

During the rooftop protest at Strangeways the cops tried to stop the prisoners and their relatives from exchanging messages and greetings. They wired up their police radios to amplifiers, tuned in to Atlantic 252, which is broadcast from Ireland, and blasted out music. However, it all came to an abrupt end when Atlantic 252, realising what was happening, dedicated 'Jailhouse Rock', 'I Want to Break Free' and 'We Gotta Get Out of This Place' to the protesting prisoners! Had the cops any sense they should have played Zack Smith singing 'My Brown-Eyed Girl'. That would have cleared the roof!

Sunday 8 April
'What a Wonderful World' by Louis Armstrong is on the radio. February 1968. Our Geraldine used to go with Joe McGivern, whose father owned the butcher's shop on the Glen Road opposite Andersonstown Barracks. Joe worked in the shop and he got me a start. I worked about two or three days after school and all day Saturday for twelve shillings and sixpence. I cleaned the chickens, made vegetable rolls and sausages and made up the parcels, which I delivered by bicycle around Andersonstown. So I had money in my pocket but I was too shy to go to dances. In the whole of 1968 I went to one ceilidh! There, I met a girl called Anne (who lived near Corby Way in Andersonstown, where I was born) and arranged to meet her a few nights later. But I was too nervous and never showed up. I have been hiding from her ever since, especially when I learnt just before Christmas that she is married and now living behind my da's!

Music which inspires reminiscences can certainly help put

flesh on the bones of the past, but we shouldn't live on nostalgia and refuse to face daily reality. Having said that, there have been times in the last ten or fifteen years when I have felt like crawling down the path of my life and into the past – had it been possible – for the innocence and carefreeness of my youth or even into the safety of the womb. This desperate yearning was usually to avoid the unpleasant reality of some extremely demoralising bombing that involved the loss of innocent life or, at a more personal level, domestic unhappiness. I think everybody's existence, and their bad experiences, must make them feel like that from time to time. Thank God, I am rarely depressed.

Tuesday 10 April
Our Margaret and Susan were up today and we had a great visit. Got a letter from Geraldine McAteer, which was a nice surprise. It's a pity you never got as far as the Hatchet Field when you went up Black Mountain for a walk on Sunday. From there you have a panoramic view of the city, and the city looks so innocent that you want to put your arms around it to cuddle and protect it.

Paddy McGrory was up this morning. Nothing new, but he heads off to Donegal for Easter and in a few weeks' time he's off to the USA. He said he recently got back the personal effects of Mairead, Sean and Dan and will have to see about approaching the families. There was dried blood on Mairead's watch, on the back of which was an inscription from the women of Maghaberry Prison, wishing her the best.

It looks as if Pat Sheehan's trial won't take place before summer – I think that's because of the appeal of Harry Maguire and Alex Murphy against their convictions for the killing of the two corporals at Kevin's funeral. That'll be after Easter.

Thank you for that sonnet. You recited part of it to me before. Do you know it by heart? It comes from Barrett Browning's *Songs from the Portuguese.* I used to be able to recite 'When I have Fears' by John Keats, 'Peace and War' by D. H. Lawrence and 'The Lake Isle of Innisfree' by Yeats. Something wiped them out. The only one I know now is Yeats's 'An Irish Airman Foresees His Death', a sort of suicidal, misanthropic piece! It finishes:

> *I balanced all, brought all to mind,*
> *The years to come seemed waste of breath,*
> *A waste of breath the years behind,*
> *In balance with this life, this death.*

Thursday 12 April

Our Margaret fits so easily into any scene; she's relaxed and makes you feel relaxed. She seemed like a veteran jail visitor, yet that's only her second time at a prison. It's because she's so naturally nonchalant that I almost forgot she has another home besides Belfast and has been away for the past nineteen years. I always felt protective towards Geraldine, and Margaret always felt protective towards me. But when she married Greg a frostiness set in between her and me which for years stood between us – probably my fault. Actually, more of it could have been in my mind than was real, but even things in the mind can seem more real than things that are tangible. As we've grown older we've grown a little bit closer. At my mammy's encouragement one Christmas I spoke to Greg on our telephone, on our *tapped* telephone! He was subsequently called in by MI5 or MI6 and told he wouldn't be serving in the North again because he was too open to compromise!

Friday 13 April

I got ten Easter cards, including ones from Mrs Brady and Paddy Kelly's mother in Dungannon (Paddy was killed at Loughgall). Also ones from cousin Liam and Rosaleen (Rosie), Aunty Cathleen and

Charlie, Uncle Seamus, Aunty Eileen and Aunty Eilish.

Monday 16 April

Cold rain and sun outside; a wrecked canteen inside. Here I am locked up, on top of being locked up. No recreation for us.

It all began several weeks ago when a prisoner, an ex-blanket man who was already on punishment, was ordered by a screw to move from the second-last row to the last row in the chapel when Mass had already begun. He refused and was charged with refusing to obey an order. He hadn't long finished serving thirty days' loss of parcels and association when he faced the adjudication for disobeying the order to move and was sentenced to another fourteen days' loss of privileges. On his way back from the adjudication the screw asked him what did he get and he told him and added that the screw who got him into trouble 'should get his . . . ' But he didn't finish what he was going to say. However, it was reported as a threat and he had another adjudication and was sentenced to another twenty-one days' punishment to run consecutively after the fourteen days expires. The Wing was in a rage because an outstanding allegation by this prisoner that a screw had set him up to be attacked by three loyalists four or five weeks ago was never investigated.

So since Saturday there were small acts of sabotage – sinks and toilets being broken, the TV smashed. Last night some people didn't get slopping out and so people started pouring the contents of their pots under the door. It's been over twenty-six hours since I've been allowed out to the toilet and we haven't been washed since Sunday morning. It was our turn for the canteen at lunchtime. The routine is that, while we are eating and locked behind grilles, the loyalists file down and collect their dinners, which they take back to their cells. But they reversed the routine and fed the loyalists first.

Later, as we were finishing our dinner, one of the lads shouted 'Fuck this!' and put a snooker ball through the television. That was it. Tables and chairs were broken, windows smashed, the pool table and snooker table were destroyed, radiators were ripped from the walls and the loudspeakers and all the fluorescent lights were broken. Then we told them we were coming out peacefully!

The riot squad was brought in but wasn't used. We went out two at a time and were strip-searched and then locked up. Then, at teatime, the loyalists were allowed down to the servery to collect their teas, whereas we were handed ours in our cells.

I don't know how this is going to be resolved. The NIO is unlikely to compromise and the mood could turn nastier. Up until today I had a quiet Easter! This is the first time in eleven years that I haven't had to speak at a commemoration! It was great.

Tuesday 17 April
Still haven't been slopped out. The lights were fused last night so we were in darkness. They still haven't been fixed. Last night most of the men smashed the glass in the flap on the door; then they pushed papers through and started fires. At times the smoke was fairly thick and I've ended up with a sore throat. Today the screws mended the glass but then wouldn't let us out to exercise in the afternoon and so the glass was broken again. I have one pair of clean socks and underpants left: everything else has piled up as dirty laundry in the basin below my bed.

Just had a number of screws at the door there – all dressed in royal-blue overalls, and the one who opened the door also wore yellow rubber gloves. They handed us our tea. Everything's two hours (or a century) behind schedule and it doesn't look like we'll be getting sheets tonight. The aisles are covered in urine, rubbish, discarded food and a million pieces of paper. Needless to say, morale is sky-high. And to think that I was so looking forward to reading *Nostromo* and *Brideshead Revisited*!

10 pm

The riot squad arrived on the Ones, and our lights have just been switched on. Eight republicans were taken out of their cells and brought over to the boards in D-Wing. Then almost all the loyalists were told to pack. They were moved to A-Wing and loyalists from A-Wing were moved to here – which seems pretty pointless. Then the riot squad withdrew.

Thursday 19 April

Hi love

I am presently in the punishment unit on the top landing of D-Wing. Last night all republicans in C-Wing were adjudicated, and I got thirty-five days' loss of association, fourteen days' loss of remission, twenty-eight days' loss of parcels and radio, etc. As a parting shot I said to the governor, 'I hope you live long.' So at 8 am I was brought over here to the PU and was charged with issuing a threat. I was doing press-ups when they came for me, and therefore I had no shirt on. I was charged again and found guilty of not wearing a shirt during an adjudication and was given the same punishment as above, to run consecutively. I kept the farce going and said to the governor as I was leaving, 'I hope you live long.' I've still to be adjudicated on charges of smashing the spyglass and pouring urine out the door. There are still six or seven republicans here in the punishment unit and we can shout to each other. I had a good wash and an hour's exercise on my own in a small yard about thirty feet by twelve. The cell is spartan. I had two books but they were removed and I was given the Bible instead. So far, I've read about Adam and Eve, Abram (who got his servant pregnant before changing his name to Abraham) and Sodom and Gomorrah! And that's just in the first fifteen pages. I'll probably be back in C-Wing on Sunday and then will be back here for another spell.

Friday 20 April
I've been given some writing paper so I thought I'd begin scribbling again. I was before the governor this morning but the adjudication was adjourned pending availability of witnesses. Though the window here is well secured, the screw has opened it for me and I have a grand new view: the full profile of Cave Hill, the grounds of St Malachy's College, two church spires, houses on the Antrim Road, part of the flats on the New Lodge Road, three industrial chimneys and some cranes in the docks.

The chaplain, Father Bennet, visited me this morning and I was bantering with him about all the fornication in the Old Testament and how full of vengeance was God. He got enthusiastic and began directing me to the best and 'most moving' parts of the Old and New Testaments. But there's too much flesh on me – and too much scepticism – for me to be born again.

That missing letter is playing on my mind. I'll do my best to retrieve it. You spend hours writing a letter only for them to withhold it just because it contains details of what's going on. I was careful not to name any prisoners or warders so that there could be no excuse for it being delayed. But I heard that they withheld most if not all of the letters.

Later
I've been shifted again. Now I can see Black Mountain and I can guess the direction of our house. I can also see the Mater Maternity, where our Ciaran was born in October 1968, Conway Mill and the spires of St Peter's, I am that close!

Saturday 21 April

I have just waved goodbye to you for another week. It was a great visit and we had two goodbyes! The traffic on the Crumlin Road probably drowned out or minced my words but I shouted out my window, 'Honey! I love you!' and three guys in cells below thought someone was calling them and shouted back, 'What is it?' 'What do you want?' 'Who's calling me?' They all must be called Henry!

I can hear the metal clang of the mop bucket arrive outside my cell door so I'll break for now and go slop out.

3.30 pm

I'm just back from an hour's exercise in a tiny yard at the back of the jail. The plumbers, in their boiler suits, visited me just there. I had a strip-search and then was moved out of the cell while they searched it. It appears to be a beautiful afternoon outside – perhaps spring proper has at long last arrived. The traffic is quite noisy; it's certainly a busy Saturday. The screws up the landing have a TV in one of the rooms and earlier I could hear the rising commentary on a horse race. It was like being in Number 37 while my da's jaw dropped as he lost yet another bet.

Sunday 22 April

Still here in the penthouse. I was handed the two books I brought over with me, thus signalling that, for today, I am not on punishment. They'll be removed tomorrow morning with the recommencement of hostilities.

I told you I was making notes and collecting material for a story. Well, if you are ever speaking to Eamonn McCann ask him does he still have a copy of a script he once read on the radio about people being charged with homosexual offences. He wrote this extremely compassionate piece in January, I think, and I wanted to study the arguments he put.

Monday 23 April

All the other lads got moved out this morning, presumably back to C-Wing, so I'm here on my own. Got exercised at about 10.30 and was then adjudicated on the charge of wishing the governor 'a long life' and 'not wearing a shirt'. I was sentenced to another three days on the boards and a clatter of loss of privileges for fourteen days (to run concurrently). But this time I was given a chair to sit on and the opportunity to explain why I was doing it! Wished the latest adjudicator a long life; he was a phlegmatic man who took no offence. I was shifted cell immediately afterwards and the view is just as pleasant as before, if not more so.

Hey, it's only twenty to six! I asked the screw for the time and couldn't believe it was still so early. When I finish this letter, what am I going to do? I've been given my supper for the night: bread and jam and tea.

Tuesday 24 April

I always make the mistake of taking people at face value. Yesterday I intimated that the governor at the last adjudication appeared a decent sort, appreciated the state of play and didn't bear grudges. Well, today I was charged again with an offence against discipline: 'You said to the governor: "And I hope you have a long life."' If I inserted the adjective 'happy', I wonder would they keep charging me! Or, 'I hope you have a great sex life.' I might just try that.

I got my exercise really early this morning, at nine o'clock. There was a busy spider that kept goose-stepping across my path in the yard and interfering with my rhythm. I happen to like spiders, though I remember you close to hysterics at one in the bedroom.

Thursday 26 April
The adjudication of my last offence has been adjourned indefinitely. I am back with Roy. You will be glad to hear that the situation with regard to letters is virtually normal. However, I never got your card. The kids told me they left in a parcel and a letter. Here is a wee poem I wrote for you when I was on punishment:

By the Stream

By the stream
Where the stream runs speckle-breasted,
Below the tall tree
Under its spangled shade,
I will laugh with you again.

I would begin with this rhyme:
Little Miss Louise (that's you)
Knelt on her knees
Eating her curds and whey,
When down came a spider (that's me)
And crept here inside her
And took her virginity away!

And I would continue
With soothing lullabies
And woo you in my arms
And promise you
Never to go away again.

I will pluck some wild flowers
And sprinkle burrs of pollen
From their souls
Into your lovely hair
Saying:
What nature has joined together
Let no cause pull apart.

I will give you my life
My shallows and depths
My dark and bright sides
And ask of you to make of me
What you will.

By the stream,
Where the stream runs speckle-breasted
Below the tall tree
Under its spangled shade,
These things I will do.

Friday 27 April
Pat Sheehan only got his letter back yesterday. They said it was
'over the top' and wouldn't let it out in its present form. I saw
the governor today on a number of issues, including getting
clearance for sending out an extra sheet (for the above poem).
I was out in the exercise yard with the lads this afternoon for
the first time since Easter Monday and we had a great time
yarning and back-stabbing!

Sunday 29 April
I am enclosing with this letter the present for you that I had a
prisoner do for me. He's in for forgery but as you can see he is

a brilliant calligraphist! He wanted to do a scroll for his girl so I gave him the words of the Elizabeth Barrett Browning sonnet, and he made me this copy in return. My effort pales into mediocrity beside this beautiful poem.

Very soon I shall be sending out a lot of my letters (or rather your letters to me) because you're only allowed so many in the cell and at some stage during a search they'll be confiscated and placed in my property. I'll have to give the censors notice so I'll do that next week some time. And don't be thinking about plagiarising them! My memory's bad but it's not that bad! There's always a freshness about new letters, however familiar the message.

Monday 30 April
Another beautiful evening here. We have the window open all day, right through until about eleven o'clock. There's a bit of a haze towards Ligoneil Hill and the sun is very hot. I just watched a seagull dive through the sky the way a turtle uses its front flippers to plunge through the sea. In an empty cell above us the pigeons are cooing. I am about a third of the way through *Brideshead Revisited* and it is a beautifully written novel. There's a magic feel to every word and sentence.

At present Roy is dying of starvation because of the punishment, which includes a ban on biscuits and fruit in parcels. He could eat about fifteen chocolate biscuits (including bars of Orange Club and Kit-Kats) throughout the evening and then polish the night off with a Galaxy and a pint of Coca-Cola. One night, in addition to the above, he ate a packet of cheese-and-onion crisps and a packet of gammon ones and rolled into bed. He groaned for four hours and then, at about five, leaped bolt upright and boked up his guts into the waste-paper bin while I rushed to his aid! He's so funny.

My bum is going to be the shape of a plank due to the amount of sitting on the edge of this bed I do. I actually think I'm getting bed sores! I'm on this bed about twenty-two hours a day and it's one long shift of tossing and turning. Okay, the moan's over from the Felons of Our Land for another letter.

Tuesday 1 May
Well, my love, the Lord is certainly spoiling all you people at large with this glorious weather. Yesterday the temperature was in the seventies and I thought this afternoon was even warmer when I caught the last half-hour in the yard after my visit with my da. It was a good visit and he seemed in excellent form. He's been very lucky work-wise and it looks like he'll be in Telephone House until he's sixty-five. I feel a lot easier about that because I was always conscious of leaving him wide open to suffer prejudices which were aimed at me. But he has lasted longer even than those who were promoted over his head.

I received a very funny letter from Joelle today with a few comments thrown in from Tom. Joelle mentioned that Trisha Ziff's photographs were in last Saturday's *Independent* magazine. Can you get me a copy?

I weighed myself today – 11 stone 2 pounds. The rate of loss is slow but I'll settle for 11 stones. And after fourteen years I've finally hammered the asthma. My lungs are as clear as a whistle and when I pound the yard it's my legs which surrender before my chest. All down to an angst-free life!

Thursday 3 May
What a heatwave! I went out in my shorts to run thirty laps but had to give up at six and lay out worshipping the sun for about an hour and a half.

I had that visit with Pam Brighton from BBC radio drama.

She's going to London in about two weeks' time to propose that my book be adapted as either a four-part play of forty-five minutes each excerpt or as the *Book at Bedtime* on Radio 4. She asked me would I be prepared to do the adaptation but I declined, and she thinks that while the BBC hierarchy will not be pleased with the proposal she can see no grounds for objection. Me? I think it will be blocked but she is enthusiastic. We got to talking about people who could possibly do the adaptation and she mentioned Jim Allen, a friend of the film producer Ken Loach, whose film *Hidden Agenda* is the British entry at Cannes. It turns out that she actually acted in *Days of Hope*, a brilliant four-part series on the history of the British labour movement which went out on TV in 1975! Anyway, when she mentioned Allen and the fact that he is shunned by the BBC establishment I had a great idea. Given that the scriptwriter for *Ten Men Dead* has had a stroke, why not suggest to David Beresford that Granada approach Allen to do the adaptation. He's more than experienced (he wrote *Days of Hope*), and his politics are sound. What do you think?

Friday 4 May
Hi! We were up in court and Barra asked for a fortnight remand to keep up the pressure for forensics and it was granted. In real terms it means very little. Waiting for Sandy is the name of the game and my confidence remains unshaken. Veronica Martin and Rosie McCorley were up for bail and were apparently taken past our cell in the holding centre in the base of the jail, but by the time I jumped to my feet Rosie had passed. But I heard that my cousin Liam managed to have a snatched conversation with her before the hearing

Going to court took all morning, so we missed the yard and the glorious sun. Hope it keeps up because tomorrow afternoon it's our turn again for the yard. (There's some fuckin' loyalists in the cell above and they keep pouring liquids out their window which strike our ledge and splash the cell. It's infuriating and pig-ignorant because it's so easy to pour just an inch or two further out, which achieves the same objective and hurts no one!)

Sunday 6 May
A cold and grey evening. Can't we moan! I heard the bands parading, presumably through the New Lodge, before heading over to west Belfast for the hunger-strike commemoration, but not having any radio I don't know how things went – shiverish, I would think.

There are two characters in B-Wing, opposite me. One apparently spends his life in bed, and the other, in the cell next door, acts as an eye to the world and continually exhorts his slothful pal to get up to the window:
'Shorty!' he shouts.
'What?'
'Shorty, get up to your window.'
'For fuck's sake . . . I'm up, what is it?'
'Do you see the rainbow?'
'What!'
'What do you think's at the end of it?'
'Fuck off!'
'Okay, Shorty, I'll see you later.'
It's even funnier when the guy is up at his window and his mate doesn't believe him:
'Shorty? Shorty? Get up to your window.'
'I'm up at the window.'
'Shorty, get up to your window.'
'I'm up at the fuckin' window!'
At this stage you can feel the raging impatience and disbelief

in Shorty's voice:

    'Shorty, there's no need to shout . . . See the clouds. Would you say it was gonna rain?'

    'Is that what you wanted me for!'

This place sure is another world. Shorty was got up to the window after twelve the other night to see a chimney on fire!

Monday 7 May

I have Theresa Burt, one of the kindest women I know, up on Friday. She's had so many troubles and has borne them heroically and she isn't even in great health. I first met her and Bobby eighteen years ago when the eldest kids, Jackie and Judette, were only nine. They are a very close family and always looked after me.

    People – I mean lovers and partners – who are close to each other grow into each other and get to read moods and gestures and the unuttered words and know how to please (as well as rile!) their lover. In some couples this can lead to sheer boredom and an unlandscaped future of weariness. But for the lucky ones, those who live love in a state of magic, the irony of the familiarity is that there are infinite surprises to it. I am well acquainted with your humour, yet you continue to delight me and make me laugh, over and over again. There's a naturalness about us.

    I have almost finished *Journey to the End of the Night* by Louis-Ferdinand Celine. It's about 450 pages long and isn't very good, but you know what I'm like: if I start a novel I like to finish it and I'll finish this one tonight. But I'm such a slow reader and I won't pass a word whose meaning I don't know without referring to the dictionary. And then, because I have such a bad memory, I might have to look up the same word about twenty times, in several different contexts, over a period of months, or even years, before its meaning is burned into my brain. Do you believe that people can actually speed-read? I mean, digest and appreciate matter to the same degree as a slow reader? Joelle says she can speed-read, and Eileen Battersby, the literary critic, told me she read *Ulysses* in a day! (It took me four weeks!) If I could read like that I'd be flying.

Wednesday 9 May

Got the clothes parcel and your letter okay and also a nice postcard in broken English from Joelle's parents in Grenoble. I got the green polo shirt and it looks great – goes with blue jeans, doesn't it? (It's okay, Roy leaves everything out on top of my bed for me each morning so that it all matches!)

On the issue of letters: the ones I have written to you are yours to do with as you will; the ones you wrote to me are *mine* and on no account are they to be destroyed, as you suggested. They are for me to mull over in my old age and to make me smile again and swell my breast. Don't touch them or take advantage of the fact that they're in your safe-keeping! If you feel tempted, just say so and I'll have them placed out of reach (you are such an incorrigible wee girl!). You shouldn't be putting things on paper unless you can stand over them, and given the amount of back-stabbing you do there probably should be a fifty-year embargo on the release of your material!

The screws have gathered at their posts and the shout 'Unlock, C-Wing!' signals the start of a brand new day in Crumlin Road Jail.

Friday 11 May

I was shocked to learn of the death of Cardinal Ó Fiaich. The last time I was here in the Crum' two popes died in quick succession – about three weeks apart – and the loyalists were up at their doors banging and whooping. But this time they were surprisingly quiet and there was no sick triumphalism.

Gerry Adams and I met Cardinal Ó Fiaich a couple of times

at his home and we were struck by his sincerity. He was absolutely opposed to violence but at least he attempted to place armed republicanism and prison protests in a historical and political context – a point I have made in a letter to the *Irish Times*, one of whose correspondents falsely described Ó Fiaich as a hate figure to extremists of both sides in the North! In fact, in 1980 he was responsible for persuading the IRA to stop shooting screws over the battle for political status for prisoners. He spent six months attempting to persuade Humphrey Atkins to make some concessions. So, in September 1980, Atkins told him that the British government would let the prisoners wear their own clothes. O'Fiaich was delighted, sent word to the H-Blocks, headed off to Rome for a conference and while his plane was in the air the British government announced that it wasn't their own clothes the prisoners were getting but government-issue civilian-type clothes. Ó Fiaich was shattered by the duplicity. The prisoners then announced they were going on hunger strike.

Sunday 13 May
All's quiet on the western front, although there's a bizarre sound in the air, like someone calling out bingo numbers.
Later
It has now been explained. Something has happened in A-Wing and the republican prisoners, it seems, have refused to leave the canteens. (We have only one canteen here, on the Ones; over there each landing has its own separate canteen.) Four prisoners have been sent to the boards (and they are shouting '*Scéal*' to our lads on the Threes). The noise we heard was a PO calling out individual names on a Tannoy, ordering each prisoner to vacate the canteens. The night is so still that his voice carried.

While I am writing, Roy – the saint – is redesigning our picture board. Until now the photos of our loved ones have been stuck down with Ultrabrite toothpaste. His scheme is to cut little angular slits on the broadsheet background so that the photos clip in flush, just like in an album. Pride of place among Roy's photos are ones of his Nissan Bluebird Turbo, which I've caught him ogling over in bed. Of course, he's not without feeling and has managed to squeeze in one or two of Donna.

I'll be writing a wee note to my da tonight. I've some money coming from Mercier and since he and I are both Danny I'm going to ask him to convert the cheque to sterling (the exchange rate has been quite good recently). I should have about £300 to give you, to either hold or use, and I'm getting Kevin and Liam passports and giving them money for clothes and for their holidays. I know this much – it would be impossible to live as a writer (unless, of course, one was supported by a young professional lady!).

P.S. The jail is alive with banging and screaming and there are a dozen different rumours. The latest is that the loyalists have managed to get on the roof of A-Wing and are being hosed.

Tuesday 15 May

I've been moved back to A-Wing, on the Twos. I'm in the dirtiest cell in the jail: the walls are streaked with nicotine stains and the mattress is saturated with stale smoke. To complete the moan, gone is the almost suburban view from C-Wing and the chattering of various forms of birdlife. The only wildlife is squawking starlings! A few yards beyond my window are brown brick gable ends with rusty leaks and a seeping leprosy of mosses. Just visible above the gables is part of Crumlin Road Courthouse – the capital and pediment upon which stands the Statue of Justice. Only one canteen is in order here (two were smashed up by the loyalists on Sunday night). Couldn't get writing last night because, although we were told to pack at five, it was half ten before we settled in.

10.15 am

Breakfasted (porridge) and showered. The early morning routine here is chaotic so I may need you to come up later on Saturday morning if I'm to get washed. If that's inconvenient for you I'll just use the basin in the cell. I can hear cheering and singing as if there is some protest on the Crumlin Road. Roy just called me to the crack in the door to tell me that he's actually two cells above me. The people on the Crumlin Road are singing 'The Sash' so I don't think they're from the Falls!

One of my great regrets about my profile was not being able to accompany you downtown, visit a strange restaurant or go to the pictures or a theatre. But who knows, maybe some day: I wouldn't rule it out entirely. The voices beyond the wall have died away and the sound of traffic has now taken over. A city just radiates noise during the day – buses and the compression of their doors opening and closing, lorries and their hydraulics, pneumatic drills and their droning. Even my cell door has a whistle, caused by the draught. I stuff paper in it to suffocate the bastard.

9 pm

Still haven't received a letter from you. Presumably it's lying over in the censor's office in C-Wing. I got the *Irish Times* okay, at 7.30, and am not long finished reading it. I could hardly concentrate because there was another loyalist solidarity protest by Screamers outside the jail, and between that noise and the singing of 'The Sash' and other songs there was quite a din. Every now and then the loyalists would scream out their doors, '"Bangers", we're gonna kill you!' and 'You're dead!' It's when they don't shout at me that I'll begin having my dinner officially tasted, otherwise they can scream to their hearts' content. At present they are banging the doors and cheering. A bus has been burned on the Shankill Road in solidarity.

I'm reading *Jane Eyre* and have finished about 300 pages. Lord, they knew how to write in the nineteenth century – incredibly fluent and precise. It's a classic love story.

Wednesday 16 May
It's a beautiful evening outside, the colour of the sky delicately balanced between white and blue. Such a contrast with this afternoon. Just after two I went to wash socks and underpants and by accident my cell door had been left open, creating a draught (there's no glass in my window). Rain was sucked in, covering my books and soaking my bed. When I returned from my visit the sky was still leaden and there was a single roll of thunder. But soon afterwards a little sunlight had sprung on the dingy wall across from my bed and the weather improved. I stood at the window and inhaled that piquant earthy smell which sometimes arises from a pavement when it's humid. I love that smell. I first noticed it when I was about five or six and I was excited when, after a sun shower, the steam quickly rose from the ground. I think I was annoyed because my friends weren't as enthralled.

On the visit Ciaran said that Mercier had sent the cheque, as I requested, to Paddy McGrory's office. At some stage in the future I intend spoiling myself. I am going to buy an old second-hand typewriter, nothing too big or heavy, but one that I can batter away at and see the results of my effort immediately. Your role will be to bring me coffee (when you are not out working!), lean over my shoulders and make the odd suggestion while planting a kiss on my head to stop me from throwing you out of the room!

Thursday 17 May

Did you see the editorial in yesterday's *Irish News*? It was so unctuous and hypocritical. It said that the television image of Gerry Adams and Martin McGuinness receiving Holy Communion at Cardinal Ó Fiaich's funeral will have been 'deeply confusing, disturbing or offensive' but that 'it is not for anyone to stand in the place of God and to judge the fitness of another to receive the Eucharist.' Then it went on to do just that!

'For those who would justify murder then to receive the Eucharist is not the simple act of hypocrisy which it might seem . . . So it is right that we should be disturbed by yesterday's image.'

Friday 18 May

I have to stop for a second and have a sip of black coffee, for you see we have access to hot water on the landing here, which we didn't have on punishment in C-Wing. There, that's better. When I write a letter to you it may sometimes appear to be in one flow. But I often sit with the blank page before me or with items uncompleted for maybe up to half an hour just to prolong the feeling of contact. I'll get up to the window and look out. Maybe call or answer someone on the landings above or below. I'll stretch myself or lie on the bed thinking. Then I'll come back to the page and write some more. As long as the page remains on the table and there are unfilled lines left, I feel I'm in conversation with you. And I can so clearly visualise you hearing and reading them, though they are committed in silence.

Anto Murray, whose letter-writing I first mentioned to you in mid-January, told me today that he regularly writes but rarely sends the letters out. He says he writes away, free-flowing, thinking 'This is wonderful', and then when he reads over the finished product he says, 'Such a lot of crap!' and bins the letter! We had a laugh last night. Rinty McVeigh pretended to be a loyalist and sang about three or four Orange songs as the loyalists kept rhythm, tapping their doors and shouting, 'Up the UDA!' and 'Up the UVF!' at the end of each song. Our side and theirs are allotted one hour to be slopped out, three at a time, between five and seven. If we go first we've to be finished by six, and vice versa. Tonight, not all the loyalists got slopping out on time so there was a crying match. They called the screws everything. One loyalist shouted 'Pour your piss out the doors!' And another voice (a republican's) shouted 'Break your spyholes!' But then they realised they were being wound up and they settled.

I'm sleeping great over here, despite the noise of traffic. I'm like a lump of concrete until I wake at about six thirty or seven. The other night there was a grenade attack and shots fired by loyalists at the front of the jail and I slept right through it!

Saturday 19 May

I am having a little anniversary party tonight. I am all pleased for remembering the date. There are no cigars or a big or even a little spread, and you are the guest. It is the story of a troubled man and a very patient woman. It begins just after eleven o'clock on a Sunday morning, when he heads to Sevastopol Street to see a comrade, Richard, about some business. Richard's wife, Chrissie, offers the visitor a can of Harp (after all, it is late in the morning), which he drinks avidly, and this sets him off on a spree. He dumps his car and calls for friend Ted and they head off to St Paul's Club. He tries to contact his friend Kevin to urge him to come and join him because he feels that this is going to be a momentous day, that the mood of abandonment will push him to resolve the agony in his soul (though he wouldn't have been able to articulate it thus). He isn't able to reach Kevin but when Ted leaves he falls in with an old jail buddy, Seando, and at teatime Seando urges him to go home (they live in the same area). They get a taxi and arrive close to home but our friend stubbornly refuses to go. He decides to go back to Sevastopol Street to visit another acquaintance and lands in with Mrs Murphy, who instantly says 'A-ha!' and feeds him tea and sandwiches – and he has a short snore out in her yard toilet. He goes out marching again, his head swarming with a thousand thoughts, and he visits his friends the Morgans, Dan and May, in Iveagh Drive. They are going out drinking (it's the national pastime) but he falls asleep for a half-hour on their sofa then jumps to attention and goes to find them in the local community centre. Our friend by this time is a quarter human and three-quarters distillery, but courage is struggling through the haze. It appears as a little bird and he listens to it.

It says, 'You've been wanting to for ages, now is the time!'

And he answers, or blubbers, 'But look at me. Look at the state of me!'

'Never mind. Do it! Do it!'

So he pulls out coins and looks at them in the palm of his hand. He sees a ten-pence piece and he goes downstairs to the public phone – which, clearly miraculously, is working. He knows the number. He is not stupid. He memorised it, you see, because he knew he would be making this call one day. So he phoned two-three-eight-five-six-six but there was no answer. He tried again – the tones rang, the house was empty: out, out in *her* world. Maybe he was just supposed to be an alcoholic instead! So he climbed back up the stairs again for more drink. But now it didn't taste as wonderful as before and the soul battled for supremacy so that he could think. 'I'm away to make another phone call,' he announced to sundry friends. And this time the coin disappeared into the slot. He got through.

Sunday 20 May

A republican prisoner, Frankie Quinn from Dungannon, who is on the Ones below, has turned his radio up loud and sat it on the sill close to the bars so that we can hear it. Pop music and sunny Sunday afternoons were created for each other.

Tuesday 22 May

I've just finished a cup of hot coffee and I'm sweltered, even though the heating has been switched off for the summer and my window is full of holes. Kevin was up on his own – just wanted to see me on his own, although Liam was disappointed and complaining. So I sent back a message to say that we'll arrange someone to bring him up next Tuesday. Can you sort that out, love? I was glad that Kevin wanted to talk to me because I was always afraid of drift setting in and he's okay now.

I am sure this week will fly by for you, given that you have the company of an old friend. Hope she doesn't stir up homesickness! I think I would find it extremely hard to live anywhere but Belfast, or, more precisely, west Belfast. My father's people are the exact opposite and he is the only one left in Ireland. The second-eldest in his family, Eileen, married Albert, an English soldier based in Belfast's Victoria Barracks, and they settled in Bury, Lancashire. My daddy's sister, Margaret, was just sixteen years of age and had won a beauty competition when, on a visit to Eileen's, she met her future husband, Ronnie, also from Bury. They now live in Virginia, USA. When my uncle Jimmy's marriage broke down in the mid-sixties it was to Bury he headed when he sold his house. He has settled there and he and Una have one son and three daughters, whom I've never met. Then, when internment was introduced in August 1971, my granny and my uncle Gerard, my aunt Harriet and their family upped and left and bought a house – in Bury, of course! My daddy was being persuaded for years to join them and kept hesitating. I don't think my mammy would have liked England or being away from her sisters and brothers.

I just feel so much at home when, say, driving up from Dublin you reach that bend on the M1, just after Dunmurry, and Black Mountain and Andersonstown come into view.

I'm plodding my way through *The Magic Mountain*: it's about twenty novels in one. Very pedantic but some good lines: 'A man lives not only his personal life, as an individual, but also, consciously or unconsciously, the life of his epoch and his contemporaries.' It is set in a mountain-top sanatorium on the eve of the First World War. The book is written from the hero Hans Castorp's point of view. In one scene he watches a woman across a room and studies her hands as she is moving! And the description of her fingers and nails is meticulous. The scene finishes with, 'But Hans Castorp sensed rather than saw this, owing to the distance.' It's as if Mann just realised his hero couldn't possibly note such detail but threw in the qualification out of laziness rather than change his good lines.

Wednesday 23 May

It's just after seven o'clock and the noise of grinding machinery in the canteen, where repair work is continuing, is piercing my ears. I think some of the lads will be moved back to C-Wing tomorrow as their punishment is up. A few days ago Roy was moved down the landing and Butch Braniff has moved into his cell. Butch keeps shouting *Star* crossword clues out the window, expecting me to give him the answers. I heard that the loyalists got just fourteen days' punishment for wrecking the canteens.

I had a good long visit with Jim. It was good to see him again. He was saying that he never goes out socialising and is content with his life of politics, studying and training. He and I should swap places! I hope my weekend letter arrived today – from the sound of yours you're getting the blues. In these circumstances there is a real dependency on letters. I suck every one of yours bone dry.

Received a short note from Pam Brighton, who's just back from London. She said the editor of the series has read *West Belfast* and thought it was 'a wonderful, lyrical book' (perhaps I should just write songs) that would dramatise very well. That's the first hurdle over and it now has to go to the Controller of Radio 4, as do all ideas for series. She'll let me know the result of that when she gets it.

Right, I'll finish now. I am being lullabyed by a lonesome blackbird which doesn't appear to have found a partner. It is sitting on an old disused chimney.

Thursday 24 May

Well, I'm off punishment! I was given two brown paper bags in which to pack all my gear this morning after breakfast. I'm now on the Ones in a cell with a Cookstown man, Brendan Neeson, whose brother Christopher was a Sinn Fein councillor. Roy, together with about ten others, has also been moved down. So, tomorrow I should have my radio back and I can receive fruit again. Brendan smokes, and for this reason I'll be looking for a cell-swap. Maybe I'll be lucky and get moved back with Roy.

I met Alex Murphy and Harry Maguire again; they are down from the Blocks for their appeal against life sentences over the killing of the two corporals. The last time I saw them was outside St Agnes's chapel on the day of Kevin's funeral but I've known Alex since he was interned in 1973 at the age of fifteen, when he was still at school.

I heard from Bernard Fox and Seanna. They've settled in well up at the Blocks. As you know, Cleaky Clarke has cancer. They said that his morale is fine and that he knows not to expect any sympathy. According to Bernard all craic is revolving around Cleaky: 'Hey Cleaky, leave us your denim jacket', 'Leave us your shoes, we take the same size.'

Sunday 27 May

As I was saying yesterday I've lost another 6 pounds and am now 10 stone 10 pounds. I am sitting here eating chocolate biscuits and drinking coffee as the loyalists parade in the yard. (I hate militarism.)

Either the light in this cell is unusually poor or my eyesight is going, because I am experiencing double vision on the page. I think I told you Pat Sheehan has been moved to C-Wing. He wasn't at all pleased. He prefers it here. You just don't know where you are going to end up from one day to the next. In some respects it's very unsettling and frustrating but in another way a change is as good as a rest. And now I must prepare to take my leave of you again. Jail makes you an expert on the passing of time and I know that there'll be a day when we'll rummage through an old suitcase and I'll point to these words and say that I know exactly how I felt when I wrote that letter, anguishing over being parted from you, and it seems like only yesterday!

I got a cell-swap so I'm back with Roy!

Tuesday 29 May

I got called for my visit at about half two and I'm sure we got about fifty minutes. I was annoyed because the screw wouldn't let Liam sit beside me. He insisted it was the rules but it was the first time I've ever encountered it and quite clearly it can't be hard and fast. For example, if two adults and two children are on a visit there is simply no room for four on one side of the table.

June or July 1982. I am in a sleeping bag on the floor of the typesetting room of *An Phoblacht/Republican News* in Dublin. I wake up and put on the radio which I keep beside me. A love song by Foreigner:

> *I've been waiting for a girl like you*
> *To come into my life.*
> *Waiting for someone new*
> *To make me feel alive.*

The office is deserted. Everyone else went home when we finished work at around five in the morning. The sky is a wonderful blue as I lie and listen to the words. I feel really good. I get up afterwards and head down to the GPO to check the *poste restante*, feeling I won't be disappointed. I sign for the letter and read it outside in the sunlight streaming between the tall columns. I stroll to a café around the corner, order coffee and a croissant, over which I spread strawberry jam, take out the letter and read it again. And all the while, Foreigner's song is playing in my mind.

Sunday 3 June
God, it was cold last night. I wore my socks and lay in the foetal position for hours. And to think that it's June! The two houses, Numbers 17 and 2, that we lived in in Corby Way were the gable ends of a group of terraces and were freezing in the winter. At least Margaret had Geraldine to cuddle up to! I got underneath about ten heavy blankets and stayed under to stop my ears from falling off. Of course, this story can't really be appreciated without violins in the background.
7.30 pm
Not long back from association in the canteen, where I played cards, a game called Fat.

We drew. The noise of the TV always gives me a sore head. I actually feel relieved to get back to the relative peace and quiet of the cell. I am listening to some classical music.

Roy is lying on top of his bed wondering what he did to deserve being punished by a hundred-piece orchestra playing the charts of the eighteenth and nineteenth centuries! Actually, he likes a lot of it. His real problem is that he has four letters to write and can't muster the energy to do them. He says he has nothing to say. A 'mystery parcel' (a shit wrapped in a brown paper bag) has just flown past our window at a velocity of 32 feet per second. In the mornings the screws force the sex offenders to pick them up.

Wednesday 6 June
The canteens on the Twos and Threes have finally been repaired so there'll almost certainly be a move soon. However, things could be delayed as a result of new measures aimed at preventing prisoners knocking down the walls between the cells using their bed-ends. Trade screws have begun welding beds together and then bolting them to fixtures on the floor.

Three new republican remands arrived today. There may well be a military stalemate but the conveyor belt shifts non-stop, the Diplock judicial system remains firmly in place, the coloniser judging the natives, a perception that traps us, prejudicing and blinding us, making us hostile to the legitimacy the passage of time has conferred on the loyalists and their presence in Ireland. And, of course, should republicans make a move there's the real fear that, in addition to it being interpreted as a sign of weakness, any republican gesture towards accommodation or compromise could actually exacerbate the situation by encouraging the mistaken view that a little bit more repression, more intransigence, will break the republican struggle. It is so tragic and there, today, another man, an ex-RUC reservist, has been killed and his wife critically injured. Nor will Brooke's latest initiative, should it ever come to fruition, prove to be a solution: it will merely be a part of the strategy of isolating the republicans. It is a critical phase and a time for cool heads and much circumspection. I haven't a great deal of time for the minutiae of political work (I've had my fill of housing and social-security complaints at constituency level) but retain a major interest in the overall manoeuvres. If I had no conscience I could easily spend the rest of my days doing nothing but our housework and reading books and then having your slippers ready for you in the evenings. Peaceful, simple, escapist!

But I don't think you would like me: well, you still would, but maybe not as much, because I would be a different person. The unreality of the way we republicans live – our lives completely and indefinitely subordinated to the pursuit of this struggle – can sometimes come home to you with a jolt which is felt in the very foundations of the political convictions which to date have sustained you. When that happens, the principles and objectives which you embraced so nobly and passionately all those years ago begin to feel like so much dead weight – an obstacle to freedom of movement.

Really, it all comes down to 'Peace With Justice'. Irish sovereignty could secure that if the loyalists weren't so suspicious and the Free State so reactionary, not to mention unenthusiastic! Peace with justice is the objective which the methods have to be tailored to meet.

Sunday 10 June
Mass was fairly packed as a large number of men have been returned from C-Wing. Pat Sheehan's back but not Gerard Hodgins.

Books. I picked up the Thomas Mann novel – which I had discarded at 400 pages – and finished it. So, yes, I'll try *Buddenbrooks* next and *Cider With Rosie* and the book Geraldine left in for me.

Tuesday 12 June

Only three and a half weeks of the World Cup left! It's simply flying by. I'm sick of it, too. We're in the canteen for three hours – from four to seven – every second day to facilitate viewing the first match of the evening.

The two novels you sent look great. I'll start *Cat's Eye* tonight, maybe. I read a really depressing book yesterday, *The God Squad* by Paddy Doyle, about a young lad who spent his life in an orphanage and various institutions.

Got a letter from Derek Dunne. That's the third! What a conscientious man, and more than a gesture because the letter was again long and detailed. Do you have his number? If so, phone him and say I'll review the odd book for *Now* if he likes.

Wednesday 13 June

Did you read Gerald Barry's review of Gerry Adams's book, *The Street*, in the 'People' section of the *Sunday Tribune*? He was scathing: 'silly and juvenile' he called it. No matter how thick-skinned you think you are, abusive comments always hurt. But, of course, that's the price of putting yourself forward.

I see Terence O'Neill, former Stormont Prime Minister, died last night. When the civil rights movement first came on the scene there were all these new words in vogue – like 'gerry-mandering' and 'franchise'. I would go down to the Falls Library and look them up in a big dictionary in the reference section to understand what Gerry Fitt and Ian Paisley were going on about. I remember working as a waiter in the International Hotel in

1968 when Fitt came into the lounge to buy cigarettes during an election count in the City Hall. Next day in school I boasted, 'I saw somebody famous!' How naive! My family watched O'Neill's famous 'Crossroads' speech on television with rapt attention, as if the end of the world had been announced. Paisley was the main villain, followed by William Craig, John Taylor and Brian Faulkner. What's interesting is that many other names from that period surface from time to time in the banking or legal worlds – bigoted cabinet ministers disguised as latter-day neutrals.

Friday 15 June
That was a great visit today and I can't remember anything that has happened to me since, because I've angels on my feet! I'm in a real dreamy mood: whatever your drug is! And I've another fix on Monday! Roy's sitting writing a letter to his wife, whom he loves, and I steal a look at him and wonder what the future holds, how the dice will fall. I am captivated by the mystery of it all and, as I wrote to you once before, you are part of the adventure of my life.

Sunday 17 June
Well, the most popular record in Long Kesh in 1973 – 'Tie a Yellow Ribbon' by Tony Orlando and Dawn – is on the radio as I write:

> *I'm coming home, I've done my time,*
> *Now I've got to know what is and isn't mine . . .*

We used to sit glued to the TV in the hut every Thursday night watching *Top of the Pops* and ogling Pan's People (semi-clad female dancers)!

My mattress is made of rubber and it stinks, particularly in hot weather. At primary school (when nits and fleas were common!) there was always at least one boy in class who stank and who was shunned when he wasn't being persecuted. I tried sharing a desk with one such lad but I had to move away within a short time. This lad didn't even come from what was commonly called a 'dirty home'. When we passed on to secondary school he still stank and was avoided like the plague.

Do you ever wonder what happened to former school pals? I can still remember where most boys sat in our class in Glen Road CBS in our last year, 1969. Some subsequently disappeared into universities, thence abroad; two or three surfaced in jail; one went off to fly for Aer Lingus; several became insurance men and the rest disappeared into the woodwork. Oh yes, and one tried to commit suicide before having a nervous breakdown. The only member of our class whom I have met in about fifteen years is Gerry Fitzgerald, a staff photographer with the *Belfast Telegraph*, and yet I'm sure that about twenty-five out of the thirty-eight all live in or close to the west of the city. If I were trying to avoid them I'd be tripping over them.

Sunday 24 June
This place is crazy. When someone in the yard scores a goal or when something to one's satisfaction comes on the news there are shouts of 'Yee-ha!' Republicans, loyalists, crims – everybody uses the phrase and nobody knows what it means! It has triumphalist connotations but also smacks of atavism.

I must say you spoilt me last week – I got six letters between Monday and Saturday. A record! I also received another Mass bouquet from Mrs Kelly in Dungannon and a postcard from Trisha Ziff, who's on her way to Mexico from Los Angeles.

We were writing about dreams and how crazy they can be.

This must be among the weirdest I've ever had. I am in a room sitting at a table and have a blond-haired male infant on my knee, clucking at him and playing. The child has a round face but his head is unusually large – a bit like those kids with water on the brain. Anyway, he is actually Adolf Hitler as a young boy, and as he sits on my knee I turn the pages of a pictorial book which shows photographs of the victims of Auschwitz and Dachau, the dead and skeletal survivors. I point to the pictures and say, 'You will be responsible for this. Now what do you think of that?' He just looks into my face and innocently smiles and I turn to others in the room and say, 'How was it possible for this child to turn into a mass murderer?' Then I wake up!

When I was a child I could never travel in my dreams. If I was in a car which drove off I would come flying through the back window and remain rooted to the same spot. But now I can fucking fly! Am I in the right institution?

Tuesday 26 June
Our Liam is going off to the States for a month. I asked him to get me his address and I would write. On a visit he sits with his head leaning on my arm and sometimes strokes or holds my hand. Despite his age he's still very affectionate. When we used to go camping he always had to sleep beside me and would snuggle up like an infant when none of his mates or the bigger boys could see. And, of course, I find him tremendously funny. I hope he's okay. Kevin will have no problem in Corsica, having been abroad three or four times with Eurochildren since he was about nine.

Thursday 28 June
I've just moved cell. Got out of that dungeon and moved to a quieter and slightly brighter cell, still on the Ones, still with Roy.

Schubert's 'Unfinished Symphony' is on the radio. The

second movement conjures up raw feeling and the sensation of being close to a revelation of the nature of pure emotion. You glimpse an almighty depth of heaven in your soul. It leaves you close to tears.

Finished *Buddenbrooks* by Thomas Mann. It was his first novel and is much easier to read than his later books. Though I don't think he was anti-Semitic (in fact, this book was banned by Hitler and burned), I have noticed in Russian and German nineteenth-century fiction that many of the characters are dangerously casual in their anti-Semitism. Such a cultural atmosphere helped to prepare the ground for what followed. But now the memory of the victims of the Holocaust is being sullied by the behaviour of the Israeli government towards the Palestinians. Last week, with temperatures in the nineties, the Israelis cut the water supply to Jiftlik, an Arab village on the fringe of the fertile Jordan valley, as part of an ongoing campaign to force the villagers to move elsewhere. Across the main road from the village are brilliant green fields and orchards of an Israeli settlement carved out of confiscated Arab land and awash with water. To survive, the Arabs have to steal brackish water from an irrigation ditch which runs for half an hour daily. A government spokesperson, challenged by a journalist, said: 'Always the villagers try to break their own water lines.' And in South Africa prisoners threw themselves downstairs and in Castlereagh they inflicted injuries on themselves.

Almost twenty past nine and the night fleets away and soon leaves us with nothing but midnight in the palm of our hands.

Saturday 30 June
Sitting here reading a Russian novel and waiting to be called for a visit. There's a lot of screaming and shouting. Somebody shouts, 'The screws beat the bollocks out of an Orangey! Yee-

ha!' Exclamations of approval. A loyalist on the Ones whose information, like mine, is based on interpreting who is triumphalist for the moment, retorts, 'Yeah, it's something you couldn't do, you Fenian bastard!' Loyalist exclamations of approval, followed by cheers from the Fenian bastards who enjoy getting mentioned in despatches.

The loyalists, one and two at a time, are let out to the yard. Prisoners are waiting for visits. They've been waiting for them since their eyes opened this morning – or since they last said goodbye. So they're waiting for their visits and they want to be cool, calm and collected. They like being triumphalist but deep down inside they know it's a fuck-up if it has to be paid for. Visits are important to prisoners and their families. The Senior Officer in charge correctly assumes that to ensure they get their visits the prisoners, understandably, will want a return to the status quo as swiftly as possible. The workings of a jail – a microcosm of society – hinge on power-relations and some consensus.

There's restricted movement but soon things return to normal. Then we learn that it was a republican going on a visit who was attacked by loyalists!

Sunday 1 July
Happy First of July! And it rained most of the day. But now there isn't a cloud in the sky. Marvin Gaye's 'Sexual Healing' is on the radio. I climbed up to my window, only a small portion of which you can see out. Between the bars lives a tiny green spider which has so cleverly positioned his fast-food shop that little flies carried on the breeze are regularly trapped. Then the spider runs out, paralyses the fly and parcels it up with his own 'stretch and seal'. Beyond, in a small, overgrown, abandoned exercise yard, tall sedge grasses sway like ears of corn on this sunny evening.

I've had two oranges for my supper but from where I sit I can see underneath Roy's bed his four bars of Galaxy and three packets of crisps! (The metal doors are shaking on their hinges. The sectarian/political/sportsmanlike score is Cameroon 2 England 1. By the way, we're the Africans.)

Monday 2 July
What about Nelson Mandela's statement calling for the British government to talk to the IRA! The Brits have no intention of doing that – not because of the specious pretext that the IRA is a 'terrorist' organisation but because they are not prepared to change policy and they have nothing to offer. And the reason they are not prepared to change policy is because the IRA has not forced them to. Were the IRA ruthless the Brits just might find that they need to talk to them. That is the tragic irony of the situation. But fair play to Mandela for speaking his mind – as he did about Castro, Gadaffi and Arafat – and not playing to the US or European gallery.

Roy came back from punishment this morning, though he's yet to be adjudicated. He asked me did I remember what our house looked like because he had forgotten until he saw photographs of his. Maybe it's because I have an eye for detail but I can remember everything, the placing of ornaments, where things are in the study, the contents of cupboards, etc. But I can also remember the contents of the cupboards in 2 Corby Way, twenty-seven years ago, a sheaf of music sheets ('Für Elise' was one) beneath the piano stool, what the oilcloth on the kitchen floor looked like. And the 78s! Mantovani and his orchestra, Mario Lanza with 'Serenade' on one side and 'The Drinking Song' on the other, and the first rock 'n' roll records. That week that I spent on the boards in D-Wing I would zero in on an incident that happened, say, over twenty years ago, and by a process of running initial recollections back through my mind again and again more memories stirred and I was amazed at the results. At times it was eerie because for a spine-chilling split second I would be able to capture and re-experience the exact mood of that chosen moment.

Wednesday 4 July

I ran about two and a half miles and then sat down on one of three narrow benches along the wall to watch the lads playing football. Sexism from the sidelines was rampant. 'Look at the big hussy!' 'You're only a slut!'

As I watched the football, sitting with legs crossed, feeling philosophical, thinking about you and me, the people here, the world, I asked Jim O'Carroll to roll me a cigarette. And so I smoked the weed and amateurishly inhaled it, deriving slight pleasure from the dry staleness it left in my throat. In a month's time I might smoke another one, or I might never smoke one again.

Saturday 7 July

Pat and I walked the yard this evening after our run. I was saying that I'll be light on my laundry over the next three weeks while you are away and might wash any T-shirts, etc., here. He said he's in the same boat – Patricia does all his washing! I didn't know that before. Outside, Pat lived with his parents and Patricia with hers (her father is handicapped from a road accident). Pat's afraid to send his clothes out in case his brother Kevin steals them!

With Roy I played chess and won, thus reversing his 'lucky' streak of the past four days. And now I'm off to read *The Fortunes and Misfortunes of the Famous Moll Flanders*, a fine girl if ever there was one! A little adage from *Moll:* 'She is always married too soon who gets a bad husband, and she is never married too late who gets a good one.'

Wednesday 11 July

There is a massive din in here right now. Earlier, we had a meeting in the canteen and it was decided, seeing that it was the Twelfth, that there would be none of the usual cat-calling during the loyalist sing-song. But when the lads got behind their doors all good intentions went out the window because there is now nothing but screams, shouts, boos, wolf-calls, whistling, drumming and beating to drown out the loyalist concert. I've no doubt that this will go on all night. One of the songs the loyalists sang was to the air of that shanty 'What Shall We Do With the Drunken Sailor?' but with the lyrics:

> *What will we do with the Fenian bastards?*
> *What will we do with their wives and kids?*
> *Burn! Burn! Burn the bastards!*
> *Burn! Burn! Burn the bastards!*
> *Burn! Burn! Burn the bastards, early in the morning!'*

Wednesday 18 July

I had a fifty-minute visit with Kevin today. He came back from Corsica last Sunday night: he had a great time and didn't want to come home. His party was returning to the villa from a disco at one in the morning in a minibus. He stopped the bus and told the driver to go on without him and walked the remaining eleven miles, enjoying the balmy air and moonlit night. He eventually arrived back at the village as the sun was rising.

Friday 20 July

We were up in court today and got our forensic reports. You couldn't ask for a better report but because of who I am it is debatable to what use it can be put. Here's the summary: '1. Nothing was found to indicate that Daniel Morrison had been in close recent contact with Alexander Lynch. 2. Nothing was found to indicate that Daniel Morrison had been recently inside 124 Carrigart Avenue. 3. Nothing was found to indicate that Daniel Morrison had been at the rear of 124 and 126 Carrigart Avenue.'

I was arrested in 126. Debris from my trainers 'was compared with the gritty substance from the footprint at the rear of 126 Carrigart Avenue and was found to be different in terms of microscopic appearance and density pattern.'

So there you have it. I'll be seeing Barra tomorrow to determine its full importance. I can't deny that it has made me perky – while the facts of the case remain essentially unchanged.

Wednesday 25 July

I'm waiting to be called for a wash. Things have been delayed because the loyalists have wrecked the canteens and the slop houses on the Twos and Threes. The big news last night was that landmine attack in Armagh which killed three RUC men and a Catholic nun. There's big flak over it, though being in here slightly distances you from the demoralising consequences.

It's Paddy Murphy's birthday today. He is fifty. We arranged for notices to be placed in the *Andersonstown News* and for him to receive birthday cards from the Press Centre and Sinn Fein councillors. He has no relatives. He was all chuffed and had the cards spread out over the spare bed and was calling passersby into his cell to see them.

Did you know that our Margaret is coming here in late August or early September to celebrate her fortieth? We must get her something. She was always the most extrovert of our family. When she was a kid she and her friend Patsy rode to school on two invisible horses, which they left grazing in a field until lunchtime, when they rode home again! Patsy's mother had bad nerves and died suddenly of a heart attack when Patsy was about twelve, leaving her to look after her father. By that stage we had left Corby Way for Iveagh Parade and Patsy used to come down the road and often stayed with us. One night she left us to go home but couldn't get in her front door as it was barred. She went to the back door but something hard was blocking it. She pushed and got in, only to discover her father dead. He had gassed himself and had a photo of Patsy and her mother by his side. My mammy was prepared to take Patsy in but an older sister who lived in Glenavy insisted she go live with her. I don't think she was happy there. As soon as she was old enough she got out, married an older mate of mine and in 1971 went to live in Australia and not once came back, as far as I know.

I have just written to an old man called James Nolan whom I may have told you about. He was a railway worker with Great Northern Railways in Monaghan. It was raining one day and he sat underneath a dripping tank for shelter as he ate his lunch. This was around 1962. He took ill and the doctor diagnosed flu and gave him a penicillin injection. Suddenly, within hours, his condition deteriorated and the doctor rushed him to Cherry Orchard Hospital in Dublin. He had picked up a polio bug from the infected water in the tank. This was not in itself very serious but the penicillin injection had the effect of rapidly spreading the polio through all his muscles and he was paralysed from the neck down. There was nothing they could do. He had three daughters, all under four years of age, and a young wife. He was never to go home again.

During the hunger strike I was doing a lot of running about and I suppose I was fairly vulnerable to whatever was going around. In early June our Kevin had diarrhoea and he turned out to be jaundiced. About six weeks after he had been sick – in fact, on the day of Joe McDonnell's funeral, I felt a terrible pain in my gut and could hardly walk. I went to the doctor, who diagnosed infectious hepatitis and wanted to admit me to Belvoir immediately. (I didn't feel that I would be safe there and would have ended up on top of an Eleventh Night bonfire, still in my pyjamas!) The doctor said that the hepatitis had been incubating for about six weeks. Dave O'Connell arranged instead for me to be taken to Cherry Orchard Hospital and it was there that I met James Nolan.

James had been in an iron lung but his chest and lung muscles had all wasted away. He had a tracheotomy, from which ran a flexible, plastic cable to a pump which made this loud, compressing clatter every two seconds. Every half-hour, twenty-four hours a day, a nurse had to insert a tube into his lungs and drain them of fluid. This kept him alive. He had been in the same bed since 1962, in the same ward, looking out on a bit of a field as the seasons changed and melted into years. But he loved life and showed no bitterness for the way the cards had been dealt. When I was there travellers' kids were racing ponies up and down the field.

James is another of my heroes. I can't remember if I was in hospital for a fortnight or a month but as soon as I was allowed up he called me to his bed. He said, rather conspiratorially, 'I know who you are. And I recognised the man who brought you in here.' He asked me to look under his pillow and there I discovered a copy of Bobby Sands's *Prison Poems,* for which I had written the introduction. James and I played chess and had long conversations, and at night a visitor smuggled a small bottle of whiskey in to him which he drank through a straw. When I was in the USA or Canada I sent him postcards; in fact, any time I was abroad I always sent him a card, which he added to a huge picture board of other postcards people had sent him from places he could only imagine. About three or four years ago I brought Gerry Adams out to meet him, and James was very pleased. In my recent letter I told him he would be getting no postcards this year and I brought him up to date with all that is happening.

Saturday 28 July

It's about half past eight, Saturday night, and by the time I finish this letter you will be back in Ireland, and by the time you read it we will have had our visit. You said that you hoped there is an afterlife – in respect of your grandmother seeing her grandchild. Of course there is! There is a good God and there is a wonderful heaven but you don't have to believe in it to get there. You just have to try your best. Although I go to Mass in here and might surprise you with the extent of my belief, I resent the arrogance of the Catholic Church (and other religions), which abrogates to itself the title of the one true faith. It is so elitist and exclusivist.

Wednesday 1 August

Well, my love, it was great seeing you again, though your candour – wishing you had stayed longer with your folks – while understandable, came too early! I can't complain. Anyway, I put in a different day from the one expected. That is only natural. The stakes and investment of feelings are high. But there is no substitute for reality.

I started the Mandela biography. It's quite a good book and the ANC certainly strikes me as being like the Republican Movement: in-fighting, splits, personality clashes and incompetence! And wrong decisions! For example, in one case they called off a transport boycott but it continued because it had public support, and because of the wrong decision their credibility was damaged. And was Nelson a philanderer! While he was married (the first time) 'he was extremely attractive to women,' writes his biographer, Fatima Meer, 'and he was easily tempted by them.' He believed in passing liaisons! His wife withstood all the affairs until it became too much.

'There was also another woman,' says his ex-wife, 'and this one started coming home, walking into our bedroom, following him to the bathroom.' She demanded an explanation but he was enraged at his wife and moved his bed into the sitting room.

Having read over this letter I think it is fairly crappy and without a swing. Maybe it's the heat. Maybe I'm feeling sorry for myself. That's no way to end a letter, Dan! Nope. Let me put my arms around you and give you a big comforting hug. We is here to stay!

Thursday 2 August
When I returned to the wing after the visit the Ones were flooded: the loyalists smashed all the sinks on the Twos and Threes as well as pulling the showers from the wall. They are also slopping out underneath their doors. Felt exuberant after today's visit – I just soared through the heavens like a swallow on the wing.

Saturday 4 August
I see the *Irish News* published my small feature on childhood summers.

Young Emmanuel Marley's girl, aged seventeen, is in Maghaberry charged with possession of a bomb on board an airport bus several months ago. You probably heard about it on the news. He got a visit with her yesterday (he was taken to Maghaberry) and came back with a black neck covered in lovebites! He is a fairly handsome youth, the same stature as our Kevin, though more muscular, and he is perpetually smiling. In many ways he reminds me of Jimmy Quigley: he has the same sparkling eyes and a thick lower lip always hanging open, as if to say, 'Right, where are we going next?' He's only nineteen and is probably facing a sentence of at least fifteen years.

I am almost finished the Mandela book. I was impressed with the man before I read this biography but his strength and humanity would leave you breathless. Undoubtedly he is a great person. But you can also see the man. A couple of letters to Winnie are quoted: 'I have been fairly successful in putting on a mask behind which I have pined for the family, alone, never rushing for the post when it comes until somebody calls out my name. I also never linger after visits, although sometimes the urge to do so becomes quite terrible. I am struggling to suppress my emotions as I write this letter.

'Whenever I write you, I feel that inside physical warmth that makes me forget all my problems. I become full of love.'

Then he talked on other occasions about his doubts: 'You come face to face with time and there is nothing more terrifying than to be alone with sheer time. Then the ghosts come crowding in. They can be very sinister, very mischievous, raising a thousand doubts in your mind about the people outside, their loyalty. Was your sacrifice worth the trouble? What would your life have been like if you hadn't got involved?'

Monday 6 August

Pat Sheehan went off the cigarettes while Patricia was away but broke at the three-week barrier, which he seems unable to get past. Meantime, however, his family continued to send him up cigarettes, which he put into the landing dump (for emergencies, etc.). The honorary position of quartermaster had been given to Paddy Murphy: there's little work involved – looking after some spare tea bags, two pounds of sugar and loose tobacco, etc. Pat is now back on the fags, and when he went to Paddy Murphy to retrieve some of his cigarettes (calculated as being about 200 in number), there wasn't one left! Jim O'Carroll told me that

Paddy's been smoking like a trooper the past three weeks and handing out cigarettes left, right and centre! What a man!

Wednesday 8 August

I hope everything goes off quietly tonight at the bonfires and that there is no trouble. I worry a great deal about Kevin and Liam, especially knowing that the cops are interested in venting their sectarianism on republicans and their relations, and tonight they can do it under the guise of 'bottles having been thrown'. Prior to the introduction of internment, 'Bonfire Night' was the fifteenth of August (Our Lady's Day) and was just a social or community gathering when wee lads asked girls for a kiss! There were rarely any cops about. However, in Andy Boyd's *Holy War in Belfast* there are references to sectarian clashes on the fifteenth of August in the late nineteenth century. After 1971 the fifteenth bonfire was subsumed into the ninth of August celebrations of resistance. The Catholic Church in the North was probably glad to see it disappear as it was an embarrassment to them. There are none in the Free State, as far as I know.

There have been fun and games in here again. At about half four yesterday a number of republicans gained access to a loyalist cell and attacked two prisoners. Then at seven o'clock the loyalists smashed up the canteens on the Twos and Threes, setting fire to our brand new £350 Hitachi remote-control TVs and pulling out the sinks. Next thing all I heard was 'Eeeee-awww, eeeee-awww' and I looked out through the jamb of the door and saw the fire brigade! Our lads kept up the 'Eeeee-awww's but in their hearts they hoped it was really super-duper IRA Volunteers dressed up as firemen come to rescue them!

More sinks were smashed this morning and the water was turned off for a while.

Roy says that Donna is looking for a contact number for that fortune-teller that Jackie and the Burts kept in wages throughout

Zack's remand period. Next time you are speaking to them try to get the number. Roy's mother and sister are both enthusiastic as well. They'll all go together some afternoon if they can arrange it.

Saturday 11 August

It's like the proverbial Tower of Babel here tonight. It seems that the loyalists have called off their no slop-out protest so they're getting dog's abuse from the republicans for having no stamina! Squeaky, effeminate voices (republicans) are declaring, 'No surrender. No surrender.' Then a thunderous voice screams at the loyalists, 'Youse have no balls! No balls!' And another taunts, 'No country, bastards!' It goes on and on and on. Only occasionally does a loyalist crack up and hazard a reply, and this incurs a greater stream of abuse.

One of the loyalists here is really heavy – very, very fat. As he was walking down the landing one of the lads shouted out the door: 'Fuck! The last time I seen anything as fat as him Gregory Peck was shooting harpoons at it!'

Did I tell you what Liam said on Thursday's visit? I said that I had just finished a biography of Nelson Mandela and Liam asked, 'Will you get any money for it, da? When's it coming out?'

I have almost finished reading *Granta 32*. Trisha Ziff got Bill Buford, the editor, to put me on the subscription list. *Granta*, as well as carrying fiction and non-fiction, also publishes photographs. In this edition there are pictures from a small village in Moravia. Two of these show a couple who appear to be very poor. In the first they are walking along a road; he is about eight feet in front of her and is looking suspiciously at the camera. She is staring in front, wearing loose slacks, and is big-bellied, well into pregnancy. (Sometimes pregnant women can look dignified and beautiful, and sometimes gross, as if their body has been invaded and colonised. This woman has all the appearance of a victim.)

But the second photograph is great! The man in his bedraggled peasant clothes, now a proud father, is holding his half-naked newborn baby aloft and has a big smile across his face. The mother, in the same clothes as before but with her body shrunken, stands a few feet away, her hands by her side and her head cocked at an angle, smiling indulgently and with such simple happiness that you can almost feel their pride at what they have begot.

Friday 17 August
The trade screws have started sealing up the jambs of our doors with metal strips. It used to be that you could see out the gap on the hinged side and pass magazines or papers through, but all that has changed this week. The gap represented no security risk – men shouted abuse, okay, or sang out of it at nights as well – but the sealing-up of that strip has made the cell more claustrophobic.

Vivaldi's *Four Seasons* is on at the Proms as I write. I am not quite sure when I fell in love with that music but it was used in a 1971 television series about the life and times of Giacomo Casanova. Jimmy Quigley and I used to watch it every week – plenty of nude scenes! Anyway, when Jimmy was interned on the Maidstone ship I bought him a book on Casanova and sent it to him. He was later transferred to the Crum' and then released but in late 1973 I came across the very book in Long Kesh with my inscription to him, almost a year after he was dead. Vivaldi published the *Four Seasons* in 1725, the year that Casanova was born. Casanova led an exciting life and once escaped from jail by going through the ceiling of his cell!

So this music brings back many memories, old ones and later

ones. It is joyous, sexy and sad – a pot-pourri of life.

Sunday 19 August
If there is one thing last year in Eastern Europe should have
taught us it was the bankruptcy of dogmatism, of communism,
which couldn't put food on the table. The lesson has certainly
helped me rethink my politics and taught me to be more
pragmatic and realistic in terms of our own struggle. If we all
lower our demands and our expectations a peg or two we might
find more agreement. Politically, we might be able to agree upon
a society in which to live in relative harmony; who knows?

Our canteen is fixed again. All metal-frame chairs and tables
have been removed and replaced with tawdry white plastic patio
chairs and tables (with little holes in the middle for parasols).
The sand and palm trees arrive next week.

In the last page of your letter you have tried to explain your
frustration and anger of late. I understand fully. Sometimes I
forget about 'the wider picture' also and it can make me ratty.
But mostly I think I keep things in perspective, otherwise I'd
blame myself rather than the British government for the situation
we find ourselves in!

Tuesday 21 August
Nothing much happened today, so instead I'll tell you about my
bedrooms! When we moved to 2 Corby Way in 1957 my
bedroom was at the back of the house, next to the gable, and
I could see south Belfast and on the Twelfth the tents of the
Orangemen at Finaghy Field (and hadn't a clue what that was
all about). I could hear the whistles of the trains approaching
the various halts at Finaghy and Musgrave. Later, I moved into
the front room, from where I could look upon the impressiveness
of Black Mountain. I was quite religious and took in far too

much than was good for me. I heard what ascetics had endured for the glory of God and secretly put on top of my bed a piece of hardboard, which I lay upon shivering all night! When that didn't chasten me I would drop salt into my eyes to make them sting! The greatest times I had in that bedroom followed the arrival of my first valve radio: a big wireless which my uncle Gerard gave me when I was about eight.

My granny Morrison, late grandad (of whom I have vague memories) and Gerard were 'dealers'. They prosperously dealt in second-hand clothes, travelling the markets, Portadown, Newry, etc.; they still trade in England but now deal in new clothes. Anyway, Gerard had picked up this radio (the first of many he gave me) and I date my fondness for music and my abandonment of asceticism from then!

Saturday 25 August

A Fleetwood Mac concert is being broadcast live on the radio right now. Their first two numbers were from the *Rumours* album and, although it was issued in 1977 or 1978, their attraction for me are the memories those songs recall of your place in Toronto in 1982. Your apartment was like a garret in a quiet backwater in which I felt very comfortable and secure and where I could have a respite from the bleak realities of my world.

Mr Brian Keenan should be back in Ireland tonight, God bless him! He has come through hell in Beirut and by the sound of him he has survived. One of the American hostages, when Keenan went on hunger strike, explained to his kidnappers that it was the Irish who invented the hunger strike. He explained about Bobby Sands and Margaret Thatcher, although it wasn't clear what concessions Keenan was granted for calling it off.

A Prison Journal

Sunday 26 August
I saw Brian Keenan on breakfast TV and was thrilled for him, especially when he raised his hands above his head, clenched them together and shook them to indicate defiantly that he had survived and that he was walking on Irish soil: it was real and not a dream – he was home.

Sean Cronin had a brilliant article in Saturday's *Irish Times* commenting on North American television's reporting of the Gulf crisis, the journalists all assuming the justice of the US's cause and becoming government spokespersons when interviewing, for example, the Iraqi ambassador to the USA. Hussein is certainly a mass murderer but he just lacks the slickness of other mass murderers.

Thursday 30 August
I wonder did you have the opportunity of listening to the Brian Keenan press conference from Dublin Castle which was broadcast live on Radio Ulster and RTE? He was very emotional and often broke down. I listened with bated breath. His diction was perfect, the description of imprisonment horrific and the anecdotes hilarious and very human. But the solid bond between him and the other hostages was unmistakable. Undoubtedly, he left part of his soul behind in Beirut. I am sure he, above all, would appreciate the quote at the front of David Beresford's book: 'We were more than blanketmen: we were brothers.'

Sunday 2 September
Sunday in here insists on putting you through every minute and every hour. Monday also crawls, and life begins with the return of visits on Tuesdays.

Tuesday 4 September

It's getting quite chilly in here. There's not a thread of summer sunlight left. Soon the heating will be switched on again and our evening association will be switched from the yard to the canteen.

I had a good visit today with Timothy O'Grady and Jim. It was good seeing Tim again. He's writing a piece about here for *Granta*. Couldn't give either of them my truly undivided attention so it was a bit frustrating.

Wednesday 5 September

About forty of us stood under the corrugated-metal shelter in the yard from ten to eleven forty-five while the rain danced around us. It was too wet to walk and because of puddles in the shelter we couldn't even play cards on the ground but we were entertained the whole time by Rinty McVeigh, whose every facial expression is comical. Rinty was arrested in Stewartstown along with Griz McKee and Jimmy McShane. Before that he served about six years in the Blocks. His repertoire consists of ridiculing himself for being so stupid as to end up in jail again. And he goes on and on and leaves everybody in stitches. He pretends to be a complete cynic: 'What are you, Rinty?' he asks himself aloud. 'Rinty, you're a dickhead. You've a brain in prime condition, never been used, never out of the wrapper. A fuckin' dickhead, that's what you are!'

We were out in the yard again from five until seven tonight. The drizzle stopped at about a quarter past six and I went running. Pat stayed with me until lap twenty-one and I carried on until I finished about forty-five. To walk around the yard on one's own is deemed an act of eccentricity or a sign that you are heavy-whacking it, but when I am running on my own I love it. I seem to be able to escape my surroundings. The only noise comes from the pace of my feet breaking the ground and from regular breathing, and there's a sort of stillness inside me, as if my mind is being gently flushed.

Do you remember about six months ago I wrote about a prisoner in B-Wing called Shorty who performed concerts out his cell window and who used to have these serious (but extremely funny) conversations with the prisoner in the adjacent cell? Well, he was sentenced, did his time, was released, but is now in again, serving six months for stealing six pairs of jeans, and is working as an orderly here. Tonight he sang 'Nothing Compares 2 U' and then he continued:

'I would now like to sing Eric Clapton's "You Look Wonderful Tonight".'

He sings the twanging guitar bit, the first and second lines, but is then interrupted by another prisoner: 'Fuck up!'

'I don't know that one . . . "*brushes her long blonde hair* . . . "'

'Fuck up, you bastard!'

'My ma and da were engaged . . . "*And when I tell her* . . . "'

'Fuck up!'

'Fuck up, yourself! If Johnny Cash can sing to prisoners then so can I!'

And Shorty continued, to eventual loud applause.

Thursday 13 September
Finished *The Book of Laughter and Forgetting* by Milan Kundera, and what a lot of balls it was. He has an infuriating habit of insinuating himself into the narrative and changing tenses back and forth in the same chapter. Imagine Alfred Hitchcock coming in front of the camera four or five times during one of his films not only to tell you that the film wasn't real and not to believe a word of it but to wax lyrical about the rough times he has had in his career. Well, that's what Kundera does.

Over 2,000 years ago the Empress of China was drinking tea

one day when a moth cocoon fell into her cup. The tea melted the glue binding the cocoon and silk began unravelling. And that's how silk was discovered. One day in a far-off land, years and years ago it seems now, I was drinking coffee when this girl fell into my cup and our lives immediately began ravelling. And that's how *love* was discovered!

Sunday 16 September
I was listening to the radio late last night and heard on the news that a number of warders and an RUC man had been kidnapped at Killeen, presumably by the IRA. It was a major talking point over breakfast and in the yard. The warders were released and I presumed that the RUC man had been killed. Nearly everyone here thought it would be far better if he was released – for a host of reasons. There can never be enough demonstrations of mercy in war.

We came in early from the yard and got watching most of the All-Ireland football final between Cork and Meath. At half-time the Artane Boys Band accompanied this fella who sang paeans to both counties. He wore a sky-blue suit, a tie made up from both teams' colours and stood on a small platform advertising the ESB! He crooned like the last singer in the Pigeon Club on a Saturday night. But he sang to enthusiastic applause and I suspect they had to drag him off so that the second half could commence. The stuff he crooned sounded really mournful: an indicator of our history. An English writer, G. K. Chesterton, once remarked about the Irish: 'All their wars are merry, and all their songs are sad.' Well, that's not true but it has a germ of truth. The only way the natives could tolerate successive defeats was to celebrate them and put a philosophical smile on the face of woe and humiliation. Republicans now are fed up glorifying past defeats and are determined to show something substantial for the sacrifices. I can't see it being resolved until, as I said before, everybody agrees to come down a few rungs.

Tuesday 18 September

Got a letter from Martin Meehan, who is in H-4 up at the Kesh. He recently produced the play *Executions* by Ulick O'Connor and part of it was filmed by a BBC camera crew for use in a documentary! I wonder was it Peter Taylor's *Inside Story* team. Anyway, Martin sent me a 'reporter's' account of the preparations and the performance. When the Block first heard of Martin's idea all the men reported in sick or developed stammers. But he was persuasive and eventually 'there were more men in the canteen than were needed for the making of *Ben Hur*. And with the money that was spent on refreshments, Charlton Heston could have been hired for the leading part.' The actors suffered stage fright but Martin told them to relax and be their normal selves. 'But Martin, how can we be our normal selves when we're acting someone else?' they asked!

Apparently, it went off with only a minor hitch and at the end Martin B. de Mechan climbed up on the stage and sang 'Take It Down From the Mast'! Nine years ago the prisoners were on the blanket protest, were denied their own clothes and stood in cells covered in their own excrement. Now, they are wearing not only their own clothes but also costumes which they made themselves and are staging a play about the IRA and the Civil War.

Thursday 20 September

I have learnt how to roll up the precious moments of a visit into a parcel of memories which I carry around and unwrap at will to savour again the spirit of your presence. That's how you keep me company. That's what I am doing now as I sit at this table writing.

I had a really rough sleep last night in which I continually replayed an agonising game of chess I had lost earlier. And in another scene I was arrested by soldiers in Derry in the most incriminating of circumstances. In this nightmare my overwhelming concern was that it was now inevitable we would be breaking up!

Monday 24 September
Shortly after I began to run around the yard today there was a heavy, concentrated downpour and I was drenched right through. But it was thrilling – like running through the waves at Iniscrone with you on that night in August 1988; the waves crashing around us in garlands of foam, tasting the brine, body goose-fleshed, conscious of your bones chilled but not caring a damn because we were free below that panorama of leadened heavens and endless shoreline.

And God pulls the clouds apart with his fingers, sticks his big face through, smiles and winks and comments in a Barry Fitzgerald accent (straight out of *The Quiet Man*), 'Dan, me man! You sure know how to tickle a girl's fancy!'

I see from your letter that the folks have offered you a ticket for Christmas. Should I still be here and if it is convenient work-wise I think you should take the opportunity to have a wee rest.

Thursday 27 September
We had a laugh in the canteen this morning and there was hardly a dry eye in the house. Shorty, one of the orderlies, was getting released today. He's the guy who does all the singing. Well, one of the lads did a brilliant drawing of a Celtic cross surrounded by the flags of the four provinces and it carried a dedication to him, which we all autographed. We called him in from the kitchen area and I presented it to him and we pretended to pose

for an official photographer. He was humbled and shattered and made a wee speech about always treasuring the scroll and he would never forget 'the men behind the wire'! Then he sang a song, a sentimental republican ballad, 'The Sniper's Promise', the chorus of which goes:

Oh mama, mama, mama, comfort me
For I know these awful things have got to be.
But when the war of freedom has been won
I promise you I'll put away my gun.

He was called for an encore and sang 'Two Sweethearts', and the words went something along the lines of:

One is my mother, God bless her, I love her,
And the other is my sweetheart.

We were speechless.

Tomorrow, to the day though not the date, is Jimmy Quigley's anniversary. I was sitting in a car outside the dole office in Frederick Street waiting on a mate of mine, Kieran Meehan, who was signing on, when news came on the radio of a shooting in the Lower Falls. For some reason Jimmy immediately sprung to mind. When we were driving back up Divis Street we stopped a fella who told us he had heard that it was a lad called Quigley who had been killed – Jimmy Quigley. I just went home and lay on top of my bed for hours.

I had first met him during the curfew in July 1970. Then, when I changed from St Mary's Grammar to St Peter's Secondary in September 1970, I found that he was in the year below me. He served nine months up in St Pat's Home for rioting and possession of an acid bomb and from the time of his release in

1971 we were buddies. He slept on the floor in my bedroom and sometimes I stayed in his mother's flat in Whitehall Row in Divis Flats. Down there it was terrifying to be stopped by the Brits late at night because you'd be routinely punched about.

Jimmy was interned for a few months and we had a great party the night of his release. He hung around Beechmount but got fed up around about July 1972 and went back down the road. It was off him that I used to bounce my moral uncertainties about the war.

The only other person to whom I have felt so close and with whom I felt a spiritual harmony was Kevin Brady. Jimmy I had the pleasure of knowing him for just two years, and I knew Kevin for about four. Jimmy and I would laugh our heads off for hours on end and my mammy used to shout from her bedroom for us to keep it down. Conversation with Kevin was just as joyous but more mature, and we had long talks on our journeys around the North. When Kevin was driving I sometimes would steal a look at him and think to myself, you're a dead-on guy, a good person.

I feel quite lonely without them, in the sense that I've lost them as close friends and confidants as well as comrades. Have you ever been so close to a friend that you felt you could touch the very heart of their goodness and that a bond other than the candours of friendship joined you?

I think that telling you all the things I miss about 'us' only upsets you . . . and you have become weary (or case-hardened) about hearing all the things I swear we'll do in the future! Tough! I haven't even started!

Monday 1 October
I'm glad you introduced yourself to Mrs Brady. Isn't she great? I remember being up with her one night and she told me about her mother's life in Donegal and how poverty forced many

people to emigrate and how some, including her own mother's brother, were never heard of again. She is very kind and without any bitterness, despite Kevin's death. And she is very strong: I think she gets that from her religion. She used to sprinkle holy water over Kevin and me when we left the house! Anyway, if you ever do call up to see her some evening you will not be bored. She can't always express herself in English and breaks into Irish, then she realises you don't understand what she means and she struggles to find English alternatives! Of course, she'll talk a lot about Kevin, and your conversation yesterday helps her rather than upsetting her. When you talk about somebody you keep them alive.

Roy is sending me (schoolboy) jets with messages written on their wings. Earlier, in the canteen, he was going around setting fire to newspapers people were reading!

Nicky Campbell, a BBC Radio 1 presenter, has just played Christy Moore's new single, 'Welcome to the Cabaret', which is Number 1 down south. He received that many phone calls that he is playing it again! What is amazing is that it is being played at all, because among those Christy is welcoming to the Cabaret are 'those on the run; Sinn Fein too'! I was telling Roy that we went to Moving Hearts concerts two nights in a row in the Baggot Inn, they were that good. He was really envious. I told him that he could look forward to camping and *fleadh ceoils* and concerts and restaurants and cinemas and standing kissing under broken drainpipes in the pouring rain and he swears he'll do all those things except jump into the Atlantic because, as he says, 'I cannay swim.'

Thursday 4 October

I had the trial papers served on me yesterday by Detective Inspector Tim McGregor and have been working on them since.

Barra needs them as soon as possible. Of course, the bulk of them do not apply to me. Nor am I mentioned in Sandy Lynch's statement. Two Brits, who were brought into the kitchen of the house in which I was arrested, say that I was the person they saw leave through the back door of 124 Carrigart Avenue. One of them said it was a man in his 'late forties'! Thanks!

By the way, the DPP has dropped the IRA membership charge (big deal). As I was leaving I heard McGregor say to the other RUC officer, 'That fella's lost a powerful lot of weight.'

I sent a short letter to the *Irish Times* drawing attention to the fact that no one from the Progressive Democrats or the Dublin government attended the funerals of the two young joyriders, Karen Reilly and Martin Peake, shot dead last week by the Paras in west Belfast, though representatives had attended the funeral of Detective Constable Louis Robinson, the RUC man abducted and killed on the border two weeks ago by the IRA. I also asked why, when referring to west Belfast, the statements from the MP for the area, Gerry Adams, always were in second place to those from an SDLP councillor, Joe Hendron! They didn't publish my last letter, which attacked the revisionism of columnist Kevin Myers. A wise old saying: 'Never let the sun go down on your wrath.'

Saturday 6 October
A little bit of a poem by Vikram Seth called 'All You Who Sleep Tonight':

> *All you who sleep tonight*
> *Far from the ones you love*
> *No hand to left or right,*
> *And emptiness above –*

Know that you aren't alone.
The whole world shares your tears,
Some for two nights or one,
And some for all their years.

Barra called up this afternoon. He says we'll be given no notice of Sandy Lynch appearing, that the Director of Public Prosecutions, without using the Voluntary Bill of Indictment, may attempt to have Lynch's statement entered without him being present and that, even if he does appear and is an unsatisfactory witness, it is highly unlikely that a lowly magistrate would have the courage or the independence to throw out his evidence. In other words, we shall be returned for trial. Paddy McGrory is still not well so I don't know if he will be representing Jim, Danny and myself.

Sunday 7 October
Roy's been a virgin for a year now and he's no closer to God. It went so quickly, he says, you wouldn't see it.

This is going to be a long week, waiting for the preliminary enquiry. The way I look at it is that if Lynch had changed his mind about giving evidence we would have heard before this, as an eleventh-hour rethink is highly unlikely. We were joking about how hope springs eternal and you just keep postponing the hour of release with explanation after explanation, after three months, after six months, the PE! Jokingly thinking ahead, Jim O'Carroll remarked (shortly before his body was discovered swinging from the light socket), 'It's a cert we'll get out at the appeal!'

Monday 8 October

Last night there was a ghost on the Twos. Roy's co-accused, Seamy Doherty, woke up in the middle of the night to discover a figure sitting at the end of his bed. It then advanced into his face, sidestepped him and disappeared. He woke up his cellmate, shouting 'Did you see that? Did you see that?' His cellmate told him to fuck off and do his whack and if he ever tried to pull a stunt like that again (he sleeps without underpants) he'd report him to the OC. Round about the same time Seany Adams (who is on the Threes) swears that he felt as if something got into his bed, and he broke out in a cold sweat. He thought no more about it until this morning, when he got out of bed – and so did a mouse.

Tuesday 9 October

Poor Donna. After her visit here last Friday she missed the train to Derry by a minute. She then rushed to Botanic Station and missed it again. A button on the epaulette of her coat came off, a button on her skirt came off and the zip broke. She had to stand in the station for two hours, and when she phoned the taxi firm that her da works in it took forty-five minutes to come to the station in the Waterside. She got home after nine o'clock, almost twelve hours after she had left Derry. That cell door might as well be a magnifying glass for how a prisoner views woe and experiences frustration.

I have had some fun with the Schubert postcard you sent me. Lads come into the cell (as occasionally happens – to view each other's picture boards), stare and scrutinise Schubert and ask who is it:

'That's a fuckin' disgrace,' I say. 'You call yourself a republican and you don't know who that is!'

'Is it Robert Emmet?'

'Nope.'

'Is it Thomas Davis?'

'Go away and don't come back until you've learnt something about your country's history.' So they shamefacedly withdraw, tossing out all the names of nineteenth-century republicans as they go!

Sunday 14 October

I heard on the news that tonight sees the last sailing of the Belfast to Liverpool ferry – the end of an era. You often used to hear the saying 'He took the boat to England' in answer to 'Where's such-and-such-a-one this weather?' There were two ferries – the Heysham and the Liverpool (for the Midlands or London). Because my da's relatives lived in the Manchester area it was usually the Heysham boat we got, arriving in England about six o'clock in the morning, when it was always freezing cold. Then there was a train journey through towns with evocative-sounding English names such as Morecombe, Lancaster and Preston. I loved that sea crossing and could never sleep, even when we had money for berths. I remember going over with my da for a holiday in 1970, and when we returned a friend of mine, Gregory Fox, had been sentenced to six months for rioting during the curfew and it was the whole talk of the district! The Heysham ferry eventually stopped because of the fall-off in passengers, and now the Liverpool service is gone.

About ten years ago on the Dublin-to-Belfast train I went to the toilet, having had a few drinks at the bar. We were approaching Portadown and the bar was closing for the customs check. There was this anxious-looking passenger with his head stuck out the window. He turned to me and said, 'Are we nearly there? Isn't it late?' I told him we wouldn't be in Belfast for another half-hour. 'Belfast!' he exclaimed. 'I thought this was the train to Dublin!' He almost had a nervous breakdown and I tried to console him. He said it was too late, he had fucked up again and his life was ruined. His wife had left him some weeks earlier and had taken the kids with her to England. They had lived in Dundalk (where he had boarded the wrong train) but he had given her a rough time and had hit the bottle once too often. He had finally contacted her on the phone and she still didn't want to know him and doubted if he had mended his ways. He had begged her to forgive him and said he was prepared to come right away to where she was. She was cynical and said, 'Right, if you love me, get the boat to England tonight and I'll see you in the morning. But I suppose you'll be on the drink as soon as I put the phone down.'

So he set out for the Dun Laoighaire ferry but was now on his way to Belfast! And this was the last train. I calmed him down and told him that it would be cutting it close but he might just be able to catch the Liverpool ferry from Belfast. We were due in Belfast at about half eight and the boat set sail at a quarter to nine. He was eternally grateful and asked me would I take him to the boat and offered me money to do it! Our train was late in getting in but we ran hell for leather up the walkway and through the ticket gate into a private taxi and arrived at the quay with about a minute to spare. He got a ticket and got the boat! He gave me his name and telephone number but I never checked up to see how he got on and if his wife and kids came back to Dundalk with him.

I have just told Roy that story and he says he didn't know there was a bar on the train and that he has only been on a train once or twice and would it be worthwhile for him and Donna to take the train to Dublin for a day's shopping as he would really love to do that . . . and he has me shattered but I don't show it. He asks me can you relax and lose yourself in the bars in Dublin and I tell him about our odysseys and how you drink draught Guinness and that though there are yuppie bars there are also those with great local characters.

Happy birthday, Cliff Richard! He's fifty today. When our Susan was about six or seven Cliff had a hit with 'The Twelfth of Never'. It was on the radio one day and I caught Susan crying and said to her, 'What are you crying about!' She replied that it was the song – 'It was so sad,' she said – and I burst out laughing. I wonder does she remember? I do. I remember all my cruelties, however small.

Monday 15 October

Paddy McGrory was up today and I had about an hour with him. He looks fine but hasn't lost any weight. He said that he had always intended taking our case and then he'll be bowing out. Let's hope his swansong is a sweet one! What I like about him is that there is no bullshit. He'll give you frank answers.

I read what you wrote about my mammy and daddy keeping well. My poor mammy – she doesn't know what's going on around her and has simple responses to all queries. When I was a kid I used to think – like all kids, I suppose – that I'd die without her. She was the cornerstone of my life. Later, arguments, especially the political arguments I had with her, used to devastate me. She tried to prevent me going out of the house on a number of occasions by pleading and crying and, while I would stall for a while, I still went out, into the thick of things, walking over her lying on the floor sobbing, leaving her with the worry and agony of expecting me home in a coffin. She was not to blame for my politics and she never boasted about her Harry. And she was truly caught between Margaret and Geraldine on the one hand and me on the other. With me she would take their part; with them she would argue for and defend me. It was all too much and she was exasperated, going through what she had seen her own mother go through thirty years before with her son sentenced to death. I think she had a really difficult task letting us kids go: she was very protective, and motherhood is such a challenge, but it is also a privilege which you have to pay for. She could be very funny – the life and soul of the party – and were she herself you and she would get on magnificently.

I am very happy that Kevin has been over visiting you and that you are getting on well. I know it's ever so slight but like yourself I am very pleased.

As for the day that D. Morrison asks you to marry him my intention is to make that a moment in our history and to spring it in the right setting when you least expect it. We might be sitting on heather on a warm evening, watching the sun's golden rays fan out across the heavens when I ask you. Or I might approach you, beginning from the soles of your feet! But you'll hear it. You'll hear it.

Wednesday 17 October
You get away with living in the unreality of jail for days, sometimes weeks on end, and then suddenly the barbed wire sharpens, the bars are cemented to the sills and the door is irretrievably locked. So it hits me now and again.

Roy was telling me a story there which reminded me of us. Shortly before he was arrested Donna had begun planting wee love letters in his lunch box. I remember once having been stopped at a checkpoint and searched and let go. Then that night, when I unzipped the side of my bag, I found a wee note from you! He laughed when I told him about the time I came back from Dublin and pulled back the duvet to find spread out on the bed the black lingerie, including the crotchless knickers,

Fionnuala O'Connor and Poilin had got you as a present – or a joke! Then I told him that when I was heading away for a few days I did the same with my vest, underpants and socks!

Saturday 20 October
That was great news about Butch Braniff being acquitted. One of the Ardoyne men had an early-afternoon visit yesterday and he asked his relatives had they seen Butch yet. He had been released about an hour by then. Yes, they had seen him: he was heading into the Highfield Club!

Sunday 21 October
Music from 1972 is on the radio. Just after Bloody Sunday I dropped out of the College of Business Studies and fooled myself into believing that if things became peaceable I could recommence my formal education.

I opposed my own nature and entered into a world of drama-filled days. I was enthusiastic, passionate and naive. Sometimes, years later, I would meet old friends, former comrades and mentors whom I had once known as assured, implacable, diehard republicans and who were now, once again, electricians and bricklayers and plumbers – or unemployed. I didn't feel resentful nor that I was superior because of my greater stamina. In a small way it enriched my understanding of human nature. But their bowing-out for me called into question the morality of the more grievous of their actions, actions which could only be justified through consistency of behaviour and irrevocable conviction (not notions or whims which time might erode, as turned out to be the case). Faithfulness and consistency are very important to me, but I am not making a God of inflexibility. Peace and justice may be defined in ideological terms but they are more important than ideology or any '-ism'.

Wednesday 24 October

One of the lads was released today so everybody was in a happy frame of mind. Martin McSheffrey from Derry beat the charges when the judge accepted his witness-box testimony that RUC detectives in Castlereagh punctured his eardrum during questioning. Martin's brother Eddie was killed in a premature explosion, along with Paddy Deery, in October 1987. I was interned with Martin's father Charlie back in the seventies.

On the radio about five this morning I heard a Traveling Wilburys song – that one that goes:

And the walls came down
All the way to hell.
Never saw them when they're standing,
Never saw them when they fell.

My pupils immediately enlarged and my heart thumped as I lost myself for a few minutes in the music, and memories of us in bed that morning in the autumn of 1988 when we first heard that song.

I worry an awful lot about you – your happiness and health. By the way, your gloom doesn't demoralise me or rub off on me. I am sorry that there is nothing I can do to counteract it. We have different personalities and different approaches. Even if I remain in jail for the next ten years, it will not be a waste of my life because I will always put time to good use. None of this, of course, is any consolation or comfort to you. I am by nature a cheerful person and I will just have to devise a way of cheering you up!

Saturday 27 October

That was a bad killing in Tyrone last night. That's the second time the loyalists have tried to shoot Tommy Casey. Tommy wrote to me when I was in C-Wing and asked for a visit. I know his daughter Annis Groogan. One day Kevin Brady and I were in Kildress in Tommy's house having dinner and I just mentioned that I admired the table. It was very old, very beautiful, round and engraved, with drop flaps. Tommy wanted to give it to me on the spot! But I wouldn't take it. It would have been too big for Beechmount Parade anyway. He was kind like that. I'll drop his wife Kathleen a line after the funeral.

We have a new prisoner on the wing, a young lad from Strabane. He was arrested at the Camel's Hump checkpoint when he was found to have a hand-drawn map of the barracks in his pocket with marks allegedly showing the best spots for mortars to land! This lad is dead naive and thinks he's a member of the old Irish Republican Brotherhood. If he is, he's the only one, as it has been defunct for over 70 years! Anyway, Pat Sheehan has christened him Adrian Mole, aged nineteen and three-quarters, because of his thick glasses and innocence. And today he has a lot of exciting entries to make in his diary. For example, one about his new friend, Jim O'Carroll.

Jim: 'Okay, everyone. Saturday afternoon, our turn for the swimming pool! Are you okay, mate?'

Adrian said that he couldn't swim but was told not to worry, he would learn quickly, and one of the other lads had a spare set of shorts.

Jim said, 'And don't forget later to bring your mattress to the canteen for the judo classes.'

Adrian might have to go through a medical but that's no problem as we have our own republican doctor!

Davy Clinton shouts from the bottom of the wing to Jim:

'Put my name down for swimming!'

Jim replies: 'Fuck off, you're barred, you were caught pissing in the pool last week.'

I think Adrian will grow up very quickly. He's been told to put on his good clothes for tomorrow night's disco. ('They let a few girls in but there's not enough to go around.') Yes, Adrian will be a new man by Monday!

Later

Got my hair trimmed this afternoon. Frankie Quinn, who used to be the barber, was shifted to C-Wing yesterday. Frankie was cutting my hair one day during the summer. Not long after he had tucked in the cover I began to complain about how much I was perspiring. The cover was completely stained but he told me it wasn't my sweat. The cover was actually red with blood and he had sliced – and I mean sliced! – through the ears of the two previous customers. Yesterday there was an election for a new barber. A young lad from Newry, Deckie Farrell, was overwhelmingly endorsed. Jim O'Carroll was the only one who voted for Jim O'Carroll. But when Deckie was cutting my hair his hands were shaking the whole time. I had to talk softly to him and calm him down.

On my way back, you will be glad to hear, I lifted the flap on Adrian's door and told him the lads were taking the mickey out of him. Later, when the cells were being unlocked for association, I asked him did he understand what I had said and he replied, 'Yes, I understand.' Then he said, 'But when do we get going to the gymnasium?' In the canteen tonight, one of the lads was pointing out the others and telling him who they were. When I was pointed out and identified he said, 'Aye, it looks like Danny Morrison, but it isn't him. I'm not stupid!' Another trick the lads play on new arrivals is to point out the OC or the IO and say, 'That guy's an informer. If he ever approaches you tell him to fuck off.'

Monday 29 October

Well, the big day has come and gone. I wore my checked shirt and pullover beneath my new jacket. I looked like I was going to a press conference! We were strip-searched before leaving the jail and being handcuffed for the short, hot journey to court via the tunnel. There was a ten- or fifteen-minute delay because Veronica Martin had not yet arrived from Maghaberry prison. The authorities claim to have found explosives up there so presumably that's what held her up.

We were brought from beneath the court up through a well of old granite steps and sat on chairs chained to the floor. The press were let in slowly, about a dozen journalists in all, includir Mr Ed Moloney (rebelliously chewing gum!), David McKittrick Wendy Austin, Ivan Little, Denis Murray and Alan Murray Then the public were filtered in, again in ones and twos. While this was all happening the preliminary enquiry had begun.

Sandy entered from a door at the back of the court, to the right of the magistrate, Mr Harry Hall. He was impeccably dressed in a smart suit but is carrying too much weight: he slipped coming down the steps but corrected himself in time. He took the stand and swore the oath. Of course, as soon as I saw him I knew we would be here for the duration. From the public gallery, which was behind us but screened off from the court by clear perspex about fifteen or twenty feet high, an old man got to his feet and shouted, 'Sandy! Sandy! Get out of that box, son! This is your father here!' Sandy kept his eyes fixed on the magistrate and refused to look around. The magistrate ordered Mr Lynch to sit down and be quiet or he would have him removed. Mr Lynch shouted, 'But I'm his father. Sandy! Sandy!' The RUC moved in and there was some scuffling and the old man kept shouting to Sandy to get out of the box. They pushed the father out the swing doors and Sandy momentarily turned around but then immediately looked back at the magistrate. Those few seconds were very tense and I felt very, very sorry for Mr Lynch, who was wretched-looking and ashamed. It's funny, but as I looked at Sandy I felt a lot of respect for us, the accused.

When Sandy got into his stride he relaxed (as did we) and gave his testimony flawlessly, although he became agitated and nervous on two occasions, both of which revolved around discussion of his lucky wife. It took almost two hours for his deposition to be delivered and typed. We then broke for lunch and Paddy McGrory called down to discuss tactics. We were held in a really depressing cell. It must have been used to hold most of the accused in the various supergrass trials in the early eighties. The prisoners had decorated the walls with their signatures. And while all of them, with the exception of Jim Gibney, eventually were released on appeal after many years in jail, what was depressing was what happened to them after their release. About twenty of them (including loyalists Jim Craig, Frenchie Marchant and John Bingham and republicans Ta Power and Gerard Steenson) were shot dead within two years of getting out.

We returned to the courtroom at two o'clock and Paddy then questioned Sandy.

'Are you a police informer?'

'Yes.'

'For how long?'

'Seven years.'

'What made you become a police informer?'

'I was sick of the violence, it was getting nowhere.'

(It was with great difficulty that we restrained ourselves from bursting out laughing.) He then said that he had told the RUC all about his criminal (sic) activities. As Sandy was leaving and walking up the steps he looked back and gave us a dirty look!

It was a touch triumphalistic, cocky, pathetic and even 'conscientious' in a perverted way! It was gleeful. He is not a reluctant witness and he behaved like a diligent police officer.

Creaney then asked the magistrate to rule that there was a prima facie case against all of us on the various charges. Some of the defence solicitors challenged this and there was toing and froing in legal arguments, but as expected we were sent for trial. No stretchers were needed. We walked proudly back to our cells! All the relatives were very disappointed and upset. Jim O'Carroll wanted to get back to the wing quickly to recover all the clothes that he had given away (after all, he had a gut feeling we were getting out!).

I saw and waved to Geraldine, Ciaran and Jim. From lip-reading I gathered that the kids weren't allowed up. However, I think Ciaran was saying that they'll be up tomorrow, and I certainly hope so because it is four weeks since I saw them last.

I don't know how long it will be before we come to trial but I should think it will be six months at the minimum. I got your letter tonight and I think you should pull out all the stops to get away this Christmas. It would be pointless me making a bail application, given that the conspiracy-to-murder charge still stands. I'm very sorry that all this unhappiness and loneliness has befallen you.

So that was Anto's fortieth-birthday present. He also received a card from the lads here. It was a drawing of Batman (Anto in the regalia, masked, wearing white knickers and suspenders) talking to Robin (me, in the regalia, masked, wearing black lace underwear and suspenders!). There is a bubble coming out my mouth and I am saying, 'Suffering supergrasses, Antoman! Do you think Sandyman will show up?' A bubble from his mouth says, 'Who knows, mate.' But another bubble shows what he is really thinking: 'Do your whack, Boy Danny, you watery bastard.'

And it's signed from 'the Jokers' in A-Wing.

Another young lad came on the wing today to join his older brother and tonight he saw the Sinn Fein doctor about dropped testicles and circumcision! There are now seven sets of brothers among the republican remands.

I hope the RUC harassment isn't getting to you. That attention they pay you is nothing but sheer harassment and of no security value whatsoever. But what can we expect? Did Paddy McGrory ever get back the photo of us in Donegal that they stole when they raided the house? I was waiting on that showing up in the newspapers.

My arse is sore tonight from all the sitting. It's about half nine and I've begun reading my uncle Harry's book, *Harry*. Life isn't so bad, you know. Fifty-two years ago, at the age of twenty-two, he was over in C-Wing breaking stones. And he hadn't got a pen pal like the one I have!

Tuesday 30 October
Lucy was telling Anto on their visit about Mr Lynch. She had to hold Mr Lynch's hand and calm him before the hearing. Obviously, he takes it personally because it is, after all, his flesh and blood up there. When he was in the public gallery he was so distraught that he didn't recognise what was going on. He asked Lucy, who was that in the witness box, and she told him it was his son, Sandy. It was then he burst into tears and began shouting.

Paddy Murphy has just shouted out his door: 'There's only one schizophrenic in this jail and I'm both of them!'

Saturday 3 November
I've been reading the book about my uncle Harry. In it he says: 'I was brought up in Belfast to regard Dublin as the promised land

and the government of de Valera the heart and soul of republicanism. But those dreams died swiftly when I was arrested at Giles Quay in 1935 and condemned to Arbour Hill afterwards.'

If you look at the treatment which even Austin Currie has received as a Northerner and a constitutional politician who has been attacked for daring to stand for election in Dublin, you can see how strident anti-northern sentiment has become. Different attitudes emerge, however, in a crisis, such as the 1981 hunger strikes, when the people down below elected two IRA prisoners to Leinster House.

Then there's the North! Did you read last week about the Ulster Unionist Party's annual conference? A young speaker proposed a more broad-minded, less dogmatic approach. He was hissed and slow-handclapped off the podium. Another speaker, Jeffrey Donaldson, was then loudly applauded when he said, 'No further concessions to the nationalists! We have gone as far as we can — no further must we go!' Could you imagine just how much more triumphalist they would be if the IRA was to give up! They've learnt little in twenty years.

Sunday 11 November
Paddy Murphy was sentenced to five years on Friday, which means he'll qualify for fifty per cent remission. I'm not sure where he'll serve his sentence. And Pat's trial is scheduled to begin on Monday the twenty-sixth of November, so he'll be away to the H-Blocks before Christmas, I'd say.

Jim O'Carroll and I are absolutely mad. Completely out of the blue while sitting at the dinner table we'll burst into song, sometimes putting our own words to whatever hit is around. Today we had the entire canteen singing 'Unchained Melody' ('And time goes by so slowwwlyyyy')!

I'm really glad you are going home this Christmas. I'll miss you like crazy but it is better that you are surrounded by your family instead of being on your own.

I loved your description of the film *Ghost*. The same theme was used to great effect in one of my favourite musicals, *Carousel*, when the hero, Billy, is stabbed to death or shot and then his ghost watches over his wife and daughter. Speaking of death, today is Remembrance Sunday. The loyalists paraded in the yard and produced flags, from somewhere, attached to flagpoles improvised from snooker cues. I am off now to London to listen to Benjamin Britten's *War Requiem*. It opens with a poem by Wilfred Owen, 'Anthem for Doomed Youth'. Owen, a British soldier, was killed just before the Armistice of 1918. And I see that the bishops of all denominations in England have taken the 'just war' theory down off the shelf and given it a good polishing in light of the Gulf crisis.

Sunday 18 November
There's a golden-oldie show on Radio 1: hits from 1969. In that year Radio 1 started a 'Road Club', which travelled around major cities, broadcasting a live lunchtime show. We used to beak school and plonk our school bags somewhere safe and then head off to it. The club came to Belfast about once every three months and was held in the Romanos Ballroom, now Leisure World in Queen Street. I can't remember there being any sectarian tension or fights, even after August 1969, although the club didn't make its second visit to Belfast until November or December. There was a great atmosphere and every record struck a chord in our adolescent breasts. There was 'Sweet Dream' by Jethro Tull, which had a dramatic guitar opening and particularly appealed to my mate Micky Connolly, who was learning the guitar – wasn't everybody! – and was a fan of Eric Clapton, John Mayall and Rory Gallagher.

Even the syrupy 'Sugar, Sugar' by the Archies was mesmerising and infectious. Like smoke curling around the high ceiling of the ballroom we moved in eddies around the dimly lit dance floor and then upstairs along the balconies with the ever-flowing tide of teenagers in search of Answers, which instinct told you lay hidden somewhere in the terrain between lust and love. You know yourself what that search is like and how you explore the world and identify (like kids today) with the contemporary music, or read poetry or listen to Leonard Cohen (!) but are repeatedly disappointed and frustrated and despairing and have no one to share the angst with. And now I can smile at those days though I still experience wee twinges of nostalgia listening again to 'Suspicious Minds' or 'Leaving on a Jet Plane' or the heart-tugging 'Someday We'll Be Together'!

I see that your visit to the Kesh to see Bik depressed you. But what can one do? It is a consequence of the Brits and our reaction to them. Prison is meant to depress, to demoralise, to drain you of stamina and confidence and conviction. Long Kesh will be twenty years old next September and, to paraphrase a revisionist historian, it represents the failure of triumph, all that judicial weight, all that barbed wire, with its message of permanence. Honey, you and I know what our options are but I can never subscribe to defeatism.

Wednesday 21 November
I had a great walk this afternoon. I'm sure we did about fifty or sixty laps of the yard. The air was chilly but there were great lemon-coloured clouds high in the sky catching the winter sunlight.

I read a line the other day by G. K. Chesterton:

'When you are rooted in a place, that place disappears.'

In my context I think that's true. When out in the exercise yard we are under the same sky as people on the outside, getting soaked by showers or caught by the same gusts of wind. And if you are involved in a good conversation during that hour and a half this place disappears. You forget you are in jail. And then you get so used to the cell door being opened for meals, recreation, etc., and walking up the landing, and taking your seat at the same table that your surroundings somehow dissolve and are not an issue. All this is happening to your body and your head. Of course, your heart is a different matter and that is actually the market place of another reality. Your love and hopes live there and they are more acutely real than the act of being imprisoned. It is the intensity of those two desires that with a vengeance let you know you are in jail doing time.

Pat Sheehan has returned the Mandela book so I'll pass it out to you. He wanted to see how Mandela got through twenty-six years in jail! Depressed? Don't be. Just remember, you'll never serve it! And I also told Pat that: 'You'll never serve it.' His da told him the same yesterday and he now wants his da to come up and see him more often!

Thursday 22 November
Oh, what a beautiful day! Thatcher, the bad bastard, the biggest bastard we have ever known, has been ousted! It's the end of an era and no replacement could be as bad or as bitter as she was. We had just come back from the canteen – it was about a quarter to ten. The song on the radio was 'I'm Doin' Fine Now, Without You Baby' by New York City, and it was interrupted by a newsflash, quoting PA sources. I smiled like a Cheshire cat.

Out in the yard we walked and gloated for an hour and a half. Everyone was in great form and even the loyalists had been banging on their doors after the newsflash. Eleven years – for half the present Troubles – we've had to listen to that unctuous, self-righteous fucker. Cream of the reaction was, of course, Mark Durcan of the SDLP, who said he feels sorry for her. That would be stretching Christian duty to its outer limit. Oh yes, it's like a blast of fresh air. I didn't think that feeling smug could be so exhilarating!

Saturday 24 November

I have had a relaxing day after a wonderful visit. When I blew you a kiss, Griz's girl, Regina, jokingly remarked, 'Here, I thought you were too old for that!' But the warder who was taking me back turned to her and said, 'You're never too old for love!' And she didn't know what to say. Coming through the search-box he told me he was fifty-five and was getting married for the second time!

I must say, you sounded really sympathetic to Mrs Thatcher's plight and full of admiration for her performance at Westminster. True, she came across as witty, but don't forget the bloodshed she has been responsible for: the hunger strikers, the plastic-bullet victims, the teenage sailors on the Belgrano, over 130 civilians in Libya and Mairead, Sean and Dan in Gibraltar, to name but a few. During her rule there was an increase in poverty-related suicides in Britain and thousands died as a result of cutbacks in the NHS. Sean O'Faolain once wrote: 'Every politician has his sentimental streak. Even Stalin had a daughter; Hitler loved his dog; Napoleon wept over the poems of Ossian.' Thatcher was hubris personified and as far as I am concerned Lee Harvey Oswald picked the wrong target in the wrong year! The best account by far of the reaction to the news of her resignation was on the front page of yesterday's *Irish Times*:

"'The bad news,' said a voice over the public-address system in a north London railway station, "is that a signal failure means another delay. The good news is that Thatcher's resigned! Hip,

hip, hooray!" And most of the commuters cheered.'

Monday 26 November
Today is the twenty-sixth, and on this night eighteen years ago I was arrested, taken to Castlereagh for a few days and then interned. About a fortnight before, my girlfriend, Kitty, and I had split up. I was out with another girl for the first time and we went to a dance in Clonard Hall. The Brits surrounded the hall, then burst in firing rubber bullets. We were taken out singly, placed against a wall and somebody (yes, another informer) in the back of a Saracen gave me the thumbs-down. About seventy or eighty people were arrested and brought to Springfield Road barracks. Then just three of us were taken to Castlereagh, then two of us – seventeen-year-old Paul Fox and myself – were taken to the Kesh. I remember the girl I was with standing at the door of the hall, and she had this look on her face which seemed to say, 'Hey, you brought me out, how am I getting home?' I never saw or heard from her again, sensible woman. But even though things were looking bad I had to laugh. I was kept in Clonard car park in the back of another Saracen and could see those being put up against the wall for the spotlight to be trained on them. A mate of mine, Seando Moore, who was on the run and who had deep ginger hair, had dyed his hair ink-black but not his eyebrows or eyelashes! When I recognised him I started laughing – his disguise was so obvious. But he got through the check. He called around to my ma's a few nights later and told her that I had sent word out for him to collect the crates of home-brew I had bottled! He took them to his billet and had a great time.

Did I tell you that years later I was speaking at a meeting in Waterford along with a Sinn Feiner, Ray Coady, who had been in the British Army but deserted? Later, in his flat, we were talking about the North and different incidents and it turned out that he had served in the Royal Green Jackets and had been in Clonard Hall on the night I was arrested! It will be Paul Fox and Laura Crawford's anniversary next Saturday. They will be fifteen years dead. I must remember to drop Mrs Fox a card at Christmas.

Roy was telling me that his cellmate before me had a strategy of spinning a sad tale of woe to his wife at least once every three weeks. Stories about cockroaches and mice in his bed, cold showers and atrocious food. He would send her away from visits with tears of sympathy rolling down her cheeks. He had the calendar marked so that if he forgot to mention his growing trials and tribulations to her on visits he would remember to write them into his letters. Anyway, it allegedly worked wonders and his wife was too preoccupied being concerned about his 'oppressive' living conditions to worry about her own!

I'm sitting here counting the slugs that are moving across the table. I suppose I could swipe them off with my towel but it has to do me until February. Three prisoners had their throats cut during the night and there were six suicides but none of this made the news. Oh Lord! The pipes have just burst and we're sitting knee-deep in sewage. Two more suicides have been announced on the Threes! Please don't leave me!

Tuesday 27 November
This morning when I got up and looked out the window I saw that the few blades of sparse grass left in the ground were sheathed in brittle frost. I was first in the showers and there the floors were dry and warm.

I wonder what sort of a prime minister will John Major make. I never even heard of him until this year. He probably doesn't even know where Ireland is. I'm sure we'll soon get his measure.

Strangers always surprise you and it is impossible to tell character from looks.

It was our turn for the canteen at lunchtime. We queue up at a servery with an opening through which plates can pass – but not fists – and which is otherwise covered in a grill and perspex sheeting, just like a post-office counter. There is always a demand for extras and sometimes the odd ruse works. A common one is to ask for 'Martin McSheffrey's burger, he doesn't want it,' and hope that the screw doesn't know that Martin was released a month ago. I laughed today: one of the lads asked for 'John Major's fish' and got it! Another asked for and was served 'Alex Maskey's cake'. Too late did the orderly realise what had been said:

'But Alex Maskey isn't in here!'

'Aye, but he will be!'

There is a totally incorrect view among kitchen staffs in jail that prisoners just love lard. Everything comes floating in grease. Sometimes if one of the landings runs short they'll shout to the screws on the next landing, 'Is there any more sausages on the Twos?' Davy Clinton, mimicking a warder, shouts, 'Threes! Threes! Is there any more grease on the Threes?' He can be very funny. He pulls that stunt regularly, calling orderlies down from the other landings or shouting up, 'A3! Send Sheehan down for a parcel!'

Our wing is quite long, with the dimensions of a large aircraft hangar. Tonight it was actually misty, that's how cold it was, and you could smell the frost in your nostrils.

Saturday 1 December

Only twenty-four more slopping-out days to Christmas! You asked about books. Any of the following: *Fabian* by Erich Kastner or *Remembrance of Things Past* by Marcel Proust, *The Life and Times of Michael K.* by J. M. Coetzee, *A Child of Our Time* or *Youth Without God,* both by Odon von Horvath. If none of these are available I'll supply you with other titles (it's great being in jail!).

Monday 3 December
Somebody fused our lights at ten last night. Then, Adrian Mole on the Threes, who has started to come out of his shell, began singing 'James Connolly'! With great pathos his voice wavered and wobbled like someone playing a saw with a bow. The loyalists must also have suspected Adrian because they were up at their doors telling 'The Proclaimers' (Adrian and his lookalike brother) to fuck up. Republicans rallied to their singer and encouraged his crowing for the Provovision Song Contest as he began 'My Only Son Was Shot in Dublin'. It all degenerated into political, sexist and sectarian abuse. One republican, recently charged with shooting a former UDR soldier, was reminded by the loyalists of what he said when he was charged: 'I didn't shoot him, I was only the driver.' Dozens on each side promised last night to 'stiff' each other. Yesterday's *Sunday World* carried a story about a loyalist on this wing whose son has cerebral palsy and who, when asked what he wanted for Christmas, said, 'My daddy home.' So to the air of 'All I Want For Christmas Is My Two Front Teeth', one republican singer substituted ' . . . my daddy home.'

After tea in the canteen tonight we had a meeting to curb the abuse from our side. Ideologically correct abuse excludes personal remarks about wives, girlfriends, kids or families – or the first two's sexual predilections. It's amazing how it suddenly flares up.

I got a letter from Pam Brighton yesterday. She said that *West Belfast* has been with three writers, 'all of whom have said no'.

'No', they won't do it, or 'no', they can't do it, isn't clear. It's presently with a Dublin writer called Peter Sheridan. She has asked me to consider writing a few short stories for Radio 4.

Tuesday 4 December
A mate of mine has come up with a master plan! He says he's going to ask his wife to ferret out her old school uniform and to wear it on a visit. Then he can tell the warders that she's really only twelve and she can come around to his side of the table and sit on his knee! I have suggested a further scenario in which she has been a very bold pupil and has not done her homework!

Last night on Radio 1 Nicky Campbell played and praised to the high heavens 'Only Our Rivers Run Free' by Christy Moore (from *The Time Has Come* album). It was quite stirring and reminds you of what is still there, how things started, the price that has been paid and the sacrifices that have been made. There are many aspects of this struggle from which I want to step back and which make me shudder, but it is impossible to ignore what has gone down and to be dispassionate and coldly intellectual.

Wednesday 5 December
The search team bounced into the cells for a lightning search at around five on customs-and-excise business but Roy and I were teetotal. We run a temperance house.

I finished *Out of Africa* and *Shadows on the Grass*. Blixen's book is autobiographical. Dialogue is sparse. There is no romance, unless you include her fondness for Africa, but she is pompous and racist. Kenya is 'a dumb nation' where 'the most inexplicable fits of idiocy might occur even in the most intelligent natives.' That observation could be applied to intellectuals in any European country without being considered remarkable. 'There are times when coloured people cannot make themselves clear to save their lives.' She never questions the assumptions – progress, enlightenment, profit – on which colonial rule is based. However, she is a good writer. I remember the big tears running down your cheeks when, in the film, Robert Redford died in the plane crash, or as she concluded her reminiscing at the end (to Mozart's 'Clarinet Concerto').

Sunday 9 December

Did you ever see anybody washing themselves with a bar of cheese and getting nowhere? Well, that's what happened to one of those new prisoners this morning!

I had a great night's sleep and a very peaceful dream, which, Rita O'Hare will be glad to hear, featured her. I was walking up Islandbawn Street, and where it meets the Falls Road I bumped into Rita, who had a big smile on her face and she came over and hugged me. There was peace and she was saying wasn't it great, it was all over. She was glad she was able to return home before her mammy and daddy died! You could easily do fifty rounds of the yard on that one!

Monday 10 December

We've been moved to a new cell on A1. The beds creak and the walls are stinking but we'll spring-clean it tomorrow. We have decided to enter into the spirit of the season; our resistance to Christmas has been broken. With a razor blade we have converted one of the paper bags, in which we moved our clothes, into a brown Christmas tree! And we spent about an hour making decorations out of coloured tissues which Donna sent Roy. We ended up in stitches because, when we hung them in a loop across the ceiling and between the two walls, Roy said they looked like a clothes line of frilly knickers

Scott Fitzgerald's *The Last Tycoon* is very good. It is about a Hollywood film mogul in the thirties, and Fitzgerald's prose is absolutely controlled and sparse yet amazingly descriptive. Stahr, the tycoon in question, falls for a girl about fifteen years his junior and this is what happens:

'Stahr's eyes and Kathleen's met and tangled. For an instant they made love as no one ever dares to do after. Their glance was slower than an embrace, more urgent than a call.'

I love the way he uses that word 'tangled'. Later, Stahr takes her for a drive and she throws up verbal barriers, not quite bordering on cynicism, the way new couples sometimes do:

'But she was deep in it with him, no matter what the words were. Her eyes invited him to a romantic communion of unbelievable intensity.'

Do you remember eyes tangling on Monday the eighteenth of January 1982!

Tuesday 11 December
This morning we thoroughly cleaned the cell but it's still a pigsty. Tradesmen came around later to replace nine missing panes of glass. Yes, at last we have clear glass and can see out.

I was saying in yesterday's letter about Danny Caldwell and Jim O'Carroll being a bit down after the legal visit, but they've come out of it now. It's amazing what a night's sleep – or maybe a night awake! – can do. Jim wrote a letter to Father Christmas but the censor refused to pass it because on the envelope was written 'c/o the North Pole'. It goes:

'Dear Santa, I'm writing to you early this year as I have changed address. I suffer more than anybody else as I have extra-large ears. A good set of ear muffs or two cushions and an elastic band would suffice. Please could you send my big friend Doc some colouring pencils as those miserable bastards on the next landing won't part with anything. Last but not least could you leave me a speedy car. Just outside the main gate. At midnight. Leave the keys in the ignition . . .'

Monday 24 December
We have moved cell yet again – this time at our request. We are in Cell 30, whose previous occupant, Davy Clinton, got bail over a week ago.

The cards are coming in thick and fast now. From aunts and uncles, cousins and nieces and nephews and complete strangers. I've a total of 150 spread across the cell. How is your Christmas in Toronto? I'm sure you've heard the news by now about the IRA calling a three-day ceasefire, the first in sixteen years! Of course, it's led to all kinds of false hopes. What else has happened? Frankie Quinn was sentenced to sixteen years, and that young lad from Strabane, Adrian Mole, got bail.

On my last visit I had Kevin and Liam up. Liam was moody but when I whispered to him and asked him what was wrong he said he missed me and would love to go back to my cell. So that gave me a lump in my throat. That's the first time whilst I've been in here that he has been openly emotional or, rather, explicit. Right, I'll go now and speak to you later. I forgot to say, Roy and I have been charged by the governor after a cell search. The charge reads that, 'You, along with prisoner D. McCool A3616, had in your cell a plastic bottle of liquid suspected of being alcohol.' But the adjudication has been adjourned until the new year.

Saturday 30 December
I had a legal visit on Friday with Paddy McGrory. We got the transcripts from the audible sections of the bits of tape recovered by the RUC in their search of Carrigart Avenue. On the tape

Sandy Lynch admits to having been paid for his handiwork: '£100 at Christmas', '£400 for Manor Street' (the arrest of three men), '£120 for the rail line' and '£30 for the New Lodge Road' (when an RUC man was shot dead by an undercover agent by mistake). I know it isn't time for being emotive but he says he got £50 for Velsheda Park – that is, he squealed on old Paddy Murphy, who's now doing five years! Of course, the importance of these admissions is that he denied under oath at the preliminary enquiry that he was being paid.

Joelle, and Tom's brother, Brian from New Zealand, were also up on Friday. She bought me two books. We also had a lively conversation about the writer Milan Kundera, whose style I don't like but which Joelle loves. He writes a lot about exile and I was wondering if Joelle feels strongly about being an exile. How often would you be conscious of being away from your native home? Possibly too bluesy a question to be putting now, when I'm trying to take your mind off your vacation! Sorry.

Well, we were spoilt on Christmas Day – lots of food, lots of variety, but it was all institutional and suffered from an insipidness and lack of personal touch. Later, we watched *ET* in the canteen and then had our party. Two lads painstakingly made party hats. I presented the *Mister and Mister* competition, during which each contestant was tested for intimate knowledge of his cellmate whilst his cellmate sat in a far corner, wearing headphones blaring out pop music. Some of the more harmless questions were:

'What is your partner's greatest fear or phobia: (a) Spiders, (b) mice or (c) getting Judge Carswell?'

'How often does your cellmate pray: (a) once a week, (b) once a day or (c) he's never off his knees?'

'How many IRA operations has he claimed to have been on: (a) none, (b) between one and five, (c) more than five or (d) more than Martin Meehan?'

'What was his reaction to the IRA ceasefire: (a) it should never have happened, (b) it should have lasted seven days or (c) they should never have called off the last one?'

'How many Christmas cards did he get: (a) between one and thirty, (b) between thirty and sixty, or (c) more than Pat 'I love me, who do you love?' Sheehan?'

7.30 pm

I am not long back from the canteen, and as I was coming out Dermot Carroll told me that on the seven o'clock news there was a report of the Brits having shot dead a man and seriously wounded his brother at a checkpoint in South Armagh. So I wonder what all that is about. We'll find out tomorrow.

Weather-wise you haven't missed anything. Out in the yard this morning we crunched through a dusting of snow upon frost. A stormy cold wind was ripping the air apart and the starlings kept trying to find roosting spots on the disused chimney stack but broke up in disarray and went crashing through the air. Anto told us a funny story as we were walking. Years ago, around Christmas, he and three mates (labourers and an electrician) all went to the old Hunting Lodge after work. One of them bet the others that he could steal a stag trophy off the wall without being caught. They placed their bets. The aspiring thief went to the bar and asked for a couple of plastic carry-out bags. In two moves he had the stag's head off the wall and under the table and its antlers covered over with the bags. Then he put the head under his coat and they all walked out, caught a black taxi to Twinbrook and got out opposite the Hitchin' Post, where the two who lost the bet went to buy a real carry-out. When the two emerged from the bar there was a small crowd gathered behind their mates. Anto's mate had removed the bags and stuck the stag's head on a hedge, tied an electric wire around its neck like a rope and pretended to be struggling with it!

It was dark and most of the crowd had a fair sup of drink. The guys told the people they had caught the reindeer on Black Mountain and were bringing it home as a pet for the kids. Anto said that you could see the stag's big artificial glassy eyes and its tongue protruding and every now and again when they pulled 'the rope' the crowd moved back a few feet in case it reared up at them. Then, they pulled too hard, and to gasps and astonishment from the crowd the head landed on the footpath. Then it was, 'Fuckin' bastards', 'That wasn't funny', 'I knew you couldn't get reindeers on the mountain.' He had us doubled up.

I think society can sleep safely in its bed at night, assured that the most dangerous men in the country are all under lock and key.

1991

Tuesday 1 January

Happy New Year Miss Universe!

So at long last we have rid ourselves of 1990 – good riddance! And, as promised, I got up to the window at midnight and whispered my wishes to you. I couldn't see a star because of the glare of two arc lights which illuminate the exercise yard but what the heck. Then I went over to Roy and shook hands with him. And then I couldn't sleep a wink.

I finished the book *The Last of the Just* by Andre Schwarz-Bart. It was quite sad. However, earlier in the book one of the characters, Mordecai, marries a fiercely independent woman and they have a dazzling sex life. He can't believe his luck. But then, 'Mordecai wondered in shame whether such delights did not contain a certain excess, a pagan undertone; did they not cut him off from God?' That sounds very familiar to me. There's something almost Catholic about it – not being happy about feeling happy! Having been raised in a secular culture you probably escaped the effects of joy-related guilt. Lucky woman. It took me many, many years to rise above those ghosts.

Wednesday 2 January

I was listening to the midnight news last night and heard that Dave O'Connell had died suddenly. Despite having several major disagreements with him I still liked him. On that occasion in 1986 when Sinn Fein dropped its abstentionist policy in the South I think he left more because of his lifelong friendship with Ruairi and because he had lost a number of important ideological battles rather than out of conviction that Republican Sinn Fein could deliver the goods.

Thursday 3 January
When we were out in the yard today the sleet turned to snow but Pat and I kept on walking. Snowflakes fell like big suds of soap and I even caught some in my mouth. The yard eventually turned white and then the clodding started. We were attacked but most of the snowballs missed. Snipers, my arse! However, I was blue with cold when we got back to the cells and I had to change my entire clothing. It's a lovely feeling climbing into warm, fresh clothes in the spring of your cell having just walked from the North Pole at its winter height!

Well, have you attempted any New Year resolutions?! Pat has once again gone off the fags, and his nerves are frayed. He says that sometimes he would smoke up to thirty a day. He'll probably last about three weeks. I'm resolved not to have any resolutions, although I'm gonna try and stop back-stabbing people! Not that I do that much, mind you. But when one's general company is putting the blade into an absent one it is so easy to go along with the slip of the knife!

Saturday 5 January
It was great to see you again and it put me in top form. But isn't it just a pity that we can't dislodge you from limbo or block your view of that appalling vista of endless pessimism. I understand your need for self-protection and your long, slow, qualified retreat. I have always been a big respecter of fate, though it delivers benefits and blows in fickle measure. But when you don't have a choice – and, as a prisoner, I don't – you have to respect it even more. If you don't accept the walls of the cell you go up them by your fingernails but will still fall down. There is no escape. I want to be as loving and carefree as ever (despite the

walls of Crumlin Road Jail) right up until that moment – if it comes – when we have to make the break. I can't be as loving as ever if you are distant. I know you are not sending me smoke signals, and it's just your way of doing things, but I don't believe I can keep excluded from my letters the subjects you asked me to. So that's another wee problem. I don't think I can put on a grave face and officiate at my own wake. In fact, for the first time in twelve months I am experiencing feelings I don't quite like. I'm sorry for this dip in composure. I apologise. But you see, I love you dearly, and I just wish you'd let me steer you, and us, through this. I know what's required. To see you sad and despondent kills me. You mistake my frivolity for a lack of realism and you should know me better than that. Just be a little less serious. I hope I'm not beating my head against a brick wall!

Monday 7 January
Just when the prisoner almost succumbs to despair and depression the avuncular Peter Brooke rides to his aid! Fifty-six years of age, a widower, and he is to marry again within the next few months. It all depends on how you view things – the world is at my feet!

Roy and I are locked up whilst everyone else is in the canteen. We were adjudicated this morning and found guilty of having in our cell a plastic bottle suspected of containing alcohol. We lost seven days remission, twenty-eight days of evening association, fourteen days of parcels and fourteen days of privileges. So, I'll have to see P. J. and go to court for a judicial review, since the punishment is out of all proportion to the alleged offence and there was nothing to show that we had any knowledge of the bottle.

I got a letter and a magazine from Dermot Healy, a writer who used to live with a friend of Sandra's. He swelled my head by saying that the guy who wrote the film script of *My Left Foot*, Shane

Connaughton, is one of my 'most ardent fans'. Dermot is moving into a cottage on a cliff overlooking the sea just outside Sligo, where he is working on an arts project. Mark it on the map!

I must have the anniversary blues – haven't been home for a year exactly – because I am sitting over these lines, staring vacantly at the wall, as a fountainhead of memories pours over me.

Imagine you questioning my sanity the other day, when you should know that there is no such thing as 'normal' behaviour! All 'normal' people have totally irrational fears, tell lies for no good reason, laugh at nothing, have the queerest thoughts, act in a way that does not correspond with their beliefs, hold contradictory views, are actually living several lives at once, and behave abnormally! I'm as insane as they come!

Saturday 12 January

I have just read in the obituary columns notice of the funeral of Freedom O'Neill. Hughie, his real name, would probably have been around my age. He was a bit of a hood as a teenager but his father was a real gentleman called Paddy the Hat (because he always wore a trilby), and Paddy was in the IRA. The family had little money and few prospects. Hughie was always being locked up in jail, so maybe that's why he was called Freedom, although when he was standing drinking cider at the street corner he would always raise his arm and shout, 'Freedom!' The IRA beat him with hurleys in early 1972 but Paddy must somehow have intervened because by about August 1972 Freedom was in the IRA in Beechmount and 'behaving' himself! Did you ever see the film *The Battle of Algiers,* where the hero, Ali la Pointe, starts off as a petty criminal but joins the FLN and quickly establishes his credentials? It is odd and inexplicable the way some people attempt to redeem themselves. Not everyone was convinced of Freedom's volte-face. But I was once in

Springfield Road barracks, spreadeagled against the yard wall, when he was arrested and brought in. Maybe all those hurleys had prepared him well because the soldiers kicked him up and down the courtyard and put his head into a water tank until he was spluttering, but he wouldn't talk.

Freedom and I and Paddy the Hat ended up interned in Cage 2 together, and Freedom and I were released on the same day in December 1973. In early January I went to England to see Sandra and we planned our wedding for Nottingham in April. Everyone else being in jail, Freedom was tentatively to be my best man. But after a few weeks he and I were back on the run again. So that's how my other brother-in-law, Brian, a British soldier, ended up being asked to be my best man (as well as the fact that he had introduced me to Sandra)! Of course, Brian didn't know I was on the run when I slipped into England.

Sometime in 1974 or 1975 Freedom fell foul of the Movement and was once again drinking and messing about and hooding. Paddy the Hat was now out of jail but was ill with a heart condition. He attended his bedridden wife Mollie but also worked for Prisoners Transport. He died in August 1978 and everybody wondered how Molly would survive. Suddenly she was up and about like Lazarus and you would often see her walking up and down the road linked to the arm of one of her daughters.

Freedom's sister Josephine was married to a fella called John Torbitt. He did time for hijacking a car, only I think the driver, who was an off-duty RUC or UDR man, hijacked him in turn. In 1981, just after the hunger strikes ended, there was a lot of paranoia inside the IRA because the RUC's tactic of using supergrasses was well under way. Anyway, John was involved with the IRA again. He was arrested by the RUC and they must have broken him because he agreed to rendezvous with the

Special Branch if they let him go. I am not sure at what stage the IRA found out about this – perhaps when they were debriefing him and discovered he was lying. Anyway, they were afraid he would 'go supergrass' so they ordered him out of the country, and he left. But before Christmas he returned to his Horn Drive home. One evening he and Josephine appeared in the Republican Press Centre and asked to see me. He said he had tried to but couldn't live away from his wife and kids. He told me that the IRA had been around and ordered him out and said that he would be shot if he didn't go. I told him he should go, it wasn't worth it. He said he didn't care, they could shoot him. They came to his house just after Christmas, I think, and shot him, critically wounding him.

Three weeks later, the nineteenth of January, the day after I was introduced to you in Toronto, he died in hospital in Belfast from his wounds. His death really upset me. He came back because he couldn't live without his kids even though he knew he was going to be shot. I see from insertions in today's *Irish News* that Molly is also deceased. I didn't know that.

Freedom's ill-repute grew and I think he was caught a few times doing armed robberies, and he was involved in drug-pushing. And then he ends up dying in a London flat of an overdose or alcoholic poisoning. He told me a lot of things about himself that I will never breathe. Paddy the Hat once told me that when the Troubles were over there was only one reward that he wanted from the Republican Movement: a second-hand car, so that he could take Molly on day outings in the country.

You know, we are very lucky people. We have close brothers and sisters. Our parents aren't in any great debt. Much of life's cruelties have missed us. Deprivation and illness have passed us by. When I think of the O'Neills, and millions like them, I want to kiss the heavens for the future I have.

Sunday 13 January
Did you see today's *Sunday World* and that ridiculous story?
'Sources close to the Republican Movement' report that Morrison
has modified his views and opposes 'economic bombings'.
Actually, I got slagged about it – and it was all favourable! Anto
says it's great publicity and will ingratiate us with the judge! And
Pat now interprets Anto being charged just recently with GBH
against a screw last year as a move to hang on to the 'hawk' when
the 'pacifist' gets out at the trial!

Wednesday 16 January
We were awake half the night glued to the radio.

It was at ten minutes to midnight that we heard on RTE's
news that reports were coming in that anti-aircraft fire had been
heard in Baghdad. I immediately tuned into BBC Radio 4. It
was relaying live the eyewitness reports from the Iraqi capital of
the CNN team based in a high-rise hotel. It was incredible –
listening to and realising that the sound of gunfire and explosions
were actually occurring at that instant. All I could think about
was what effect it must be having on the civilian population –
on terrified women and children. I fucked the Brits and the
Yanks, aloud and often.

Then this morning it was sickening again to hear the
commentators give false credence to the claim that the bombs
were dropped with 'pinpoint accuracy'; that they were 'laser-
guided', etc. These would be the same bombs – 'smart bombs'
is what, I think, they are called – that the US Air Force dropped
on a Libyan barracks in 1986, hitting the French embassy and
a working-class district. On that occasion 113 men, women and
children – and *one* soldier – were killed.

Saturday 19 January

It's Saturday night at the war movies on the radio. Talk about saturation coverage. I have just listened to a Pentagon press briefing and all the initial euphoria has evaporated.

I think there is an onus on us to view or attempt to view this conflict from the perspective of those who have no power, who are most oppressed and who are dispossessed. How many UN resolutions condemning Israel for its systematic occupations of the West Bank in 1967, of the Gaza Strip and the Golan Heights in 1973, and of Southern Lebanon in 1982 were backed up by sanctions or the mustering of the biggest amount of firepower since the Second World War? The US has ignored all UN resolutions calling for a Palestinian homeland. The World Court at the Hague called upon the USA to lift its blockade of Nicaraguan ports and it ignored that ruling. The Iraqis *believe* that Kuwait is part of Iraq the way Cornwall is part of England.

Of course, Hussein's attempts to fragment the coalition's Arab sponsors by attacking Israeli cities indiscriminately is totally immoral. To make sense of this crisis you have to remain sceptical and cynical and remember history.

Sunday 20 January

Father Bennett told us at Mass that the body with head wounds found in Twinbrook or the Stewartstown Road yesterday was that of Shorty (Brendan Short), who used to be an orderly here. He was originally from the Whiterock area. Do you remember I told you about him singing out the door and when the loyalists shouted abuse he replied that if Johnny Cash could sing at San Quentin he could sing to prisoners in the Crum'! He was only twenty-four. We said prayers for him at Mass.

I see that there were four fatalities in Israel after those missile attacks. A three-year-old Arab child died as her parents tried to get her gas mask on, and three elderly Jewish women, alone, helpless and confused when the strike came, suffocated in their gas masks. And the propaganda battle on both sides continues apace. The Iraqis have a station broadcasting disinformation to the Allied troops. One of the presenters is a sexy-voiced Baghdad Betty, but one of her statements backfired. She told the soldiers that while they were stuck in the desert their wives were having it off with other men. Betty named two of these men as Tom Cruise and Bruce Willis. Lucky women!

Wednesday 23 January

I laughed at your description of rushing breakfast, doing your hair and reading my letter all at once. Although I am not rushing to go anywhere I have been known to read your letter from start to finish whilst four peas remain on my fork, suspended in mid-air. Both Roy and I have the habit of reading funny bits out of letters from Donna and you, and as we do so the other automatically stops eating as well! He now addresses me as 'Honey-Bunch'!

Saturday 26 January

It seems that as a result of our trial being postponed half the jail's cases have been brought forward! Pat is now up on Monday the fourth of February, and the trial of Eugene McKee, Rinty, etc., will begin two days later. Rumour here is that Jim Donnelly and Rosaleen McCorley are going to get hammered – possibly life. Yesterday, in the courthouse, we were brought from the cells below up through the public corridors and stairs. We were each handcuffed to a warder and there were clusters of cops at strategic points. As we were passing a number of civilians I noticed a middle-aged man walking towards us and I shouted back to Anto, 'Watch out! There's Jack Ruby!' Anto caught on but the young cops hadn't a clue.

As I was saying about Lord Chief Justice Hutton, he bounced spritely into his seat. He uses every muscle in his face to communicate and has a reputation as a workaholic – which I wouldn't doubt. I'm looking forward to working alongside him!

I didn't read that article in the *Guardian* but I heard its author, Alan Rusbridger, on Radio Ulster. Years ago he was the *Guardian*'s diarist and it was the best and funniest column in the paper – very droll. I gave him a couple of items, which he used. He also came to Belfast to cover the funerals of Mairead, Sean and Dan and his article on the Milltown attack was incredibly vivid. He wrote that he was hiding behind a headstone as the shrapnel was flying, terrified for his life, when this man came bounding across the graves and ran towards the source of the gunfire and exploding grenades. Then he named the man – Martin McGuinness.

Sunday 27 January
The air in the yard was nippy this morning. We were paged for Mass at about a quarter to eleven and when we went into the dining hall the priest hadn't arrived. We soon learned that he had called Rinty McVeigh out to tell him that his mother had died in hospital this morning. Poor Rinty was shattered and came into Mass not quite managing to stem the tears. Apparently, Sadie, his mother, was in her early sixties and her husband is in his late seventies so her sudden death came as a complete surprise.

Wednesday 30 January
Roy and I have just finished an extremely tough game of chess, which lasted well over two hours. I was in front and then suddenly it appeared as if he had turned the tables on me. He

was one move away from queening a pawn. I didn't know how to stop him and sat sweating for about ten or fifteen minutes. Then he declared that I was two moves from checkmate and there was nothing he could do to stop me. I looked and looked but couldn't see the moves. Then he showed me. So both of us were satisfied.

You were asking me was it our first anniversary together. It passed peacefully on the nineteenth of January! Not one argument or a cross word the whole time. And if his trial goes ahead next week as scheduled he'll be away in seven or eight days' time. He's a good young lad – as, of course, are most of the people here. Occasionally he plays football in the yard then comes back to the cell and complains that I shouldn't have let him! On those days that he doesn't play – which is most of the time – he and a group of friends stand in the far corner of the yard, which receives a bit of sun, just chatting and laughing and only do a few laps of the yard towards the end of exercise. I just love to walk the whole time.

7.30 pm

I was called for a legal with Barra this afternoon. He says that Judge Nicholson will be delivering his judgement at ten in the morning on our application for a separate trial.

Saturday 2 February

Roy sends his thanks for the 'Good Luck' card. I was very pleased at your letter, which just bubbled with humour and love. It capped a brilliant visit. Even though it's a lonesome Saturday night I feel on top of the world, like a young fella who has just left a girl home and jumps into the air and clicks his heels as he walks away from her door.

Monday 4 February

A fella called Brian Henry got a suit sent in for his trial, which begins next week. When he was slopping out last night Jim O'Carroll stole the suit and quickly changed into it. Brian would be about 14 stone and Jim 11 stone. The cuffs came over Jim's hands and the jacket and trousers of the double-breasted suit were baggy. Brian was at the sluice emptying his pot when Jim came dandering in nonchalantly carrying two pisspots. It was a real scream because, of course, everybody then told Jim what an appalling suit it was: 'Is it second-hand?' 'Is it your grandfather's?' 'Fuck, you're sure to get twenty years if you wear that in court.'

Last night after lights out I was listening to a programme about the life of a Swedish soprano. She requested 'The Pearlfishers' Duet' and I sank into a tranquil, dreamy world until the fading of the last note, which was followed immediately by agony! The song itself is actually about reconciliation and the renewal of friendship (you actually get the feel of it) between the two fishermen, who had both fallen in love with the same goddess and quarrelled.

Tuesday 5 February, the Condemned Cell

Well, he's lost two games of chess in succession (not one of his better nights), his face is pure white and I swear I can see him visibly balding before my eyes. His palms are clammy, his eyes dilated and his heart is palpitating. And there is nothing I can do to help. His co-accused had a legal visit this afternoon and suffice it to say that sentence-wise things don't look too good, even though Campbell, the trial judge, today sentenced a loyalist to just six years for conspiracy to murder Butch Braniff's father, who was killed in Ardoyne in 1989.

We've been joking all night but reality continually intrudes. It's Donna whom we are both thinking of the most.

Roy is very self-conscious about his baldness. In fact, he refuses to head the ball in a football match! His two brothers, Gary and Brian, went into the Blocks with heads of hair and came out with heads. I was showing him a very funny newspaper article about a man who for twenty-five years avoided going any place where he would be required to remove his cap. He couldn't stand anyone being behind him when he had his cap off – he felt their eyes boring into his bald head. Nearing retirement age he bought a toupee and it changed his life. For the first time in years he and his wife could go to the pub, to the pictures or to a dance. A guy who specialises in hairpieces said: 'Some fellows don't care what it looks like once they've got something on top of their head.'

And that's absolutely true! Do you remember when we were on our camping trip, a tourist walked into that café in Clifden with the gerbil on his head? You and Chrissie laughed so much that we had to leave.

I hope your cold has receded. I loved that description of you emerging from the bath! Do you know the feeling in your heart when you see a newborn baby first smile or when you see the splendid sun surrender itself to the horizon? That's the joy I feel each time you walk through that door.

Wednesday 6 February

Well, Roy is back with me for another day or two. I fixed his Paisley-patterned tie for him this morning, firmly shook his hand and wished him the best and said a wee prayer for him when the cell door was shut. His mouth was dry and he seemed nervous but told me later that the feeling disappeared when he was in the tunnel on his way to court. He was offered seventeen years if he pleaded guilty but said no. He's expecting between eighteen and twenty years. The whole time he was away I was thinking of him. He returned in late afternoon, over the worst part, he said. He's putting up no defence or fight but is forcing them to prove the case – 'not guilty, no defence', in jail or court parlance. So his strength returned to him.

Whilst all this was happening Dermot Carroll from Armagh returned from his visit in what can only be described as a state of shock. Last night his wife of forty-five days, his brother and brother-in-law were all arrested in connection with that arms find in two cars at the Birches, County Armagh. I had a good yarn with him but there wasn't much I could say. However, by later afternoon he had partially rallied and overcome the initial shock. You always think you are badly off until you hear of someone else's woes.

Pat Sheehan arrived back, smiling, boasting that he was only getting life but that it didn't matter since it would all be over in three or four years. 'The signs are there!' he said. Finally, as you know, Jim and Rosaleen got twenty-two years each. Jim sent back word with Pat to 'tell the lads I took it on the chin!' He then told Pat that if Pat's three- or four-year prediction was wrong and he met him in ten years' time during a wing shift in the Blocks he'd kill him!

Our judicial review before Carswell on the 'Scrumpie affair' is supposed to be heard on Friday, I think. I had to fill in a legal-aid application form. Two of the questions were: 'Does anyone besides you live in the place where you live?' and 'Do you own the place where you live now?'

There is a beautiful piece of music on the radio at the moment – Prokoviev's 'Montagues and Capulets'. I used to do a lot of recording on three-quarter-inch tape (as I think it's called). In 1971 our Geraldine lent me money to buy a four-track Grundig tape recorder. I taped pop records but also news items – for example, all the bulletins for the ninth of August 1971 as internment was being introduced and the first reports of 'six people' being shot dead on an anti-internment march in Derry on the thirtieth of January 1972.

'Montagues and Capulets' I taped around about the time my friend Stan Carberry was shot dead by the Greenjackets. A few hours after his funeral I was arrested and taken to Castlereagh and this music kept going through my head. I always associate it with death and mourning. I used to visit Stan's grave in Milltown and place flowers on it. I experience the same kind of inner peace in a cemetery as sitting on a deserted beach watching the waves roll in. Enough about cemeteries!

Thursday 7 February
I was in the shower when a prisoner, Decky Farrell from Newry, shouted in that there was a newsflash on the radio stating that three mortar bombs had exploded at Whitehall. My first thoughts were of Donna, who I was sure would be convinced that fate was conspiring against Roy, who is charged with possession of mortars. Then, at twenty to eleven, on my way back to the cell, Danny Caldwell said that it was believed that the mortar attack was on Downing Street and I remembered right away that the Cabinet meets on Thursday mornings.

Roy came back at half four and we flocked around him like hacks seeking his response. He was philosophical about it and had been told of the attack by a defence solicitor shortly before they went into court. He and his co-accused at first laughed and thought the solicitor was joking! The trial will finish tomorrow. Pat Sheehan is up for sentencing tomorrow for definite.

Saturday 9 February
Poor Pat. Twenty-four years and he doesn't begin serving it for another two years because of his licence from his last sentence.

Did you read the review in the *Guardian* of the new Kevin Costner film *Dances With Wolves*? It said: 'What the film achieves in keeping the eye happy is more than balanced by the still, quiet voice at its centre. This insists that we live in a largely corrupted world but that individuals can still do something about it from inside themselves.'

I like all expressions of hope – and good endings! I think I read novels for religion or edification. I'm serious! Of course, there's the entertainment value. But what I mostly seek are those nuggets of wisdom or truths about humanity and existence and relationships and love which fiction appears best able to communicate. History, biography and documentary are too restrictive. I read somewhere that fiction is a medium which unites the spiritual with the material worlds, or it's at least where they meet. And I think that is correct.

Sunday 10 February

On our good mornings, which is when we eat breakfast in the canteen, we carry out what is called a 'dry slop'. That is, empty our pots and just do a quick brush-out of the cell. A 'full slop' includes clearing the floor of lockers and chairs and mopping out the cell. Well, Jimmy McShane gets slagged because he will only wash his hair once a week. He must have some phobia about it falling out if it sees shampoo. He showers – if you can call it that – on alternate days, and he stands about four feet away from the spray and emerges as dry as he went in. So people say to him in the mornings, 'Well, Jimmy. Is it a dry slop today again!'

Poor Roy is dying. He says that when he was about thirteen he helped his mother dismantle a heavy bed and creaked his back. Since then a sharp pain returns to haunt him occasionally. It has been hurting him for the past three days. Then his muscles became sore with an impending cold, and now a cold sore has broken out on his lower lip. He's lying in bed right now and has taken painkillers. He would need to get up later and write Donna a letter. He has just woken up and said: 'Honey, I think there's somebody downstairs trying to get in to the house. Would you go down and check?' But I assure him that it is only an orderly polishing the brass handle of the lock on our cell door.

Out in the yard forty prisoners of the Queen are marching around in circles, and on my radio, at a quarter past two on a sunny February afternoon, is a nocturne by a dead French composer. And we are all flying around the sun at 108,000 kilometres per hour, and it and the rest of its solar system are travelling through space at 200 kilometres per second! How can we be sane, or how can any of it make sense!

8pm

Roy has been given a brown bag – a large one – so he is doing half his packing tonight and then I'll finish it off tomorrow afternoon. Here he is to say cheerio:

Hello, Leslie, just wee me here! Well, this is it. Time for the hardest day of my life, time for everything to come crumbling around me. I'm completely shattered! I mean, how can I possibly live without Danny! I'll tell you this, he'd make a great nurse, for he has cared for me and my sore back all day, not to mention the few times I regurgitated my Mars bars and crisps at 3 am! By the way, Leslie, there's a song on the radio now called 'Feel Like Making Love', and Danny isn't half giving me some funny looks. Maybe it is time I was moving on. Anyway, I'd like to say a very big thank-you to you both, you've been more than good to Donna and myself. I'll say bye-bye for now. Take care of my honey-bunch, I'll miss him! All the best. Roy.

Well, let's hope he misses me and I don't join him! And now, my honey-bunch, I shall leave you until tomorrow. Came across a beautiful expression in a book: *coup de foudre* – love at first sight.

Monday 11 February
Twenty years. Poor Roy and Donna. Your Valentine's card and letter took the edge off my desolation. I see that his conviction has depressed you. I spoke to a fella called Gill who saw Roy at lunchtime, and he says he was okay. Just as Roy had added a paragraph to my letter to you last night, I wrote a piece in his to Donna with words from an old song I once quoted to you:

> *Somewhere the sun is shining,*
> *So honey don't you cry.*
> *We'll find that silver lining,*
> *The clouds will soon roll by.*

It's a pity you missed Donna after Saturday's visit. I can't understand where she went, unless she was offered a lift in a car. It's now after seven and, like you, I am on my own. I've just tried out Roy's mattress and it is much firmer than mine so I think I'll have it!

Tuesday 12 February
Well, I had a good visit and collected your parcel and letter immediately afterwards. Liam leaned across my lap, almost in the foetal position, for the whole visit! Ciaran was up also and I explained to him that I would be in court all next week, so they could forget about Tuesday's pass. The kids are off school next Monday, Tuesday and Wednesday on a mid-term break so they will be at the trial on those days. It will probably be boring enough to disillusion them about courtroom dramas. I am glad that Mark Mahoney and Jim Harrington are coming over. That is very kind and loyal of them. Does Jim Gibney know? The

reason I ask is that it is up to Sinn Fein to chaperone them and provide some transport.

With six weeks to go to the seventy-fifth anniversary of the 1916 Rising the Dublin government has still not decided how to commemorate it! For the fiftieth anniversary there was a big splurge. Patriotism was okay, in theory, back then. But even the theory is now gone. The divide is even greater with the promotion of a twenty-six-county nation state, and fuck the North. As the Proclamation says, we have to rely 'first and foremost on our own strength'. We should probably also rely first and foremost on our own negotiating skills and intelligence. When the hunger strike was called off in October 1981 without the achievement of the five demands, the men in the H-Blocks were still able to exploit their strength of numbers and use their ingenuity to redeem the situation.

Wednesday 13 February
I've just heard on the news that several hundred civilians were killed in Baghdad when two missiles hit a bomb shelter. Hopefully, these deaths will at last force people in the West to realise the extent of civilian slaughter carried out in their name.

Thursday 14 February
Seany Adams and Gill returned from court early today in a bad mood. The prosecution is now claiming that the firearms residue found on their clothes came from an AK-47 and not a British Army weapon and that they can distinguish between the two because powder from an AK-47 contains traces of a tin compound. Up until now their defence had been successfully making the point that both of them could have been contaminated by the soldiers or RUC men who arrested them. So today Seany wasn't pleased about getting called Rin Tin Tin.

Seany went to court wearing a black (charcoal) suit whose jacket has huge shoulders and he was told it would be a good idea if he took the coat-hanger out! 'It is fuckin' out, it is fuckin' out, okay!' He gets all confused when he's recounting what happened in court:

'When my barrister had the cop in the witness stand he was cutting him to pieces during cross-contamination!' he said, before realising he was obsessed with forensics!

Anto was telling me that they were all prepared for him at the dining table this morning and when he took his seat they all immediately stuffed their ears with huge lumps of dangling toilet paper! But he takes it well (I hope!).

Monday 18 February
I had a legal with Paddy. He sounded as if he had a cold coming on – I hope he doesn't fall ill at this stage. But to be truthful, even if Dessie Boal lost his voice for the next month I would still feel I was in competent hands with this junior barrister Charlie Adair. There's no shit with him. He cuts through trash and can isolate the relevant point in seconds. Very impressive. And he's only forty! I expect he'll go places over the next few years. Roll on the future, with its flood of answers. I am a good swimmer and will not drown.

I heard that Roy arrived in H-6 safe and sound and with a bag full of biscuits! He lives on chocolate biscuits!

Tuesday 19 February
The clock on the wall says ten past two and I am sitting on a most uncomfortable chair, bored stiff. I am in the dock. On my left, but separated from me by a waist-high wooden partition, are Erin Corbett (who is charged with allowing her house to be used by the rebels) and Michael Maguire (who let his car be

used). On my right is Anto (who is dressed for digging the garden), then sit the people with ties, Jim O'Carroll and Gerard Hodgins, and in the next dock, Danny Caldwell and Liam Martin (wearing some kind of Masonic earring for Hutton's benefit). In the seats behind Danny and Liam are Liam's mother and father, Jimmy and Veronica, who at least can sit together whilst we are in court for the next three or four weeks. Ciaran and Jim were here this morning but the kids weren't. Many other relatives were present.

As I write, Charlie Adair is quizzing a police mapping officer about the street lighting in the entry to the side of the block of houses in which we were arrested. Things liven up when the defence barristers cross-examine.

There was an ass on every press seat this morning as Creaney made his opening remarks, but now they are gone, leaving behind a woman from the Press Association. It hardly matters because this is all boring stuff, largely. Mark and Jim and another attorney from New York are in a bench to the left of the judge.

We had our lunch in a holding cell called 'the safe', where we will spend all lunch hours while at court. I noticed a statement scribbled on the wall of this cell, written by someone obviously waiting anxiously on a verdict: 'I spent a week in this cell one day.' Tomorrow we are moving to Court No. 2 for the day to allow the Kelly et al. appeal over the two corporals to finish, then on Thursday or Friday we will be back in Court No. 1.

Tell Mark and Jim that I noticed how scrupulous they were in jumping to attention when Higgins entered the court and 'God Save the Queen' was declared!

7.30 pm

Back in my cell. I arrived back to a beautiful letter from you and three 'Good Luck' cards. Your words have been of great consolation: aside from being my partner, you are a true friend and supporter. Thank you for going through all this anguish for me and, of course, for us. I am extremely proud of you.

Wednesday 20 February
Courtroom tension and excitement drains the very marrow from your bones. And today was fairly exciting because of the number of times the RUC witnesses were found to be telling lies, covering up God-knows-what – presumably their secret intelligence operation on the seventh of January. They have also admitted forcibly removing Sandy Lynch from the house.

Of course, Mr Fenton also gave evidence about his son's voice being on a tape played to him in a Sinn Fein office. That's the whole purpose of the Fenton shooting being intermingled with our case.

Given the bits of excitement today, I am sure Kevin, who attended with Ciaran, was not too bored.

Thursday 21 February
Extremely boring, apart from some more RUC witnesses being revealed as liars. However, others subsequently took the stand and have – with the help of Hutton – attempted to correct and synchronise the times of arrival, of Sandy being taken out and of the arrests. Hutton dashes in and out of court like a ferret. He sits with his glasses perched on the end of his nose, his lower lip pushed into his upper in a permanent grimace.

I have now seen the document I referred to yesterday. It is a statement Sandy made at Chiswick Police Station, England, in March 1990, to Detective Chief Superintendant George Caskey. In this statement Sandy is a little angel, running to a phone each time he smells explosives or sees a rifle, to tell his handlers and save lives. On one occasion, though, he couldn't get to a phone, but before blowing up Shortt's Airport he sabotaged a couple of the bombs!

Caskey and I know each other of old. He coordinated the raids against *Republican News* and the executive of Belfast Sinn Fein back in 1978. Nearly everyone was arrested, apart from myself. I was very careful about my movements. However, I was eventually caught around September. I met with Gerry Adams in the Lake Glen Hotel on the day he was released, having been acquitted of IRA membership. Later, I bumped into Jim Gibney at the bottom of Beechmount Avenue and we went to Sandra's to get some dinner. But the undercover agents, it seems, were following Jim. Brit jeeps came flying into Beechmount Parade and sealed it off. They raided the house and took me to Castlereagh.

There, Caskey was in charge. Throughout some of the interrogations he was smoking Ritmeester cigars so I, being a cheeky bastard, asked him for one! Before the seven days were up I had smoked quite a few. He charged me with IRA membership and conspiracy to pervert the course of public justice. I conducted my own defence and got bail after about a month in the Crum' because of a statement he made to Judge O'Donnell. The evidence against me was my fingerprints on telexed IRA statements and claims of responsibility that had passed through the Republican Press Centre and the *Republican News*. But I pointed out in court that on that basis I should also have been charged with UVF membership! Hadn't I spotted, during interrogation, an article in my handwriting, written for the *Irish People* in the USA, which contained a statement from the UVF claiming responsibility for blowing up a Catholic pub. O'Donnell thought about it and then said, 'That's a good question, Mr Morrison. Mr Caskey, why isn't Mr Morrison charged with UVF membership as well?'

'Don't be ridiculous!' said George.

And at that, O'Donnell gave me bail of £1,000. Sheila McVeigh and Miriam Daly cheered in the public gallery, so he upped it to £3,000.

The charges were dropped about four months later. George was also in charge of the Kincora Inquiry. A few years ago I was arrested and brought to Grosvenor Road barracks for a couple of hours. Before letting you go they usually clear the yard of personnel you might have an interest in. And as I was walking out, there was George getting into his car. He turned and saw that I saw it and its number plate and said nonchalantly, 'Oh well, I was fed up with the colour.'

Sunday 24 February
Well, I see that the war is under way. God help all those soldiers, especially those at the front. I woke up about a quarter to four, put on the radio and heard on the five o'clock news that the ground assault had begun at 1 am. I then dozed until eight o'clock, when I got up.

The loyalists are on some form of protest here – over what I'm not entirely clear. They've been smashing sinks and ripping out pipes. They're probably also trying to provoke us but we're in a pacifist phase! They threatened the orderlies not to serve in the canteen, clean in the wing or leave out mops and buckets for slopping cells. So some of the warders have had to take on these duties. One orderly, called Maxwell, was released yesterday after serving his short sentence. But when he was here he seemed to be the one who did everything. All that you'd hear from warders was, 'Maxwell, clear those plates!', 'Maxwell, get the mop buckets!', etc. We were in the canteen tonight when a warder who's particularly grumpy was huffing and puffing and sweating, trailing the heavy tea urn. As he dragged it into the canteen all the lads were shouting, 'Maxwell! Leave that tea in the corner!' and 'Right, Maxwell, that's it for now!'

Monday 25 February

I got your letter. It was very moving and I felt honoured by the sentiments and devotion you expressed. In fact, I don't know how to handle it at all and there's no point just now getting into a definitive position but court today was not good. I know Sandy will be in the witness box all day tomorrow and probably Wednesday but he has been perfectly tutored.

He has repeatedly stated that he was getting killed and he has flatly denied shooting Peter Duggan in Downpatrick and carrying out the Girdwood bombing. When asked to explain actions which tend to support our defence – such as not declaring that he was held against his will when the RUC raided the house – he says he 'doesn't know'. Unless he is broken down under subsequent cross-examination (and remember, he has now found his feet and his confidence), the Crown's case stands and we fall. That's how it is at this point in time.

I don't care about anything but your future. I find little difference between a fifteen-year sentence and a twenty-year one. There are better ways of spending *your* life than running to a jail for even five or six years. Maybe things will change tomorrow, who knows, but I doubt it. Sandy is motivated: his prosperity turns on his ability to deliver us. Plus, he's full of revenge! In common parlance, Sandy is a bastard! And I admire his ruthlessness. He is enjoying his role! He's sorry that he has been found out and has to emigrate, etc., but he is savouring this last 'operation'.

The boys were glued to the TV last night watching the film *Days of Thunder*. Jim O'Carroll and I disrupted the viewing of it by continually asking dumb questions and mixing it up with other films. It was great! You could see their fury mounting!

'Have we missed the part where Dustin Hoffman counts the matches as they fall?' I asked. Jim wanted to know if Michelle's surname was pronounced 'Effer' or 'Peffer' and then said, 'What exactly is the plot of this film, I was playing snooker and wasn't really interested?'

Tuesday 26 February
Hello, my love

Well, today was a bit better, though what effect it will have on the judge I just don't know. The barristers seemed pleased anyway. It seemed clear to me that Sandy was lying – his lies hung in the air for minutes on end but he gripped denial like a terrier with a bone between his teeth. Maybe that's what made it worse; that is, his ruthlessness, which I had so much admired, was certainly exposed. And then, suddenly, the barristers pulled off, content that his credibility and motivation had been called completely into question. Again, I suppose it all comes down to what it means legally. The warder sitting behind me commented: 'It looks like he's trying to stitch youse all up.'

I forgot to say that Veronica Martin has pleaded guilty to aiding and abetting unlawful imprisonment. It doesn't affect us in the least and, in fact, it's good that she's not facing a big sentence. She is pleased enough with what she has heard.

Wednesday 27 February
Well, I'll not get too far tonight because I am absolutely exhausted and feel like climbing into bed and sleeping for a week. There was very little happening in court today concerning me – apart from a statement from the cop who arrested me. So whilst sitting there I wrote Roy a fairly long letter sending him our regards. Maybe this tiredness I'm experiencing will result in a good night's sleep. I think I think too much! I'm obsessed – not frantically but inescapably – with this case. Oh well, it'll not

be long before it's over. I didn't realise it would be such a drain physically.

I'm still humbled by your words the other day.

Thursday 28 February

Court has just begun. I was the last to arrive in the dock, having just came from a legal visit with Dessie Boal and P. J. It lasted about forty-five minutes and was very satisfactory and reassuring. By that I mean that they expressed confidence in me. We will be meeting each day, covering all areas thoroughly. It is fairly nerve-racking. Do you mind me sharing all my anxieties and apprehensions? Monday night's letter was a bit gloomy perhaps and yesterday's was brighter. That's how it goes. I am afraid to hope. I think that's where the terror lies – knowing that the case is still open and that you could walk free. Before, I thought that with Lynch's testimony we would know for definite by his performance if we were finished. But its value for convicting us – or perhaps me – can probably be countermanded by me in the witness box. It gives me butterflies the size of bats!

At the moment Jimmy Martin's statements are continuing to be read out. There are two reporters in court, only one of whom I know by sight. He has a gingery-brown thick beard and combed-back, greyish hair. Perhaps he's from the *Belfast Telegraph*. Ivan Little has just arrived. His eyes look beady. I wonder where he was last night! The cop in the witness box has a monotonous voice, which is lulling everyone to sleep despite the fact that this is an account of a Castlereagh interrogation.

Yesterday additional evidence was presented against me – and such a joke it is! Listen to this:

'I am a Chief Inspector of the Royal Ulster Constabulary presently stationed at Lurgan Police Station. Between the first of August 1984 and the twenty-sixth of November 1990 I was stationed in the west Belfast area serving respectively in Andersonstown, Woodbourne, Springfield Parade and again in Andersonstown. I know Daniel Morrison of 37 Iveagh Drive, Belfast, and during the course of my duties have observed him on numerous occasions entering and leaving the Sinn Fein office at 51 Falls Road, Belfast, and appearing on the platform at Sinn Fein rallies at Connolly House, Andersonstown Road, Belfast. Signed, S.T. Ormsby.'

P. J. says to Boal: 'We're fucked! Our client never told us he was in Sinn Fein!'

Do they think I'm going to deny being a full-blooded republican!

There's just been an outburst of laughter from everyone in court – cops and barristers included. A detective is giving an account of Jimmy being questioned about 'Danny Morrison and Sinn Fein'.

'You described Danny Morrison as a politician. What do you mean by that?'

'I thought he was Adams and that.'

'To what party would this boy Morrison you refer to belong?'

'Sinn Fein, I think everybody knows that.'

'What in your view does Sinn Fein stand for?'

'Looking after the people of west Belfast, their social problems, advice centres and that.'

'Have you ever heard the statement, "The ballot box in one hand, the armalite in the other?"'

'Aye, I think it was Margaret Thatcher said it.'

The detectives then asked him who he voted for.

'I vote for Sinn Fein, for housing and that sort of thing.'

'What about the SDLP?'

'They're too middle-of-the-road for me.'

A few seconds later the cop says, 'What about the Workers

Party, they're not all doctors, they seemed to be for the working man?'

The Sticks find support in all the right quarters!

Our Ciaran is up in court today again so I have to hand it to him for his solidarity and loyalty. Most of the time it is as boring as death.

7.30 pm

Another beautiful letter from you. Thank you. I'm into the second part of the 'Indian' novels that Jim and Mark left me: *Tracks* by Louise Erdrich and *A Yellow Raft In Blue Water* by Michael Dorris. There's a funny part in the Dorris book when a priest comes on the reservation and is attempting to evangelise. In order to sound friendly he asks an Indian how do you say 'Hello' in their language. The Indian gives him the phrase and the priest thinks he's doing great because when he says 'Hello' everybody laughs at him. Little does he know that he is really saying 'I smell like dogshite'!

My friend Schubert is on the radio with one of his bequests to me – his Symphony No. 5. I once watched you sleep whilst this played on the radio as we drove out of Galway on our way to Kilkenny.

Saturday 2 March

Still glowing. A very satisfying and contenting visit. Afterwards, when I was queuing up for dinner, one of the lads said, 'Smell the perfume!' Sure enough, it was me.

'I always wear Chanel 19,' I said. 'What about yourself?'

I got your letter, and one from Geraldine, a card from Theresa Burt, a 'Good Luck' card from Leila Burt and another from Chrissie. Chrissie's card featured two gangsters throwing their chained victim (whose feet were encased in concrete) over the edge of a cliff into shark-infested waters! Did you see the great photo of Sandy Lynch in the *Sunday Tribune*? He looked like a pimp, the Boston Strangler and a dickhead all rolled into one.

Sunday 3 March

I fell asleep early enough last night but woke up with a jolt at the terrifying noise of a man screaming, howling, as if a ghost was strangling him; then there was whimpering. It lasted for about half a minute. Then there was a deathly silence. It must have worried the night watch because a warder came around, lifted the flaps and switched on the lights in every cell as if to check that no one had hanged himself!

Monday 4 March

It is twenty past two and Margaret Boyce, a forensic scientist, is on the stand and I suspect she'll be there for the rest of the afternoon, if not longer. She has an English accent, sounds thoroughly proficient and yet is only in her late twenties. Ed Moloney, Jim Gibney and our Ciaran were in court this morning but have now gone. Wise men. At lunchtime we got dinner in a long, poorly lit cell which is below the dock. Afterwards, four of the lads played cards, Jimmy twiddled his thumbs and I got called for a legal with Boal and Paddy.

Well, I wonder how the Birmingham Six are feeling, back in the dock? A lot happier than us, I'd say! I think their appeal is due to last two weeks. It will be a very emotional occasion, as you said, when they step out into freedom.

So the Gulf War is over. The Iraqi dead can be counted in scores of thousands and the Allies' in hundreds, if even that. The *Sunday Times* had an article on the 'Jeremiahs' – which included the *Guardian* for its editorials, Robert Fisk, Tony Benn, Bruce Kent, etc. – showing how grossly inaccurate were their predictions and quoting from them. I am certainly in that camp and don't intend revising my position. There are a lot of gruesome stories emerging about the treatment of Kuwaiti civilians by Iraqi soldiers and the looting and wanton destruction carried out by those soldiers. There is no excuse for what they did but it sickens me to see the West beat its breast so sanctimoniously. In a year's time or five years' time let's see what changes there have really been: a democratic Kuwait! a settlement of the Arab-Israeli conflict! a neutral Gulf!

Oh Lord, what a weary afternoon this is. All of us have dried up. There's little chit-chat, and we're fed up chewing sweets. It could be another week before the prosecution has finished its case. No wonder people plead guilty! There are eight large windows in this courtroom – Courtroom No. 1 – where all the video equipment is assembled, but the heavy green drapes are permanently closed so there is no natural light. Instead, the room is illuminated with formal, soulless, artificial lighting, which is sore on the eyes and burns holes in the screen of your vision.

M'lud must have been caught in yesterday's shower whilst out on the green. He has sneezed about four times, continually blows his nose without disturbing his glasses and, worse, he is now picking it like a child.

Ms Boyce has just given details of my 'hair combing' and doubtless there must be some mistake! It consisted of six short light-brown-coloured hairs! Not a grey one in sight! Anto has asked me whom am I writing to. He says it's a pity you can't come to court, otherwise he could blow you kisses. This would be in retaliation for me showing him how to blow kisses to Lucy.

That was a bad shooting in Tyrone last night . . .

8 pm
Back in my cell. I was saying about that shooting. When I came back somebody said that from the names given out on the radio it seems that one of those shot dead is the brother of Frankie Quinn's girlfriend, Pauline Quinn. She's on remand in Maghaberry.

Tuesday 5 March
Do you know what is satisfying about writing a letter? It is an act of creation, forming words to communicate thoughts, and your character and mood rub off on those words. The satisfaction is all the greater when it is a love letter you are writing because the recipient knows you intimately and can feel the glow of affection and the ache of longing from your words.

I was in deep discussion in the legal boxes with Dessie Boal and Paddy at about ten this morning when I heard a rap on the glass panel of the door. I thought it was the court being called; I turned around and a girl smiled and waved. She had been ushered away before I realised that it was Frankie Quinn's girlfriend, Pauline, down from Maghaberry, applying for bail to attend the funeral of her brother John tomorrow. I must drop her a letter of sympathy. Manuel Marley's girlfriend was sentenced to ten years in court today after having been convicted of possessing explosives. Maghaberry is filling up rightly.

The forensic scientist, Margaret Boyce, has turned out to be a right shit! When being cross-examined by the lads' defence barristers she was coy and evasive or did her best to paint a blacker picture than was presented in her report. But she was caught out and was forced to concede all the points they wanted. I brought Paddy's attention to what you said last week about certain aspects of press coverage – 'the Morrison trial', etc., when Joe Fenton issues – nothing to do with us – were before the court. Not only that! The indictment reads from 'Jimmy Martin' down, so it should be 'Martin and others'. But on the exhibits the tags even read 'Morrison and others'. When I told Boal and Paddy this they appeared to be completely nonchalant, even slightly proud that we were to the fore.

Erin Corbett and Michael Maguire changed their pleas to guilty and have been released on continuing bail, which is sound. Susan and Ciaran were in court most of the day. Susan shouted that she couldn't hear a thing.

Thursday 7 March
It was very funny yesterday when a detective was reading out the notes of Jim O'Carroll's interviews in Castlereagh. Generally, Jim refused to answer any questions, except one, when he told them he was separated from Kathleen and talked about his kids. Anto remarked, 'Fuck, he even squealed on his kids!' Then a fingerprint expert spoke of finding Jim's fingerprints on the inside pages of a *Woman's Own* magazine! Everyone was straining their eyes to see if it was the astrology page, the problems column or the recipes! Anto said it was a knitting pattern!

You mentioned your walk home from work in the city centre. I used to love that walk when I was going to and coming from the College of Business Studies in Brunswick Street when I was doing A-Level English and history in 1971. Although redevelopment had begun, most of the old streets around the Grosvenor Road still stood, including Blackwater Street, where my uncle Harry was born in 1916. The front of the road had a pub or old shop at each corner – pubs and shops with character, atmosphere, ghosts of past generations. And all of it was bulldozed to make way for unsatisfactory housing estates. There's hardly a decent pub in all of the Falls now.

I would walk up the Grosvenor, then cut through the grounds of the Royal Victoria Hospital and emerge onto the Falls at the

Children's Hospital. Back then, at nights it was impossible to study because of the explosions and shootings, which had dramatically increased after the introduction of internment.

I'm glad that you phoned our Margaret and that she's keeping a lot better. I forgot about her daughter Marie reaching the age of eighteen, an age when we thought we were adults but were still really children. She was born when I was interned. I don't think you have ever met her but she is a beautiful kid, though tall and skinny. Gilleen, the other daughter, whom you may have met, is a pure tomboy! Margaret must have reared those two on her own because Greg seems to have always been on a posting somewhere.

I'm listening to a programme on Radio Ulster at the moment called *Caschar*. It is presented in Irish (which I still can't speak) and the song by Edith Piaf is in French! It is old and crackly and there's a swirl of cigarette smoke rising from a silhouetted figure in the corner behind a table upon which sits one glass of wine. She is all alone but she is waiting.

Monday 11 March

I think my ordeal is over! I don't think there'll be rebuttal evidence so it looks as if I'm finished in the witness box. I know I should feel elated but I am wound up tight and don't know how to uncoil. I was in the box from about twenty to eleven until about twenty to twelve with Dessie Boal doing the questioning. Then Creaney took over until 1 pm. Finally, I gave evidence from two until four. The tension was incredible. I swear to Almighty God that the hatred in Hutton towards me was palpable. I sought his permission at one stage not to comment on things that I had subsequently learnt in jail from my co-accused. With glee he ordered me to answer the question.

Creaney was jubilant but, of course, it backfired on him

because I then went on to explain what everyone had told me they had been doing there and this tended to alibi them without them having to take the witness stand! I didn't think Creaney would have pulled out so early. I suppose I can't relax because I can't believe it's over and I expect them to conjure up some pretext in which to recall me. In the middle of my cross-examination I noticed our Kevin had a big lovebite and I remember wondering who did that on my son's neck!

Anyway, I returned to my seat in the dock with the lads all winking at me. When the court adjourned both Boal and Charlie Adair came over and congratulated me and said I was excellent, never put a foot wrong. When I got back to the jail and went to the canteen I got a big cheer from all the lads.

It's after seven now and just before lock-up I saw Anto on the Twos. He was still beaming and said that he was still full of excitement and hadn't eaten yet. I've just stuffed myself with four headache tablets and three chocolate biscuits!

Although Walter the censor – whom I like – has gone missing, his successor has been efficient: your letter was through the censor and awaiting me. You would have laughed tonight when Jim O'Carroll got his parcel. Anto, Danny Caldwell and I were standing behind him when he was signing for it. He pulled out two magazines to see what they were. Can you guess? *Woman* and *Woman's Own*! He got some slagging and everybody shouted, 'Jim, *don't* lend me them after you!'

I wonder how our Ciaran is getting on. I'm praying hard that that blister on his lip isn't cancerous. I can't believe he has had it for a year without taking any action. I think it's tonight that you're visiting him so I'll probably hear about him in tomorrow's letter.

Tuesday 12 March

Creaney never put in an appearance today but left the summing-up to his deputy. I met with Boal, Adair and Paddy this morning; they all expressed satisfaction with yesterday. Boal said, 'Creaney never put a glove on you.' He said that he has his legal submissions prepared, that our defence was bold and our strategy perfect. It's now a straight case of prejudice, that is of the judge overcoming his prejudice against me. So we have all done our best. Hutton can choose to believe Sandy and declare his disbelief in me and simply convict (probably not on the conspiracy to murder but on the unlawful-imprisonment charge only) and there's not a thing we can do about it. Tomorrow the defence barristers make their submissions.

The court finished at twenty to four today and when I got back to the jail I was called for a visit. It was Ed Moloney and David McKittrick, and we had a good yarn. Aine, Hodgies' girl, was in court and he was over the moon.

You were right not to listen to the news. Naturally, the media focuses on the most sensational aspects and does not accurately reflect legal developments. Our Susan must certainly have got a shock. I got a shock myself when I saw the *Irish News* tonight – 'Morrison defends IRA "right to kill"'! I wish I was a nonentity!

Wednesday 13 March

This morning the prosecution finished its submissions. Arthur Harvey, on behalf of Jim and Dan (though actually covering us all), was on his feet all day and was simply brilliant. He took Sandy apart limb by limb and heavily criticised the RUC's 'forty-minute' investigation of the allegation of Lynch's involvement in the attempted murder of Peter Duggan.

Harvey said that the RUC knew, and Lynch admitted in court, that if Lynch was the one who shot Duggan then the case against us fell apart because Sandy would have been proved to be lying. You can detect from Hutton's interventions that he is resisting like mad the defence's propositions and that he is anxious to convict but is being frustrated. Today was a good day for me and my mate, Mr Boal, who has yet to put my case!

I wrote Pauline Quinn a letter of sympathy. And I received a letter from Derek Dunne, a fairly consistent correspondent, so we'll always keep our door open to him.

At about a quarter past four we were back in the wing, in the canteen eating our tea, when there was an almighty roar. You have to come through a gate, kept locked by a warder, and then two sliding grills (one is closed before the other is opened) before getting into the canteen. One of our lads was waiting at the last grill for it to be opened, when two loyalists came in behind him. They immediately jumped him, punched him and kicked him to the ground. We were going crazy because we could see this through the grill but couldn't help him. Two more loyalists arrived but before they could join in warders came running in and pulled the loyalists out. The prisoner – J. J. from Turf Lodge – was badly shaken and suffered mostly bruises.

Thursday 14 March
Heard the great news about the Birmingham Six being released and later watched them on TV stepping out to freedom. What a day for those men and their families! The entire canteen was hushed as we watched.

Arthur Harvey, representing Jim and Dan, completed his submissions this morning; then Reggie Weir, on behalf of Anto and Hodgies, began. Up until today he hadn't impressed me but he put up several very good arguments. He's a bit flamboyant and cut the judge down to size when Hutton more or less stated that anyone who didn't answer police questions whilst in custody must be guilty. Weir pointed out that it's part of the political culture in republican areas for people not to talk to the police. He said that if what the judge was saying was true then the aerial man (who erected an aerial on Jimmy Martin's roof on Saturday the sixth of January) would also be charged with conspiracy to murder and unlawful imprisonment had he been arrested and exercised his right to remain silent! The judge made a comment about Anto and myself along the lines that if my testimony was true then wasn't it possible that we two were guilty of aiding and abetting unlawful imprisonment because Sandy was being unlawfully imprisoned *until* we arrived and *for* us! Boal got up and quoted legal precedent after legal precedent from the top of his head, demolishing Hutton's remarks! He spent about forty-five minutes making his case and then said that he would begin my submissions tomorrow and sat down!

Boal is quiet, authoritative, ponderous, cogent, humorous and fucking brilliant! There is no doubt about it – all that remains against me in particular is the prejudice of Hutton. He is bursting to convict but is being thwarted at every turn. And my big advantage – besides the facts of the case – is that Hutton is outmatched by Boal and appears to defer to him. All this has left me a nervous wreck. I have been up since half five this morning, unable to get back to sleep. The temptation of thinking about freedom.

You were asking what you thought you should get P. J. present-wise. I haven't a clue! Maybe Barra could suggest something that he would like – a tiepin? He said he'll not be coming to the court for the judgement because his heart couldn't take the excitement. Boal is looking forward to his submissions tomorrow because he will be attempting to push back the frontier of some law, plus, of course, there is the prestige of the case and its unique features. He came up with a fantastic idea yesterday which he let Harvey pursue. He quoted a case when an IRA man, charged with armed robbery, pleaded that he was under duress from the IRA to carry out the act. A judge had ruled that when somebody joined the IRA they surrendered their will to that organisation and couldn't then plead duress of actions committed. Sandy had admitted surrendering himself to an IRA debriefing a month prior to the Carrigart Avenue incident – so he accepted the rules of the IRA and the IRA's 'right' to carry out security checks. Harvey argued that after Sandy entered into a deal with the IRA on the Saturday – to do a press conference – then he was no longer unlawfully imprisoned against his will but was detained with his agreement and that that explains why he didn't declare himself when the cops raided. That's just one of the issues Hutton has to rule on.

Have you noticed the pale, lingering light these evenings? Spring is here and everything is budding and the birds are singing again.

Monday 18 March
Anto's lonely. Rinty and Ceefax are away to the H-Blocks and the humour has gone from A2 with them!

You were talking about our letters – speculating about the volume of what we had written and how we could have a bonfire when I get out. No chance! In my old age I will tramp up to the attic, unlock the trunk, lift out a ribbon-tied bundle at random, come downstairs and go out to our conservatory, sit on an armchair with my feet up, pour both of us brandies and ask you if you remember the day you wrote this or that! One's wealth is the sum of the past and the purpose or meaning you read from it.

Saturday 23 March

I had a good long yarn with Jim Gibney yesterday. Despite all the visits I've had with him throughout the last fourteen months, yesterday's was really the first occasion when we actually had a thorough discussion about the political situation. He is a good, independent thinker whose opinions I respect, though obviously I don't always agree with them. For example, I remember him expressing the unorthodox view after Raymond McCreesh and Patsy O'Hara died that the hunger strike should be called off or stopped. Republicans were at a total loss as to how it could be stopped without the Brits crowing about 'victory'.

I like Jim's pragmatic brain, only today I think he was at a bit of a loss to cope – even confidentially – with the pragmatic scenarios I was feeling him out on. Obviously you are very isolated in here – although, it could be argued, more clear-headed as well – and he helped correct my thinking and my calculations somewhat. At the moment I'm in the middle of reading *The Uncivil Wars* by Padraig O' Malley. He's a revisionist, but the book isn't as bad as I thought it would be. The most depressing aspect of it, however, is his assertion that the only conclusion you can reach about our political problem is that the problem is insoluble!

The most frightening realisation is that were the IRA to say tomorrow, 'Okay, we are prepared to compromise and will accept arrangements which fall short of our ultimate demands', unionist leaders would still reject power-sharing and – for want of a better phrase – an Irish dimension. So it would be back to the slog. And, in anticipation that this would be the outcome, and in the absence of any overtures, the IRA is unlikely to call a ceasefire. In the meantime, we have death, injury and long-serving prisoners.

Brooke's talks are actually meaningless because the unionists are looking to get rid of the Hillsborough Treaty and even if –

miraculously — they were prepared to be magnanimous, the *quid pro quo* required from the SDLP could destabilise the SDLP if the deal represents a retreat from Hillsborough. Everybody's caught in their own trap — personal, political and historical. Yes, lucky is he who can spend his nights gazing at the stars and wondering how many speckle the heavens. He is a happy man!

Monday 25 March
Morning begins with the light being switched on at around seven and if you're in a deep sleep (as most innocent prisoners aren't!) you'll not notice. However, the arrival of day staff is like the arrival of football fans outside a stadium, there's so much noise. They don't seem to realise that the most dangerous men in the country are still trying to catch up on beauty sleep! They are full of shouts and laughs and they crack bawdy jokes, which could just as easily be told an hour later. At about a quarter to eight the orderlies are let out and then begins the clattering of mop buckets, the orderlies competing with each other to see who can clang the buckets over the tiles loudest and longest. Sometimes, if there has been a leak overnight from the toilets or showers, a suction machine is hauled out. It wails like a choir of banshees. I'm not sure if I can think of anything else to moan about just at the moment but if something comes to mind I'll not hesitate!

I finished *Under the Volcano* by Malcolm Lowry. It is a very sad story set in Mexico on the Day of the Dead and is about an ex-British consul, Geoffrey Firmin, who is an alcoholic. Probably because it is semi-autobiographical the descriptions of Firmin's/Lowry's drunken mentality are more moving and fascinating than they would otherwise be. His wife, Yvonne, had left him for a year but comes back and is with him for only a day because the drink now has him in its fatal grip. Yvonne, Geoffrey and his brother go out to a festival and they think he has rallied and is enjoying himself but within he is destroyed and can't cope with reality. He says to himself: 'Nothing is altered and in spite of God's mercy I am still alone. Though my suffering seems senseless I am still in agony. There is no explanation of my life.'

That walking stick sounds like the ideal present for P. J. He also needs eyebrow tweezers! They're like grasshopper legs overhanging his eyelids! If I were Phyllis I'd pluck them in his sleep.

Saturday 30 March
Hello Tragic Face

There's a fella in here on a Mickey Mouse charge – that is, he'll get a suspended sentence but will spend about eighteen months on remand. He's married, is in his early twenties and is incredibly naive. On Thursday he complained to Griz and Anto that the warders were giving him dirty looks and were telling him to hurry up when he was slopping out. Anto told him that that was because he hasn't got a star on his prison card.

'What do you mean "a star"?' he asked.

'The screws probably think you are a hood,' said Anto, 'and not under the umbrella of the Republican Movement. You have to get a star stuck in your card. Then, when the screw opens your card and sees the star, he knows to respect you. You'll probably get an extra ten minutes on your visits as well. Go down to the PO tomorrow and tell him you want a star.'

'Right. I'll do that.'

Yesterday afternoon at the table in the canteen he said: 'I wrote a long letter to my wife this morning. We had a couple of problems to sort out.'

Griz said, 'Aye, I know.'

'What do you mean, you know?'

'I read it.'

'What! What do you mean, you read it? I only handed it to the screw this morning?'

'Listen,' said Griz. 'We have to check what's coming in and what's going out of the jail. Every day, after the mail's collected, I go down to the censor's office and select three or four letters for spot checks. It's an agreement we have with the NIO. Yours happened to be one of the ones I checked today.'

The fella shook his head and complained to Anto, 'That shouldn't be allowed.'

'Don't worry,' said Anto. 'When you get your star he's only allowed to check an individual's mail once a month.'

Talk about innocent!

I finished the O'Malley book. Some of the things he wrote were similar to what I was saying to you. He said: 'If the IRA called a halt to its operations, there would, of course, no longer be an overt conflict, and therefore there would be a less pressing need for a "solution". Indeed, were the IRA simply to cease and desist, the impact could be retrogressive, since there would no longer be any reason for loyalists to make any concessions to nationalists when their "unreasonableness" no longer carried with it the threat of greater instability. It is improbable to assume that they would make concessions in the future if the IRA put the gun away, in view of their demonstrated unwillingness to make concessions in the past, no matter how menacing the IRA gun.'

I think that's true and it is also one of the reasons why the loyalists will not do a deal with Dublin and the SDLP in the forthcoming Brooke talks. They would be afraid that if they reached 'a settlement' it could subsequently be 'improved on', to the benefit of nationalists, if the IRA were to cash in its chips (concessions for an end to the armed struggle).

Tuesday 2 April

Our lights were fused for about an hour last night and when they came back on, around ten, I was in bed listening to a golden-oldie show. One of the records was 'Arthur's Theme' by Christopher Cross. During that week in January 1982 that Owen Carron and I were in jail in Fort Erie Penitentiary we had a radio and that song was played regularly. I latched on to the lyrics right away because I had just left you and was heading for New York when we were arrested:

> *If you get caught between the moon and New York City,*
> *I know it's crazy, but it's true . . .*
> *The best that you can do is fall in love.*

Well, there was no mail today so I've no idea how you spent Easter. The weather was poor although this evening the sky is completely clear and the sunlight is striking the far wall in the exercise yard. By the way, I think the lyrics went, 'If you get *lost* between the moon and New York City . . . ' but I got caught. And I did fall in love.

Wednesday 3 April

We were out in the yard this morning when I heard that Martin Meehan Junior's seven-month-old daughter, Natasha, had been found dead in her cot a few hours earlier. He had been called out and given the bad news. So I walked the yard with him when he came back. Needless to say he was absolutely shattered. A month or two ago the child had pneumonia but it seems this was a cot death. He later had a visit with his wife. She gave up their house after his arrest and the certainty of conviction and moved in with her mother. His cellmate spent the lunchtime lock-up with someone else so that Martin could have privacy. I think he is going to try for bail tomorrow. Martin Senior, who has only three years left of his sentence, might get compassionate parole. Young Martin's mother died of cancer when he was twelve.

I see Graham Greene has died. He used to be my hero. As a teenager I read all his novels. The heroes faced moral dilemmas amid whiffs of sex, religion, politics and cordite! I went off him after he wrote a novel called *The Honorary Consul* about a political kidnapping. This was in the mid-seventies. And I was right. In May 1981, around about the time of Bobby Sands's death, he visited Belfast on an NIO-sponsored propaganda trip, and he then went off and wrote a tirade against the Republican Movement. Before Greene shuffled off this mortal coil he described the Belfast-born author Brian Moore as his favourite living writer. I reckon he was long brain-dead when he made this comment. Moore's novel *Lies of Silence* was one of the favourites for last year's Booker Prize. I have just read it. Honey, I am in the running for the Nobel Prize for Literature, given these standards. It was appalling.

Roy wrote to me. He thanks you for the Easter card and says Donna sends her love and best wishes. He's in with Bernard Fox and Gill, who was sentenced with Seany Adams. He says the Blocks are great. People with one leg always tell you they have no problem walking about!

Thursday 4 April

Martin Meehan applied for bail today. Some people thought he wouldn't succeed because he is so close to his trial on attempted murder charges. Anyway, he's got from nine in the morning until five tomorrow night, I think. I've lent him my good trousers and jacket, even though he's stouter than me. He tried them on tonight and they fit okay.

Saturday 6 April

Jim O'Carroll has organised a sweep for this afternoon's Grand National. For a bar of chocolate you can pick out two pieces of paper containing the names of two horses. I drew 'the Thinker', which had been shot dead on Thursday after a serious fall during training. I asked for half my bar of chocolate back but Jim told me to do something coital with myself. My other horse is called 'Solid as a Rock'. The raffle leaflet describes in glowing terms the various packets of crisps and chocolates which make up the winnings: 'Yes, fabulous, yum, yum'; 'Everyone's a winner with D. H. [Dick Heads] Bookies'; 'Tell a friend about our great prizes' and 'The sky's the limit with us'.

Later

If you ever come across a horse called 'Solid as a Rock', shoot it! It wasn't seen or heard of before, during or after the race! Nevertheless, the atmosphere in the canteen was great as we cheered tiny adult men and one or two token women in silky pyjamas with numbers on their backs (so that their mammies could find them) as they whipped horses to run around the same track twice and jump man-made fences whilst being filmed by other people in speeding cars.

About an hour ago I shaved off my 'half-beard', as Inspector McGregor described it when identifying me from the witness box. I have put on weight and now look like Broderick Crawford of *Highway Patrol* (probably before your time).

By the way, I didn't know that Timothy O'Grady was doing a profile on me for the *Guardian*. He came over here last July or August to write a feature on Belfast, including me, for *Granta*. But Jim and I had so much business to discuss that he hardly got to say hello.

Monday 8 April

I received your letter this afternoon, and boy were you in a mood when you wrote it! I make a good pincushion or voodoo doll! We are so close to this business being resolved and yet the tension has us turning in on each other. There are a couple of things I would like to say but they can wait. The good thing about hardship and crises is that one's character really emerges! Dissimulation comes to an end! I don't think you realise how much you and I need each other and suit each other. No, that's not true. You do. And I'm just trying to paint my motives for calling things off if I get convicted as noble and unfairly trying to depict yours for needing 'time to calm down' as being selfish and not facing perhaps more unpalatable truths. I am a joke. I tell you to tell me how you feel and then when you do I find a soapbox. Fuck it. I don't even know if I am being coherent. This waiting is the cause of most of the tension. That and the fear that we will discover that our relationship has changed even if I do get out.

Here, it's been nice knowing you . . . what's-yer-name! Am I the man you know?! Haven't changed a bit! And I know you better than anyone else because – I haven't told you this before – you've been talking in your sleep over the last few years. Boy, are you crazy! You're a basket case. I would be doing your parents a favour taking you permanently off their hands. To put it crudely, I think we are well and truly fucked for life!

I remember you telling me that you always quickly read the end of my letters to check that everything was okay. Everything is okay. You made me touch happiness, not just on the border, but its capital.

Thursday 11 April

There was a rumour doing the rounds that we were going to be up in court tomorrow, and immediately Jim O'Carroll's legs went like castanets! Most of the time he's like Dr Pangloss and has an over-optimistic and cheerful view of the delay. His theory is quite simple – if Hutton was going to find us guilty he would have found us guilty by now! If you think you are frustrated by the delay in judgement then in my case you can multiply that tenfold. Every day some prisoner or warder asks, 'Any word yet?' Even the priest called into my cell yesterday to find out what was happening.

I'm sure my da is not looking forward to retirement. He has always liked working. My abiding memory of him when he was at the painting was of him coming home from work. He always wore a long dexter and a cap, had a lunch box under his arm and smelt of linseed oil from putty. I never saw him rush. He always had a steady, dignified walk. It was only when he took up that sedentary job in Telephone House that the lard collected.

Monday 15 April

I was down in Walter's office and have just collected and read your weekend letter.

So, you dry-roasted the chicken on Sunday. It's a wonder it didn't burst into flames and blow open the door. When I was a kid I loved fire. I used to steal candles and matches from a cupboard and play with them and toy cowboys, Indians and a stagecoach in my bedroom. Once, I had a lighted candle underneath the bed and was acting a night-time scene outside the Wells Fargo office. Margaret or Geraldine shouted up the stairs that *Top of the Pops* had started. I ran downstairs and was glued to the set for a half-hour. When I went back upstairs and opened the door my bedroom was billowing smoke. Below the bed the plastic stagecoach was ablaze and the linoleum was starting to melt. I doused the fire with a shirt, burning myself in the process, then took out my window – which was on a sash – and dispersed the smoke.

Then I got down on my knees, cried and thanked God for getting me back to the room, instead of going out to play, before the house had been burned to the ground. Wouldn't you love to have had me as a son?

Night is starting to fall outside. I need a good court with you! I'm getting fed up kissing the pillow. I'm beginning to talk precisely and poetically like Brian Keenan – though I haven't arrived just yet at thoughts of wanting 'all the wine and all the women in the world'! Soon, out in the visiting boxes I'll be snatching a baby from some passerby and holding it up before making some profound statement about the meaning of life. Everyone will stop in their tracks, they'll be wide-eyed and marvelling and they will say:

'Can that poor cratur not do his whack?!'

And the doctor will reply, 'That poor cratur has been in here for the past twenty-six years since he set fire to a stagecoach under his bed which burned down the house. You should hear what he has imagined has happened to him since!'

Wednesday 17 April
As you know, I used to be in charge of the 'Campaign To Have Jimmy McShane Wash His Hair'. He had this fear that shampoo would make him go bald. Anyway, he's gone to the Blocks but we've begun a new lobby – the 'Campaign To Have John Doherty Kiss His Mother When She Comes Up To See Him'. He's nineteen and is the lad whom you were astonished to see in with us big boys and whom you referred to as a child. He can't explain why he doesn't kiss her at the beginning and the end of

a visit. The woman sets out from Derry and travels 140 miles all-round to see him, we point out. She would be over the moon if he was to surprise her with a peck on the cheek. He blushes when we put this to him – but we're serious. Yesterday morning at breakfast in the canteen we forced him to go through a simulated visit. The TV was switched off and I wore a towel draped over my head (long hair) and tiptoed (high heels) up to his table but the bastard still wouldn't kiss his mother! We're working on him.

That was tragic about that taxi driver last night. He had only started working for the firm a few hours before and the woman he had married had been widowed before when her first husband was killed in a similar sectarian assassination. After news of the UFF/UVF ceasefire we had a short meeting on the Ones and decided that there was to be no slagging the loyalists. But as we were returning to our cells from the canteen around seven, our lads on the Twos emerged from their canteen shouting 'No Surrender', and I saw from the exercise yard today that some republican had hung out a white flag from his window. If it means even one less life lost then their ceasefire – when it takes effect – is to be welcomed.

Thursday 25 April
I cut myself in about ten different places when shaving tonight. My face is now chalky with diluted toothpaste, which cools the skin and feels antiseptic. I have the radio off for a change, so the cell is relatively silent. But there are other noises. There is the sound from the TV in a room where a warder is sitting, country and western music from somewhere down the wing, the soft chords of a guitar being strummed in a cell nearby and from the yard the echo of laughter from a cell on the Twos. The laughter is incredibly happy, not at all irritating.

Sunday 28 April

Sometimes at Mass, especially if it is our 'good day' and we are in a hurry and anxious to return to the yard or the priest has another Mass to say, the priest doesn't bother putting on his vestments or give a sermon. This morning, the fella sitting next to me, a maniac called Jimmy (the one who lost and later found his false teeth last week), said to me that he would like to do a reading. Oh yes, I forgot to tell you . . . I'm a lay minister in my spare time and set the altar and arrange the readings. I know. Such a hypocrite. But hypocrisy makes the world go round.

Anyway, I award Jimmy the second reading and I go and light the candles and return to my seat. The priest puts on his cassock and surplice, etc., and your man says to me:

'He's going the full hog. He's putting all the gear on today.'

I ignore him. Then he bends forward and whispers to me, 'Here. You don't believe in all this, do you?'

I reply solemnly, 'This isn't the time to get into it.'

'Oh right.'

This afternoon I joined in with the football. Griz McKee kicked the ball over the wall and, as is the convention, he was seized and put under the tap, to shouts from Anto: 'For fuck's sake watch the big lad's hair!' Then a false rumour was spread that we were up for judgement tomorrow and had tried to keep it quiet. Anto, Jim, Danny and I were then surrounded and dragged to the water tap, where we were drenched. Well, at least that's the traditonal going-away present over and done with!

I am still basking in the warmth and intimacy of you laying your head on my hands yesterday. Simple but magic – like a long adolescent kiss which you live off until the next date! So, my childhood sweetheart, I shall leave you for a while and I'll end with lots of kisses with the old yet fresh and forever message that I love you.

Tuesday 30 April

Well, the talks started today and the sun shone. Yesterday was so wet and dismal that during exercise in the yard we had to stand the entire time under the shelter, plundering our brains for entertainment we hadn't already exhausted and counting the sheets of non-stop rain dancing in the puddles and putting their tongues out at us! But now it is bright and although it was a little blustery this afternoon it looks quite peaceful and pleasant. I haven't heard the latest news but it seems all the political leaders are asking the media not to probe too much. There is no way politicians can keep their mouths shut.

Thursday 2 May

Almost the end of another week. Well, I don't know if we can read anything into Hutton's granting Veronica Martin compassionate bail to attend her mother's funeral in England, but he's back on the bench and the big delay remains a mystery.

Sunday 5 May

Well, my love, this is probably my last letter from the Crum' to you! I bet that you have a good bonfire's worth of correspondence since I first wrote you on the tenth or eleventh of January last year, thinking that I'd be away for only a few months. And you were right the whole way along about how bad it could be.

Monday 6 May

Have just learnt that we are in court for judgement on Wednesday.

Wednesday 8 May

Well, love, I don't know what there is to say and I doubt if I can console you.

I think it was when I was on my way over to court and going

through the tunnel that I realised exactly what was going to happen. I had absolutely no thought for myself, just for you and how devastated you would be. As soon as Hutton pronounced us guilty of the charge of unlawful imprisonment I nodded to Jim Gibney to immediately get to the phone and let you know before you heard it on the news.

It was only later, in the afternoon, when going into detail, that Hutton said he found Anto and I guilty of 'aiding and abetting' unlawful imprisonment, which, sentence-wise, probably makes little difference. Anyway, you'll know what we've been given by the time this comes tumbling through the letter box. I spoke to the lawyers and they were extremely cynical about Hutton's judgement, one describing it as 'a patchwork quilt'. Hutton gratuitously even offered an explanation for Sandy's behaviour in the living room which neither Sandy nor the prosecution advanced! He said that perhaps Sandy thought that he couldn't approach the RUC because he had just informed on his handlers to the IRA! The whole tenor of his delivery was very aggressive and he angrily rebutted several of the barristers when they were making pleas of mitigation. For me, Adair simply stood up and said: 'I've been instructed by my client to say nothing on his behalf', or words to that effect, and I felt good then because I was politely saying, 'Fuck you'.

The courtroom was packed with relations and friends and, of course, with press hacks. Surprisingly, the cops weren't what you'd call triumphalist. Inspector McGregor asked me how I was doing, a pleasantry which I reciprocated, having been taught manners by my mother. Perhaps they expected us to go down on the conspiracy-to-murder charge, but even they must have seen that it wasn't there.

We got back to the wing at 4.15 pm and I am back in Cell 30, which I thought I had vacated for the last time this morning after a fairly restless night. I have sent out excess clothes, including my good jacket, which earned an accolade on Radio 4! ('Mr Morrison was smartly dressed in a casual jacket.') After sentencing at three o'clock tomorrow we'll be brought to D-Wing but it will probably be too late for a committal visit. Hopefully, Anto's Red Book status will be our passport to an early shift to the Blocks. All the others are fine. We've been up and down so much that it's a relief that the whole thing is over.

There's the media flak to come and then that will be it. The burden has fallen on you to explain all this to your relatives – your father would have really liked me, you know! – and to come to terms with this major blow to our relationship.

Friday 10 May
Hello, my tired, swollen-eyed lover! You're simply the best. Thank you for your words of comfort and support.

Sentencing was even more nerve-racking than I supposed. As you now know we weren't brought in as a group. Jimmy Martin was taken up first. As it turned out, Jimmy, who got twelve years, was in the dock with his wife Veronica (three and a half years) and their son Liam (suspended sentence). Jim, Danny and Gerard were next in and were together; Anto was on his own; and then me last, on my own. The reason Gerard was given twelve years (two more than Danny and Jim) was because of his previous conviction. Anto and I got eight each because the charge had been reduced to aiding and abetting.

When I was brought up to the dock Hutton began a lecture and I looked at the clock, then the press, then the cops and public gallery. I was more tense than I had expected and the only way of release would have been to have shouted something back at the hypocrite but we had all agreed to say nothing. Everybody – with the exception of Gerard – is relatively pleased with their

sentences – with the emphasis on 'relatively'. Anto thought that
I would have got six years because Hutton claimed he had played
a more central role. My mind was just full of you and what you
would be going through.

We were taken straight to the base in D-Wing and I spent last
night in a cell with Jimmy and Anto. I was called for a visit but
when I came back Anto, Jim, Dan and Gerard were gone! They
had been taken to the Blocks. I was in a foul mood. I saw a governor,
who asked me a stupid list of questions, and I was then told that
I was being put up on D-3, the assessment unit, for two weeks.
What a cynical pretext for what is really punishment! I later saw
the NIO story on page 2 of the *Irish News* – that crap about seeing
if I wanted to conform. Can you get Richard to contact the press?
Jimmy is also here so in that respect I am glad to keep him company.
However, why move Danny, Jim and Gerard – Anto is a different
case because he is Red Book – straight to the Blocks without an
assessment and keep me here on twenty-four-hour lock-up and no
exercise unless I integrate?

Jimmy and I are in the same cell. He is relieved that Veronica
got off so lightly. We still haven't been given our clothes. Before
Hutton even gave our judgement Dessie Boal said to me, 'I know
this sounds crazy, but I'm telling you now that we will have
several major grounds for appeal.' Later, Barra said the same,
having talked it over with others overnight. I won't be placing
any hope in it even though I listened to Hutton stitch me up.
I'll do my whack and begin another book. This letter's a bit of
a ramble, I know, but I can't relax just yet, though I was relieved
to hear from Siobhan that you are fine.

Sunday 12 May

Two things, honey. You looked really great yesterday – in fighting form – and you left me feeling very strong and optimistic. And to see Liam with you was brilliant.

But what an astonishing development regarding Peter Duggan: that when he saw Sandy's photo in the paper in relation to our case he contacted the RUC, alleging that he was the man who shot him and left him for dead! I hope he doesn't disappear into the woodwork and get frightened off by the publicity. Two points immediately arise. Firstly, in the trial, Sandy, under cross-examination from Harvey, said that if he was lying over the Duggan shooting then his entire testimony fell. Secondly, the DPP in its summation said that its case rested on Sandy's testimony in this trial being a truthful account of what happened that weekend. Duggan's statement implies that Sandy lied in the witness box and that he cannot be believed when he stated that he did not enter into a deal with the IRA on the Saturday to do a press conference. Of course, there are other ramifications: the RUC covering up an attempted murder and the RUC and the DPP suppressing evidence and denying that evidence to the defence.

Today's *Sunday Times*, which Duggan first contacted, played the story down, but I hope that more effective publicity is forthcoming in the weeks ahead. It has the potential for being a big, big story.

Jimmy is very quiet; he tries to sing to records on the radio, though, but is tone-deaf. He just makes up his own words and his own notes. He also snores. It sounds like rough sandpaper scraping through the bones of his nasal passage. But then, who am I to complain!

Tuesday 14 May, H-Block 7, Long Kesh
Here I am, settled in at long last in my new home – I mean room!
But first things first. What a day I put in yesterday. They say
it never rains but it pours. P. J. called me for a legal visit and
began by telling me about Kevin's arrest and that he had been
taken to Castlereagh. My heart stood still. I felt very frustrated
and a bit frightened and I just hoped that he had been listening
to me and no one else. You can never help the RUC with its
inquiries – just dig a grave for yourself or someone else. I was
glad I was told – I always prefer to know what's happening. If
you are not told, you're a victim anyway to endless, gnawing
speculation. I had a restless night but learnt on another legal
visit, this time with Barra, that Kevin had been released and I
was overjoyed. And just before being told that, I was informed
by the PO that I would be going to the Blocks in the afternoon.

The one sunbeam yesterday was your letter, which I received
mid-afternoon.

We left the Crum' at about three o'clock today. There were
two Tyrone men, Jimmy and myself in the prison van. We were
handcuffed and locked in cubicles which had small windows
with a tiny view of the outside. The journey was bumpy but
interesting. We could see the shoppers in Royal Avenue. I caught
a quick glimpse of Kelly's Cellars and of Castle Street! Then we
went around the side of the City Hall and down Linenhall
Street, I think it's called, on to the Dublin Road, then up past
the University and out the Malone Road. Once we left the city
I just sat down. We arrived at the Blocks at a quarter to four.
I had to choose which clothes I was leaving out because there
is a quota of items allowed. I also discovered in my personal
property that a hardback book had been sent to me over a month
ago by a British publisher on Tim O'Grady's recommendation.
I was never told about it.

Jimmy went to H-3. I believe Danny Caldwell and Hodgies are in H-6 and Jim O'Carroll in H-5. I came here, to H-7, from where the 1983 escape was launched. I climbed out of the minibus, that brought us from reception, into sunlight. The sky was huge after the enclosure of the Crum'. Huge and bright blue and filled with fresh air. I came through all the security gates and into a large canteen, where Anto and Tom McAllister ('Ceefax') welcomed me. Brendy Mead from the Rock Streets is also here. He is the barber and gave me a haircut. Also here in B-Wing is Kevin McMahon. I am in a cell on my own. This place will take a while getting used to. I seem to have touched lucky for a very laid-back republican community, and the courtesy and banter between the warders and prisoners is disorienting. When the warder was locking me up at half eight tonight he said, '*Oíche mhaith*'!!! My cell looks out over 'no man's land' (which in some of the Blocks would be 'no person's land'!) to D-Wing, which is occupied by loyalists, including Michael Stone, who killed Kevin Brady. Apparently we travel in the same minibuses as the loyalists to the visiting area. Everybody's official ID is contained in a passport-size book, which is stamped with a security classification: 'Red Book', 'High Risk', 'Medium' or 'Low'. The likes of Anto will be moved every six weeks and I will be moved every six months, presumably, being classified as 'High', which isn't too bad.

I'm not sure which blocks Roy and Pat are in. Maybe we'll see them out on the visits on Saturday. The cell is neat and I control the light. I've a good solid table to write on. I have almost finished *The Odyssey* by Homer, which was written 3,000 years ago!

Odysseus went to fight in the Trojan War, which lasted for ten years, but it was another nine – and after many close shaves – before he found his way back to his patient wife, Penelope. In one encounter, when he is begging someone for help, he offered them the following blessing in return: ' . . . may the gods grant you your heart's desire; may they give you a husband and a home, and the harmony that is so much to be desired, since there is nothing nobler or more admirable than when two people who see eye to eye keep house as man and wife, confounding their enemies and delighting their friends, as they themselves know better than anyone.'

Isn't that nice! May the gods grant you your heart's desire!

Thursday 16 May
There is a library which comes around about every three weeks that is amply stocked with the latest best-sellers and quality hardbacks. You can take out six books at a time and order specific titles, which come from the main libraries in the North.

Because the cell door is open most of the day there is a great temptation to spend a lot of time wandering about, watching TV, playing cards, just chatting or playing ball in the yard. Plus, we can eat whenever we want and there is no shortage of bread, which means there's a lot of toast being constantly eaten.

Friday 17 May
Dear Penelope, it was wonderful being with you today. I came back whistling and beaming. 'He had a good visit,' said one lad to another as I passed! I had a good yarn with Kevin McMahon. When he was in Portlaoise Jail Kevin Brady used to write to him from the Carrickmore Sinn Fein Advice Centre while I was sitting there doing constituency work. Kevin teaches Irish and I'm in his *rang*. It's very basic stuff.

I went down to the big pitches for the football. I prayed that nobody would kick the ball to me and occasionally hid behind the referee when I thought this was becoming a possibility. We also play tennis in the yard – the court is marked out in white with a bar of soap. I must be conceited: I just know that after a few months here I am going to be good at tennis!

Saturday 18 May
The kids and I got about forty minutes. I had a good yarn with Kevin. He was at school on the day that that RUC man was killed in Beechmount and he says that all those other kids have been stitched up. Anyway, he didn't speak to the cops and, of course, they slagged him about me and said he would end up in jail. He apologised for not coming up last week and said he had been studying hard and was fairly wrecked. He is not looking forward to moving to north Belfast. He doesn't know what he wants to work at so I told him to get a job in Corsica if that trip comes off.

Did I tell you that I got weighed: 10 stone 12 pounds. Don't know how long that will last because I am eating like a horse. Did you know that we can have our photograph taken together on a visit? It's a couple of quid for three black-and-white shots.

Monday 20 May
I heard that Pat Sheehan has had Patricia up once or twice, on a friendship basis. He says she's going out with someone else. He also sends you his regards.

I was looking at some of the Open University literature and it seems that, unless you cram, a degree takes six years. They don't start until January. I may just do a foundation course, which takes one year. I met the Open University tutor, Jenny Meegan, and later, one of the education officers, Frank. I would be reluctant to get into anything too long-term and too distracting from my ongoing reading and writing.

You said in your letter that your mind is at rest, knowing that I am in such good conditions. Well, I actually feel guilty about it! I said something along those lines to Tomboy Loudan and he reminded me that what we have was fought for and men died for it. I know that, but the truth is that our loved ones on the outside are bearing the brunt of things now.

Saturday 25 May
The sun has gone right across the sky and its last creamy-coloured reflections just manage to strike obliquely and illuminate the concrete slats inside the window which act as bars. It is unmistakably evening: morning light has a fresher hue and a different character. This afternoon was hours ago. We will be experts on time when all of this is over. Today we laughed perhaps more than on any other visit and observing proprieties was like courting a girl in her mother's parlour!

(The sun has gone down – its light strikes the cells on my side of the wing for about twenty minutes only.)

I am very pleased about that cheque from the *Independent* for that piece I wrote about the Crum' and I hope it covers Kevin's fare to Corsica. I am all excited for him. By the way, I think I need some money in my tuck shop. Our 'earnings' (a couple of quid) are pooled for the commune to buy tea, sugar, etc.

Monday 27 May
You would sure like it here! Some of the lads sunbathe in the nude! Wasn't the weather fabulous today. I hope your outing was a success. As the sun beat down I thought about you and pictured you in the company of friends strange to me.

I have been thinking of writing an article about the lack of republican understanding of the unionist/Protestant people so I have started making points or headings before I begin. Although I don't want to be too controversial I would like to provoke a debate and take it from there.

I've put my name down to see the dentist and the optician. I don't think I've had my eyes tested since I was about thirteen. I had a look at the Arts Foundation Course and I'm waiting to see the Open University tutor. But if I do it it's going to consume a lot of time. What would you do without the present number of letters! I got weighed again. Guess what? Eleven stones seven pounds! Anto must have misread those scales the other day!

Tuesday 28 May
I can't get that shooting of Eddie Fullerton in Buncrana out of my head. I'll get a sympathy card from the shop and send it off to his wife. Eddie was always concerned about 'the people of the North', without realising that he himself was just as much in danger as they were. He was great craic at the *ard fheis,* always passionate, always running over his time at the podium and always apologising in the most disarming way! Every few years he would announce an expedition to Rockall to repudiate the British territorial claim to it!

Wednesday 29 May
After I finished last night's letter I began reading the *Irish Times* and saw an article announcing the death of Captain John Feehan, the founder of Mercier Press. He was a quare character and it seems he died suddenly, though he was seventy-five. It was with him and his daughter Mary that Kevin and I had dinner in Cork a few days before my arrest. He treated us. Kevin had the full course, which included breast of pigeon! But the subsequent long journey to Dublin upset his stomach and he had to give it up. We laughed over that because the meal came to about £85!

Today I lay in the yard on a blanket sunbathing and reading. Above the yard about a quarter of the sky is in view but it is still vast. There were a couple of white wisps astray in a windy stream high above and I was reminded of that poem which begins, 'I wandered lonely as a cloud . . . ' The sun was like a pure-white exploded asterisk. Occasionally, jets would cross the sky at a fairly low altitude and the silver glint of the sun would, for a few seconds, run along their curved fuselage and then disappear. Tom McAllister would keep rolling over. He says he doesn't tan but gets burnt. Both his legs are withered from the time he was shot by the Brits in 1978 and again as a result of the hoods trying to kill him in 1986 when they ran over him in a stolen car. He has been doing weights and asked me today if I thought the muscles in his legs had thickened. They would serve a sparrow. I said that he'd soon be progressing to calipers! What my lack of hair had to do with his vitriolic reply I'll never know!

Thursday 30 May
I got your letter and a nice card from Mairtin O'Muilleoir and an article from Gerry Adams which Tim O'Grady sent. Gerry has known me for nineteen years and he still doesn't know how to spell my surname: he uses two 's's! In his card Mairtin was comparing the RUC's policy in Beechmount of arresting all the first-born males and dumping them in the Crum' to that of King Herod!

It was the Feast of Corpus Christi today so we had Mass again. It was the first time I had met Father Murphy, the chaplain, who is referred to as 'Silvertop' in the hunger-strike comms in *Ten Men Dead*. He is a very nice man and I had a long conversation with him.

I got the receipt for the £25 you left in – thank you, honey.

Friday 31 May
Again the sun dominated my day. It was a bit cloudy at first but by about eleven the sky had cleared and the sun-worshippers were out with their blankets and pillows.

This evening in the yard, sizzling in the sun, listening to the golden oldies on the radio, we were reminded by the loyalists across the circle of the conflict. They were out parading in the yard with their flute band and drummers. We couldn't believe that on such a glorious evening they would be out beating their refurbished waste-paper bins. Such dedication!

Saturday 1 June

A new month! It's ten to one and soon you will be leaving work to come and see me, and the butterflies of excitement are flitting across my stomach!

This morning I received a copy of Peter Duggan's statement. He was arrested by several men belonging to the INLA in January 1988 in a house in Downpatrick. They were claiming that he gave names to the RUC. He alleges that Sandy Lynch was 'the fat man'. Wait till you hear this:

'I was interrogated on and off by various people, including the fat man. At times I was blindfolded and sometimes not . . . After two days I was blindfolded again, stripped and moved once more. I think this occurred about 11 pm. By this time I had got to know their voices and recognised the voice of the fat man. I could also see through the blindfold, which was not very effective . . . He led me out of the house, banging my head against a wall on the way, causing my nose to bleed. I was pushed under something and into a room and told to stand in the corner. I turned round and saw him move back and heard a clicking noise. Very shortly afterwards I heard three shots and fell to the ground. I looked up again and saw the fat man, who stood for a short while before moving away. I lay bleeding for a while before crawling out of the house . . .

'When interviewed by police following this incident I gave a full description of the man, who I called "the fat man" – the man who shot me. I also drew a photofit of the man for the police while in hospital. I gave this to Arthur Lusty, a policeman, Sergeant Hanlon, a policeman with an English accent, and Billy Hetherington, a DI at the time. When I gave them the photofit they all appeared to know the man and laughed, saying that it was a very good likeness. I asked them if they knew the man but they said they didn't, which I thought odd.

'I was then kept under police protection, which I did not ask for. I was told that I would have to give evidence. When I let them know that I did not want to give evidence they indicated that they would make my life very difficult – that they would charge me with a number of offences, like collecting information for terrorists because I had associated with them . . . They also said that they would spread it around paramilitary circles that I was an informer and that there would be a race to see who would "get me first". I felt intimidated by all this and felt like a prisoner.'

In May 1988 Duggan gave evidence against the householders where he was first questioned, and they were sentenced to about two years each, I think. He was then put in some sort of protective scheme in England.

'Policemen also lived in the complex; they kept a constant watch on you and wouldn't let you out of the building without their permission. I was given all sorts of promises and began getting very frustrated and angry. Eventually they gave me a passport in a new name and put me on a plane to France. It took some time before I got any money from them. I had set myself up in France with the proceeds of my NIO claim, £36,000 . . .

'After the arrest of Morrison and others I was made aware that the man they were accused of holding was the man who shot me. I did not know his name, however. I was told this on the quiet by one of the police minders with whom I had become particularly friendly. I do not wish to name him as our friendship greatly annoyed his superiors.

'Some time later, roughly a year ago, I was approached by police and asked to make myself available at Earl's Court police station. I thought this was finally to settle my dispute about my relocation money. I kept the appointment and was met by three policemen – Ciaran Lagan and two others. It turned out that they wanted to talk about my shooting. They were particularly interested in my description of the man who shot me. They indicated that they might have had somebody. I told them all about giving a detailed description to police at the time and about the photofit I gave to Hetherington at the time. I knew by this time the circumstances and suggested to them that they were protecting a man working for them and that they knew exactly who he was. They went very pale and cold towards me. They sent me out of the room. When they brought me back they asked me if I would attend an ID parade and look at photos. I agreed, on condition that they sort out my other grievances. Not long after that an officer came over and gave me £4,000. I still have never been given a full ID – like a history, birth certificate and so on. I did bring up the matter of identifying the man who shot me but he would make no comment. I never heard any more about it.'

On the day of my conviction Duggan was watching TV news in England and saw the photos of Sandy Lynch, the man who, he alleges, shot him. He phoned C14 – that is, the relocation unit of the RUC – and left a message on the machine to that effect.

'I also got a police officer at Ballymena RUC station and told him. He panicked and said he would look into it. In the next few days I contacted Mr Barbour, a solicitor in Belfast, who advised me to go to a police station in England and report the matter, which I did. I asked for a superintendent and told him who I was and what I wanted to say. He went off to check but when he came back he told me that he had been told by the RUC not to take a statement and that they were looking into it. Before this I had contacted several journalists – McKittrick, Clarke and others.'

If Duggan comes to our appeal we'll walk it!

When I came out of the legals I was put in a waiting room, where I saw Bobby Storey and Danny and Jim for a short while. Bobby is keeping well. He still has three years to do and has served ten already. I came back to the Block with a loyalist who was muttering under his breath about 'the fuckin' screws' because the gate wasn't opened quickly. I said to him we had little to complain about:

'If you'd been here ten or twelve years ago you'd know all about it.'

'I was!' he said. 'I'm doing life.'

From what I can gather the loyalist wings aren't as well organised. They argue a lot with the warders, sometimes refusing to lock up at half eight, and some prisoners bring their paramilitary status on the outside in with them; this leads to tension among them. On our side, I've had several lectures explaining how the commune works, the necessity of comradeship, the channels which exist to resolve differences and the progressive approach to the jail community. There are other talks on how to listen and allow a man to make his point and how to articulate a point you want to put across.

The lads are slagging me for being 'a starvo' – always eating. When I walked into my cell just now at lock-up, the door was quickly slammed behind me. They had spread on my table bowls of boiled eggs, tomatoes, poached eggs and boiled rice! Then the flap was lifted, there were roars of laughter and I was exhorted to 'Get it into you, Danny. You need it!'

Monday 3 June

What a violent weekend: three UDR men and three IRA men killed, that woman in Lisburn seriously injured and several bomb attacks. It just renders you sad and frustrated. For a few days I've been trying to write a political article but I keep postponing it or find it getting postponed because, ironically, there never seems to be a spare minute.

I went on a vegetarian diet today and was starving about twenty minutes after dinner, which consisted of macaroni and cheese sauce! Dinner, the main meal, arrives here at half eleven – the same as in the Crum'. You always feel like a siesta after it but I find that that is a waste of time. Lock-up from half twelve to two is normally a quiet time when you can read, write or study.

There are films shown on video two or three nights a week from 6 to 8 pm in an event which is called a 'party'. Coke or lemonade from the communal dump is laid on, along with crisps, wagon wheels and bars of chocolate. I'll just have to avoid them!

Friday 7 June

I was at the dentist's yesterday. I didn't need any repair work, just a polishing. Throughout, the dentist talked, mostly to his assistant, about the expense of cars and how a brand-new Citroen that cost £12,000 could be got second-hand for £6,000 a few months later but that a second-hand car 'didn't have the smell of a new one'! The dentist's surgery is in the prison hospital and I got a real chill going through its doors.

I had been there visiting Brendan Hughes when he and six others were on the first hunger strike in December 1980. The smells emanating from his body were ghastly, nauseating. I was with Sean McKenna two nights before this hunger strike was called off. Sean was going blind and hallucinating and his mother was in pieces. The following day I had a visit with Bobby Sands – a humbling experience. But after the visit I was banned from the jail. However, during the second hunger strike, and after the first four deaths, the British government opened up a secret contact with the Movement. I was allowed into the jail just once to see the remaining hunger strikers and Bik, who was the OC. Bik was brought over to the hospital to meet with me and discuss demands.

It was a Sunday afternoon in July and I came into the jail through the gate used by warders. One warder said to a PO, 'What's that bastard doing here. It's a fucking sell-out, isn't it?' but he was ordered to keep quiet. In the hospital all the hunger strikers were awaiting with expectation. Joe McDonnell was in a wheelchair and had gone blind or partially blind and couldn't see me properly. He was laughing and I sat beside him. There were two days of life left in him and he insisted, in between being given sips from a glass of salted water, on smoking cigarettes from the supply I had brought with me. Martin Hurson must have been there, though I can't recall where he sat. Among the others were Micky Devine, who'd be the last to die, Tom McElwee, over whose grave I would speak a few weeks later, Kevin Lynch, whose hair was cropped short, and Kieran Doherty TD, 'Big Doc'. We discussed the proposals from the Irish Commission for Justice and Peace and whether the Brits were still engaged in brinkmanship, even in allowing me into the jail in such unprecedented circumstances – building up the men's hopes only to send them crashing. I then went into another room and met Bik and we were given a phone to talk to Gerry Adams, who with others was in a house waiting on our call. The prisoners didn't trust the Brits nor the ICJP and there were some issues which we wanted clarified through our contact with the government. But before the answers came back, an assistant governor, John Pepper, bounced into the room and declared that all the meetings were over and pulled the phone away from us. It was as if the NIO had been divided and the camp which supported criminalisation and intransigence had assumed dominance after a short lapse. This governor, by the way, is now in the Crum' and was the one with whom I had my first row last year, which resulted in me going to the boards.

As I was leaving the jail that day, the screw who had protested at my presence was smiling. Leaving the place and men who were almost certainly going to die I naturally felt extremely sad but also, guiltily, I had an overwhelming sense of escape: 'Thank God it's not me who's there.' It's hard to describe but I tasted my own life and good fortune in that relief.

Monday 10 June

I wrote to Pat Sheehan a week ago and enclosed an *Irish Times* 'Simplex' crossword. I received his reply today. He said he hasn't done the Simplex since he left the Crum'. He wishes us well and was glad to hear we're together. He said, 'God love her.' I'm not that much of an ogre!

I'm not sure if I know Frank Quigley's friend, Bill, but I do know Fitzy, whom you mentioned. I was driving through Bundoran at about eight o'clock one morning when I almost knocked him down. He had come running out of a cottage. He leapt into the car and shouted, 'Quick! Get me out of here!' In July 1971 he was wounded in a gun battle but the IRA went into the Royal Victoria Hospital, where he was under armed guard, and rescued him. Later, he was recaptured, tried to escape from Long Kesh, was charged and was brought to Newry Courthouse, from where he finally escaped!

I was on my way to Dublin when he jumped into my car. I thought the Task Force was after him and asked him what was wrong as I burnt rubber on the road. 'My family!' he gasped. 'It's my family! They came down from Belfast to see me. They hired a house and they're all lying in there drunk. I'm getting away from them. They're crazy!' So I turned off the main road and drove into Mullaghmore. The tide was in and the sea was sparkling. You know what I'm like when I see water. We stripped off and dashed like children into the waves. A month later – September 1983 – he was shot at Roundwood and was in jail until recently.

Thursday 13 June

The wing smells of the menthol fumes of a muscle rub. The lads put it on their thighs and calves before going to football.

I am the most disorganised person in the world! I work at this table, just under the window. *Everything* is on this table or else on the floor at my feet. Just like how I would have the study! Here, I have three different exercise books, an art pad, unfinished typed articles, unfinished handwritten articles, a couple of tapes, a rubber, a ruler, a plastic spoon, a cup of cold coffee, a dictionary, a date book, a radio, the *Radio Times* and a typewriter, and they are all gasping for space! I spend hours trying to write short stories but when they don't come alive I throw them to the side and start something else. How long have you heard me say that I'm writing an article on loyalism? I add a paragraph or two each week to it. It'll be published the week I get out!

I was looking forward to reading a new novel tonight but was asked to edit an eighty-page article on extradition. This piece of work is pressing: I have to have it done for tomorrow.

Sunday 16 June

I went to the optician's this morning – his office or surgery is based in an empty room in H-6. I was with a fella called Richard who is serving six years for holding a dump. He has a severe speech impediment. A warder came in and asked him his name. He got the first sound started and then there followed a stutter and I became embarrassed. The warder then must have recognised me and as he said to Richard, 'It doesn't matter', he got the rest of his surname out. I asked him if he knew when he was stuttering, which was probably a naive question. There are times when his speech is perfect and other times when he seems stuck on every other word. He says it happens when he tries to rush a word which he thinks he is going to have difficulty with but that while in here he is going to see a speech therapist because it can be cured or substantially cured.

I was then called into the optician's. He put on me these goggles – all that was missing was the motorbike. He switched on the light which illuminates various charts and put me through my paces, not in terms of 'What letter is this' but 'Are the words sharper with the lens like this or like that?' Honey, it was incredible! I saw the world again and my eyes felt so relaxed I couldn't believe it. He says I have a slight astigmatism and need glasses for reading and perhaps watching TV. I asked him would it affect my lovemaking and he said not for four years. So I've ordered glasses, which I should get in about two or three weeks.

Back in the waiting room I met Seany Adams and Rinty McVeigh. Seany had Gerry up here a few weeks ago, which I don't think was wise. His brother Dominic, who got married, then divorced, in jail, is due for release in seven weeks' time. He was sentenced to fourteen years in 1984. Rinty is trying to grow a goatee beard. He says that Anto won't recognise him on the visits but not to worry, he'll come over and identify himself. His wife will make him shave it off. In the republican Blocks there are Irish *rangs* (classes), history *rangs*, Marxist *rangs* and socialist *rangs*. Rinty, who is full of refreshing common sense, was asked which *rang*s did he want to attend. (They're voluntary but you earn brownie points for going to them.) Rinty replied that he was okay, as he had organised two of his own:

'That's great,' he was told. 'What are they?'

Rinty said, 'A *Brookside rang* and a pipe *rang* for smokers.'

He is so funny. There are other organised, consciousness-raising *rangs*. One is the TFT meetings.

'What's that?' I asked him.

'Talk for the sake of talk,' he said.

It actually stands for 'Training for transformation'!

Monday 17 June

The door has shut behind me and I'm in for the night! At six o'clock I went out for a walk on my own. There was a bit of a shower but I had my new jacket on and tucked a Walkman into one of its breast pockets. I had the pleasure of a full orchestra inside my head whilst I dandered around a prison exercise yard! Then I came in and Anto and I cleaned the wash-house and toilets. It only takes about fifteen minutes but I was sweating at the end of it so I jumped into the shower. Then I brought a cup (our blue plastic pint mugs have been exchanged for half-pint cups) of hot water back to my cell, banged the door closed, changed into fresh, clean clothes (cords and a T-shirt), made my black coffee and sat down at my table to talk to you!

My cell and another are opened a few minutes in front of the others each morning. Two of us then go to the dining hall, put cartons of milk on the six tables for cereal, dilute other milk in a churn, make a big pot of tea, finish off any dishes from the night before and leave out bowls and spoons. But on Mondays, Wednesdays and Fridays I don't eat breakfast until about half nine because I spend the previous hour in the weights room!

Roy's back down in the Crum' for his appeal. I've sent him

a sympathy card and added a P.S.: 'Gerard Hodgins is innocent.'
And a P.P.S.: 'Ciaran McGiolla Gunna knows where there's more
rifles', so that should ensure that he is found guilty!

Thursday 20 June
What a beautiful evening – I'd love to take you for a walk.
Remember the evening we walked across Dublin from Franklin
Avenue to Christ Church and then back towards the canal,
where we stopped off in a pub for some Guinness? You wore a
long dress with a flowered pattern.

Anto leaves for another Block tomorrow. I can't believe that
we were sentenced six weeks ago. By the way, I'm writing this
letter with the sight given me by my new spectacles.

I was speaking to one of the Open University lecturers the
other day, Kate Campbell, and she asked me did I like plays.
'Free books' was my first thought! I said yes, and by that
afternoon she had sent me four books containing nine of Brian
Friel's plays, including *Translations* and *Dancing at Lughnasa*.
She also gave me two of Frank McGuinness's plays, including
Observe the Sons of Ulster Marching Towards the Somme. It would
be some feat to get the lads to perform that play. I told you that
I was writing a short story, which I am about three-quarters-
way through. Pam Brighton encouraged me some time ago to
do a piece for Radio 4's *Morning Story* and it's this slot which
I have in mind.

Sunday 23 June
Listening to music from 1969 when I was sixteen and studying
for my O-Levels. At night I worked as a waiter in the
International Hotel. My schoolmates drank like fish. The Tudor
in Fountain Street was famous for serving under-age drinkers
and we used to go there some afternoons. I think it was there

that I was first drunk. I came home but didn't have to face my parents because they were at the wedding of the girl next door, Marie McKavanagh. Around the spring of 1969 I worked in the Hayloft Bar on the corner of High Street and Victoria Street as a junior barman (what a joke – I was a skinny child!). It was patronised by sailors and prostitutes and I hadn't a clue. I left there and started work in the White Fort Inn on the eleventh of July 1969. The Field at that time was in Finaghy and on the twelfth of July there were the Orangemen, some in their bands' uniforms, drinking in the White Fort Inn in the middle of Andersonstown!

I said to my da last week that I would like to see my mammy at some stage, if she was able and it didn't upset her. I remember the day that she took ill. It was on a Wednesday afternoon in late October 1981, a few weeks after the hunger strike had ended. I was being interviewed outside the Sinn Fein offices by London Weekend Television when Sheila McVeigh, I think, got out of a taxi to tell me that my mammy had just collapsed. I went up to Iveagh Parade. Mrs Fox told me that the Brits were raiding the street, had just hit big Ted's and were on their way to do ours when my mammy got all excited and collapsed. The ambulance took her to the City Hospital and Sheila and I were the first on the scene. My mammy's face was purple and she was completely confused. It turned out she had had a brain haemorrhage. She had to be brought to the Royal Victoria Hospital for an operation but the damage was already done and she lost her ability to memorise. She was fifty-seven at the time. Anyway, she's an angel.

I see Cathal Daly is claiming to have spoken to republicans in the H-Blocks who are debating the armed struggle! Make sure my friends know that he wasn't talking to me! And I wonder what documents he is referring to?

Tuesday 25 June

The lads climb out of bed between half eight and half ten and some run around all day in shorts, and if they've no visits they may not wash until the afternoon. I did that yesterday because I spent my time revising that short story and then typing it up. I posted it this morning.

Wednesday 26 June

I received your Monday-night letter and you say that you return to Ireland on Friday the sixteenth of August at 10.30 am. Even if your plane landed on schedule you would be too exhausted to come up here that afternoon so perhaps we should just rely on a regular pass for the afternoon of the seventeenth.

   I also received a letter from Gerry Hanratty in Germany. His and Gerry McGeough's trial is now into its tenth month! The judges go off to Sweden for a few days to hear evidence and then they're off to Belgium. He said it should be over by October – then he faces extradition to the North and another court battle! Both of them are now in the one prison and have association together. Gerry's father died about six months ago and he is now allowed to phone his elderly mother in Belfast once a month and speak for ten minutes.

Saturday 29 June

How frustrating that short visit was. When I got back some people were genuinely asking me had I not been called yet. I wonder did the checkpoints for the visit of Queen Elizabeth add to the problem of a possible rush on oversubscribed jail visits. We had been tortured with helicopters for the past four or five days so it seems this must have been part of a very thorough security-clearance operation.

   I read a review of *Open Letters* by Vaclav Havel, the president of Czechoslovakia and former playwright who was jailed by the communists because of his stance. He wrote many essays about the use of power and one on politics and the conscience. Last year in England he was asked: 'Do you still think that you can reconcile morality with politics?' to which he replied, 'Yes, I do. If I found out it was impossible, I would quit politics.' When he was an essayist he had described Czechoslovakia's lucrative arms-exporting industry as simply 'blood money' which should be rejected. However, ending the arms industry would produce high levels of unemployment, particularly in Slovakia, and this would only strengthen the hand of the separatist movement and threaten the unity of the state. So instead, Havel has quietly agreed to the delivery of Czechoslovak tanks to Syria and is negotiating a similar deal with Iran. I really sympathise with him and the quandaries he faces. Politics is dirty and the connection between the 'greater good' and morality is extremely tenuous, to say the least. Havel denies that politics is dirty and says, 'Politics is simply a job which calls for exceptionally clean people because while doing it one can exceptionally easily besmear oneself; so easily, that a less vigilant person might not realise it at all.'

The most fascinating book on this subject was written by Machiavelli almost 400 years ago – *The Prince*. He candidly argued that the acquisition and effective use of power may necessitate unethical methods. Another great book about power, though written as fiction, is *I Claudius* by Robert Graves.

8.30 pm

This is when my night begins. However, I don't know how long I will have privacy. There are twenty-six prisoners in the wing but there are only twenty-four cells, so two cells are doubled up at any one time for up to three weeks.

Wednesday 3 July

I'm listening to a documentary about Jim Morrison of the Doors, who died twenty years ago today. What were you doing twenty years ago? I think I was hitch-hiking around Ireland. This music is taking me back! Long hair! Bet you don't believe I used to have long hair! Johnny Reid, who owned the White Fort Inn when I worked there in 1971 and with whom I got on well, called me aside one day as I was shifting crates out the back. He said he was embarrassed about broaching the subject but that my hair was too long – that it was unhygienic and he wanted me to get it cut. When he saw my reaction he pulled back from what I had considered was an ultimatum. Nevertheless, I decided to get my hair cut really short – but at a price. I typed up some sponsorship forms and went back to him and approached the well-heeled – and not-so-well-heeled – regulars, asking them to sponsor my haircut at so much per inch. I can't remember how much I raised but I gave the money to the Morning Star hostel in Divis Street, which looks after vagrant alcoholics. Part of the proceeds – or all of them, I'm not sure – went towards the purchase of silver candlesticks for the altar of the chapel in the hostel. And they are still there. At least I was told they were still there when I met the retired director of the hostel, Joe Acheson, about two years ago. It was he who reminded me of this story, which I had forgotten all about.

Well Penelope, I hope you are over your cold and that your nose has stopped running. You make my breast beat like that of a seventeen-year-old discovering love for the first time.

Thursday 4 July

So, the breakthrough talks, the historic talks, are over. They can't now accuse the IRA of being responsible for the Troubles here when they had the opportunity to compromise, reach some sort of settlement and attempt to use it to outlflank and undermine Irish republicanism. But to tell you the truth, I wish they had reached some kind of agreement because later it would be shown not to have brought a settlement: there will be no settlement until republicans are included in a solution. I think Sinn Fein moaned too much about being excluded and it revealed a lack of confidence. I think the loyalists have been the net losers and there is a possibility that their intransigence has added to British disillusionment with this place. Meanwhile, the dying and all the tragedies continue. What a mess.

I can't wait for the Twelfth to be over, and I wouldn't like to be studying for my exams over in C and D Wings in this Block. The loyalists have us deafened with their almost daily, mostly monotonous and extremely loud band music. They have a limited repertoire, so occasionally they break into the theme tune from *Z Cars* (a soap from the sixties) or 'The Fields of Athenry'.

Sunday 7 July
I've just heard on the news that two republican prisoners on remand in Brixton Jail have escaped this morning. The reports are still very sketchy. I bet Commander Churchill-Jones has lost his appetite – as well as his captives!

Have you been following events in Yugoslavia? It's in some mess – and that's putting it mildly. Serbia, which dominates the federation, is drafting all the able-bodied young people into the army, and those Serbs who don't feel Serbian enough to go to war and aren't falling over themselves with nationalistic fervour are in a minority. Several of them were interviewed: a group of friends in a bar where the music on the jukebox was from the Doors, Van Morrison and Dire Straits. Some of their mates had already fled the country to escape the draft. One of them remarked, 'You know, we are all in dire straits now.' Another mused, 'Will we see each other tomorrow? I don't know. Is there going to be a tomorrow for Yugoslavia or for any of us here?'

Tuesday 9 July

Pat Sheehan sends his regards. I met him down at the legals. He's keeping well and had Siobhan up visiting him last week. Barra saw Danny Caldwell, Jim O'Carroll and myself all together. He was speaking to the clerk of the Appeals Court, who said they are booked up until December, so he doesn't think we'll be in court until January. However, I am taking the RUC to court over my two diaries (1972 and 1973), which they have denied confiscating on the night of my arrest. So I should be down in Belfast for a day in September or October!

Some bad news. Peter Duggan, who we hoped would appear for the defence at our appeal, has failed to make contact and has disappeared completely.

What am I going to do while you are away? I'll think about you constantly. I must also try to finish all the books in the backlog and I must make a stab at chapter two. I shall also have to begin some initial reading for the Open University course, even though it doesn't start proper until next February. I am always busy, my mind is always occupied and with each passing day I am eating into the track of this orbit which brings me back to you.

Saturday 13 July

Did you feel a sense of relief when your plane touched down and jails and Diplock Courts and bombs and Orange marches in Pomeroy and elsewhere all dissolved? We occupy two strange worlds at the moment, though in actual fact even the M1 in Belfast separates two different worlds.

I had a good laugh at your description of your father being impatient! You were describing yourself! He has problems with the traffic; you have problems with late taxis!

I got a letter from Pam Brighton yesterday saying she enjoyed my short story and that it will be recorded for Radio 4's *Morning Story* slot before the end of the year. She asked me to consider writing a play but I don't know where I'd find the time.

Wednesday 17 July
I'm just back from my visit with my mammy, daddy and Susan. We got over an hour and a half but the conversation never flagged. My mammy was very affectionate and sat with her arm around my shoulder most of the time. When I asked her how long did she think I had been in jail she replied, 'Two weeks?' God bless her, what an innocent. Susan was telling me that she and Margaret are on the phone to each other every other day! She keeps her calls short so that they don't appear as metered readings on the bill!

I saw Cleaky before the search and he looks well, considering. His brother is on his way home. He served fifteen years and got married in the Crum' and they survived, so good for them.

Chrissie and Richard will be up next Wednesday. Chrissie's father, Sam, will be operated on next week and only then will they be able to determine if the cancer is so serious that he will lose the leg or have the muscle removed. Sam is originally from the Shankill but worked for *An Phoblacht/Republican News* and some of Chrissie's cousins were in jail for the UVF! Richard was joking that the last time we corresponded like this, he was in here and I was out there.

Saturday 20 July
I am writing at a rickety table: I had to put the other, larger one out of the cell to make room for my guest! I am doubled up for the next fortnight with a lad called Joe McQuillan who used to work in the Beechmount Sinn Fein advice centre.

Jim was up on Friday and we got almost two hours! I was making some political point and gesticulating like mad – using my arms, hands and fingers – and I stopped in mid-track. I said to Jim that the first thing I noticed outside when meeting recently released prisoners was their propensity for gesticulating and now here I was at it!

Brendy Mead was moved to H-4, so bang goes good company. I thoroughly enjoyed his craic: he was always entertaining and never tiresome. Anto was over from A-Wing today. He said he was talking to Rab Kerr out on the visits. Rab is in the same wing in H-8 as Rinty. Rinty spotted Rab with a couple of textbooks in German and asked him was he learning the language. Rab said that he was but that it was proving difficult because, unlike with French and Italian, he had nobody he could talk to and practise with. Rinty then boasted that he could speak German and suggested that they lock up together in Rab's cell between half twelve and two. So Rinty landed in with his cup of tea and the door was locked. Rab was all excited and wanted to get started so Rinty suggested that he would begin.

'Vat is your name and ver did you live before?'

Rab was not amused! He had to put in another hour and a half with Rinty, who said in consolation, 'Here, I know a bit of Irish if that's any good to you?'

Tuesday 23 July

I tramped the yard for about two hours. When the sky is grey or all mixed up and doesn't know what it's going to do, you walk looking up most of the time and your mind soars right over the fence and the barbed wire, fascinated by the play of sunlight against and through the clouds, and you imagine you are elsewhere with the one you love. When shafts of light plunge dramatically through broken clouds I feel I'm standing in a cathedral below a stained-glass window. I experience elation, I feel a desire for life, my heart roars with love for you. As long as I feel this I will never be old.

The big news here is that the UDR is to be amalgamated with the Royal Irish Rangers into the Royal Irish Regiment, and the loyalists are screaming. The new RIR will have eight battalions, only one of which is for overseas duties, the other seven to be based in the North and used in much the same way as the UDR. Although this represents no substantial change it is certainly of symbolic significance, and the potential for further change is there.

Saturday 27 July
Kevin and Liam (still tired from travelling) were up yesterday afternoon and we got almost two hours, which was sound, because I hadn't seen them for over five weeks. Kevin says he enjoyed Corsica, wrote some poems and songs and read a lot. But I was disturbed to hear what happened to the party of kids when they were invited to a barbecue. It was held in the grounds of a chalet rented by Vincent Gaggini's nephew (also called Vincent) and his Arab girlfriend. About half-past ten at night, after the kids had moved indoors, they heard shouting outside. Suddenly, the door was kicked in and a masked man carrying a pistol came in. He cursed the kids and fired two shots into the TV. Kevin said he felt the bullets whiz by. Another kid kicked a table over and the gunman ran out and joined two colleagues, one of whom had a rifle. They then beat up Vincent before fleeing. The cops came and interviewed everyone and three guys were later picked up and charged with possession and discharging firearms, etc. They had been sent by the owner of the chalet (a French colonialist), who had warned Vincent to keep Arabs off his property! A couple of nights later the

Corsican National Liberation Front blew up the chalet and two others owned by the Frenchman! I said to Kevin, 'And to think I sent you there to get away from trouble.'

Despite the incident they all had a good time. Vincent Gaggini got on really well with Kevin and offered him a job and lodgings. I am enthusiastic about that and intend checking it out thoroughly. It would be a great experience.

Some other news: six paratroopers are to be charged in connection with the shooting of those two teenage joyriders, Karen Reilly and Martin Peake, on the Glen Road last September.

I was in a bad mood yesterday, despite the good weather. I was called out to the grille to speak to Frank Burns, the assistant education officer. He told me that the NIO had turned me down for the Open University on the grounds of 'no proven aptitude for studying' and that I was 'only into the jail'! Did you ever hear such nonsense. I intend to appeal against the decision.

Saturday 3 August
Theresa Burt, Jackie and Zack were up yesterday. They all looked well and asked about you. You are invited to Leila's wedding later this month. Theresa says that Liam hasn't been out of Beechmount since Sandra and the kids moved to north Belfast. His base is my da's and every day he gets a taxi into town and then one from town to Beechmount. I hope he's okay and not too unsettled. When he starts his new school and makes new friends things might improve.

Monday 5 August
The weather here has been preparing itself for your return: dull, overcast, cold and windy – the traditional Irish fare! I wonder how you feel about preparing to return? Is there ever a knot in

your stomach – a nervous twinge distinct from the apprehension of leaving the home you grew up in? I'm sure it would be quite natural if there was.

Sunday 11 August
On Friday Tom and Joelle and Timothy O'Grady were up and we got almost two hours. They brought me up a packet of cigars so I had a great time smoking my head off and slagging Joelle over her miniskirt. They left me in two books. We had some lengthy exchanges interrupted occasionally by Tom, who was as attentive as a restless child. I really like Tim.

I met a member of the Board of Visitors, Mary Gilpin, the other day, and I was telling her about being turned down for the OU. She came back to me and said that she had been up to the NIO and they are reconsidering my application.

Friday 16 August
Welcome back, my love. It was great seeing you again despite your state of perplexity. You must know that the only thing I want is to see you happy. And I think you also know that I feel very guilty about being away from you and leaving you on your own. Is love enough to get us through the next few years; who knows? I have confidence in any decision you take because I know it will be taken for the best of reasons and after everything has been measured. Plus, do I have to tell you that I am a great believer in the future?

This evening I went out walking in the yard and fortunately I was on my own, as I needed the solitude. It was raining and I was wearing a cap (manufactured from part of a prison blanket) and my long, cream-coloured coat. At first I stepped around the growing puddles but as I got progressively wetter and my trainers began to leak I ploughed straight through the pools. There was no useful physical purpose in walking to nowhere through such weather but it made sense inside my head, turning over our future, or futures, memorising sensations that I hammered like stakes into my consciousness, knowing that if I didn't they would disappear into the past, such does time rob us of life.

I delighted in how the cold mizzle occasionally was rolled by a ball of wind and struck my cheek like a piece of wet gauze and yet, I thought, at this very same moment the happiness I have known is in the balance. The wet lining of the coat pockets stuck coldly to my hands and drops of rain in the horns of my ears rolled about ticklishly. I was drenched, loving every minute of it and wanting to share it with you because it was so reassuring, so fresh and boisterous, and cleansing, as if it would wipe away all the worries. But I can only share it with you through description.

This is make-or-break time. You can't go home this Christmas and return in the same mood. You are torturing yourself. In Toronto there will be peace and prosperity, all of your family and all of your old friends. You'll have to decide for yourself. I want you to stay but I don't believe that would be the right decision unless you felt the weight of conviction in your head and not your heart. *You* will be able to identify that feeling. And if it's not there soon, send me up the hankies!

Saturday 17 August
This afternoon's visit was very settling and I am in excellent form. I was happy to have seen such a dramatic change in your mood – without compromise, by the way, to the decision you have to make.

I got a huge parcel from Pam Brighton containing specimen manuscripts of radio plays, which was very kind of her. My short story has been accepted but I have just read in the *Independent* that the BBC is axing *The Morning Story* this autumn, so where does that leave me?

Wednesday 21 August

I'm sorry to see you still in an anguished and indecisive state but I do know something of what you are going through. You may not like being reminded but I was torn in a similar way in December 1988, when I felt guilty about missing the kids and not being with them. I am not saying that you would be making a similar mistake by going back to Toronto to be close to your parents – the two are not analogous. But you have my *total* support for whatever decision you make. I had myself psyched up anyway for such an eventuality were I sentenced. If you have to go, you have to go, and we'll both survive. Your mother was right when she said that hesitancy will result in you being swamped once again in your life here, but if you go you might find that you won't get what you want and need because, as the title of the novel explains, *You Can't Go Home Again*: it isn't there, it is in the past.

I walked the yard alone, listening to a tape of jazz music by the cornet player Bix Beiderbecke, who died sixty years ago this month, aged just twenty-nine. As a rule I don't like jazz. These recordings are from 1927 and are rich in atmosphere; the music is tender and bitter-sweet, full of the romance of that age. A contemporary described the effect of him performing:

'Beiderbecke took out a silver cornet. He put it to his lips and blew a phrase. The sound came out like a girl saying yes.'

The blurb on the tape cover, referring to his premature death but the immortality of his music, quotes from *The Dead*:

'Better pass boldly into that other world, in the full glory of some passion, than fade and wither dismally with age . . . '

That sounds almost like a eulogy to youthful suicide! Thank

God I'm passed that stage of my life. My poor love – she would like to fade away into anonymity and have security. Am I even addressing her? I have just felt a sudden rush of insecurity and sickness in my stomach and the thoughts were given free rein. (The truth is that some of my composure is false.)

I wrote a long letter to Kevin which he should get at my da's. I talked about his and my relationship, about the relationship I had with my da and about life. The visit I had with him the other day was really good – he impressed me. I gently lectured him: I see no value in a drilling. A shower can be more valuable than a downpour – the roots can only absorb so much.

Friday 23 August
Hello sweetheart

It's lunchtime and I was going to lie down for a wee siesta but was restless. So I picked up my glasses, cleaned them with a piece of lint and took out some writing paper from my folder. Natural light is sluggishly streaming from a dull sky onto my page.

I had just finished a book about Thomas Mann and his family and was entering notes in a journal I use for that purpose when I was interrupted by a fella called Sean, whom you don't know. Characters from each of our separate lives enter our letters. And God help them! They have no faces and only the identities we choose to give them. Sean once lived in Toronto and Prince Edward Island, having emigrated, but came back a few years ago. He gave me a detailed, very personal account of his parole and swore me to secrecy. I told him that the only guaranteed way to keep a secret was never to confide it.

About three months ago his father sent him family snapshots taken at home last Christmas. Sean pondered them and thought something looked out of place or was missing. In the middle of the night he woke up, rose and switched on the light. He took the photographs out of his locker, looked at them again and then realised that his youngest sister, Patricia, aged eighteen, wasn't in any of the pictures. On the next visit he asked his parents about this and they said, 'You know what Patricia's like: she avoids everything!' He said he would like to see her but when she didn't turn up the following week he was told she had an exam at school, and the next week he was told she was lying in her bed! Finally, he challenged his sister and she explained that Patricia had run away from home eighteen months ago. She took no clothes, left no message and has never made contact. Apparently it wasn't the first time she had run away, though on a previous occasion Sean's father had traced her to Dublin. This time, however, the family have had no luck, despite having contacted the RUC, the gardai, the British police, the Samaritans, etc. Isn't that weird. Sean, of course, was angry with his family for having treated him like an invalid and I can understand that.

Marcel Reich Ranicki, the author of the Mann-family biography, makes a number of observations about the duty of a writer, some of which I have read before and which I doubt I would have the stomach for. Simply stated, he says that the truth must come before compassion. You have to state things as you see them and paint people as you find them. My concern is that without tact there is cruelty. Everyone reads fiction as auto-biography: 'She must have done that to him in bed!' etc.

Goethe said, 'If one wants to leave something worthwhile to posterity, it must be confessions; one must show oneself as an individual, with all one's thoughts and opinions . . . ' George Orwell said the same: 'Literature as we know it is an individual thing, demanding mental honesty and a minimum of censorship.' And the author of this biography says: 'It is undoubtedly the right and duty of a serious writer to expose his inner depths, even at the risk of being accused of exhibitionism.'

Inner depths? It's difficult enough to expose one's inner depths even to the person we love, without going public with them! Publish and be damned is okay if it is an authority whom you are embarrassing but what if it is a poor soul whose life you are laying bare? Will friends forgive you if they recognise their none-too-disguised improprieties in print! Of course, on the other hand you could wreak some revenge! So just be careful, Van Slyke!

I'm being called out to see someone from education. Speak to you later.

4.30 pm

It was someone called Bill – a dapper, bespectacled, pleasant man to whom I let off steam. I accused the head here of being responsible for blocking my OU application because he had never come to see me nor done an assessment. He went away and later I was called to the grille, where a warder said, 'You've been accepted for some course or other.' When we move to H-3 I think I'll try for an end cell, which is the quietest place to be.

Saturday 24 August

Did you read Martin McGuinness's statement – which was a follow-up to Gerry's? I found it strange. He said Sinn Fein was ready to set aside its criticism of Britain and risk 'everything' to create 'a real peace agenda'. It is too open to interpretation – perhaps the wrong one – and by that I mean a sign of weakness, though the Brits have chosen to be cynical. On the other hand, the Republican Movement will be able to say, 'Well, we tried to talk and you weren't interested, so . . .'

8.30 pm

It is always good seeing you and I enjoyed the visit because holding you is like being plugged into a source of happiness and joy, even when we are in a trough. Liam was a scream. I dote on him and it is very good of you taking him over the weekend. That Kevin and Liam and you are friends is brilliant but it is ironic that I am not there to see my dream fulfilled.

I get so much pleasure from floating in the currents you have set up in my life. Will we ever understand our emotions? Actually, I'm nude as I write this!

Wednesday 28 August
We have moved to H-3 and I am in D-Wing, my cell overlooking the front court of the Block, through which everybody going on visits, warders going on and off duty and the food lorry passes. It's noisy. After tea I went across into C-Wing and played volleyball in their exercise yard. I'm just watching the day get sucked into the sky, and although it is dark I can hear the Brits still practising at the shooting range.

Did I tell you that Patricia has been up seeing Pat a few times? From previous conversations with him I understood that he would find the transition from a relationship to friendship too painful, but men in need soon change their creed! Pat has an optimistic – or wishful-thinking-induced – analysis of the struggle, or rather its resolution, which will see everyone out of jail sooner rather than later. I think there are some grounds for that opinion, although in his circumstances I believe his views are partly inspired by the psychological need to remain sane and maintain hope in the face of such a withering sentence.

Saturday 31 August
I hope the sun is still shining when you get this. It was a beautiful evening. After our visit I came back to my cell, but when I was unlocked at half five I had a cup of coffee and a bowl of vegetable soup and then went out to the yard. The yard fencing is made of heavy wire mesh, to which is bolted high corrugated-iron

timbers so that (unlike in the old Cages) we cannot see out of the Block. It also means that when the sun drops low in the sky it is soon eclipsed by the top of the fence and three-quarters of the yard falls into shadow. However, it was a warm and pleasant evening and I walked with a friend who is in love with a married woman who is in love with him. It is based on years of friendship, several jail visits and two nights of passion on parole. Now the husband suspects and he gave her a bit of a beating. I put to him some radical scenarios – they end the affair or she confronts her husband with the truth and leaves him, to await my friend's release, but he ran a mile from that. I then asked him to tell me some annoying habits she has and when he couldn't come up with any I think he realised that he was far from knowing her. I said he was viewing things through testicle-tainted glasses.

We then came in, though I could have walked until midnight. I cleaned my teeth, then filled up an empty Coca-Cola bottle with cold water, as I do each night. Approaching half past eight – when lock-up is called – is always a rush: bottles and flasks being filled, the tea being brewed in a big urn, sandwiches and toast being made, anyone who wishes re-heating the day's leftovers and any excess cartons of milk being distributed on a rota basis so that you get a pint at least every three or four nights. I usually share my milk and only use half for a plate of cornflakes.

A piano sonata is being played on the radio.

I am trying to tear my mood away from my morale, if indeed they can be separated. I am thinking things over and trying to put things into perspective. It's like accounting. I am in good health: my asthma has disappeared for over a year now. My hair is irreversibly and swiftly greying – unless I choose the fraud of dyeing! Really, on most fronts – almost all fronts – I haven't an awful lot to complain about. I am still very lucky. I am luckier than Pat Sheehan or Roy, luckier than Tom Hartley or our Ciaran and luckier than any member of my or your family. I am even luckier than you because I know my mind. I am trying to draw strength from my position. It's not entirely futile, though it's not entirely working. I can feel the grounds for a big debate beginning to accumulate inside my head, or rather my selfishness beginning to assert itself where I grab the reins from you. This letter is actually a rewrite and it isn't Saturday night but Sunday morning. I've had to rewrite it because the one I wrote last night was full of lies: I realised that as soon as I got into bed. I was going to let it stand but then realised this morning that that would have been too hypocritical. You see, it was full of assurances and patient understanding of your predicament. I can feel the bastard rise in me now because I am being brutally frank. It satisfies my pride. I'm away for a walk. I don't want to let my smugness run away with itself.

Later

I'm laughing at the fact (even though it is no laughing matter) that you are apparently able to cope quite adequately with a crucial decision which you can leave unresolved for months whilst I find it difficult to tolerate indecisiveness. If I could view it all as a joke, or be frivolous, maybe I could cope. You are not being serious. You have lifted the hopes of your entire family in direct proportion to mine sinking! But none of us is any the wiser! I think you should take stock fairly quickly. Forget about your work prospects. Forget about my appeal. All the facts are before you. What I can offer you lies in the distant future (though it is very tangible to me because it is *my* future), and even then it is laden with insecurities of who I am and what I am. But you have an example of it: the chunks of our past together. You know what being together tastes like. You know its worth. And on the other hand, you know what life back home in

Toronto is like – and I am not going to fight for it by describing its undoubted attractions. I am telling you now, this debate is going to go on and on, in every letter, on every visit, until it wrecks us. There is no validity whatsoever in your view that we can (or should) simply avoid it and put everything on hold.

You are probably cursing me for not showing restraint but even conversation during visits is inhibited because the place is so public. This letter is a moan, but it's how I've been feeling.

Monday 2 September
Empty lines stretch before me because of a feeling of awkwardness, given what I wrote yesterday. I lay out in the sun most of the day, occasionally turning over to make sure I didn't get burned. There were about three different radio stations blaring pop music from radios. A couple of stalwarts sat against the wire fence sanding down to a smooth surface parts of harps or Celtic crosses, and two men played six games of chess in succession. The guy next to me told me about his parole and his girlfriend. I remember rolling over on my blanket and unfocusing my eyes into the rough surface of the yard to escape a feeling of frustration and to bite on the bullet of the present tense – the master of our lives and the potential wrecker of our future. The pitted and scored tarmac surface had a metal smell, distinct from the odour you get from the street, rising in steam after a sun shower. I can't get you out of my head and it can be a tribute or a curse, depending.

I can hear dogs barking, cars travelling, prisoners coughing, a 'barley-banger' frightening night-prowling crows in the fields beyond, the heating pipes creaking, my light humming, my strength returning.

Tuesday 3 September
We're like two swings in a park – one's going up and the other's coming down! Your improved mood has rubbed off on me even though you are suggesting what I find hard to do – putting the uncertainty out of our minds. Part of my problem, of course, is that I occupy such a tiny space so I have few things to distract me. I know I prefer fiction but that doesn't alter the fact that I'm a deadly realist! Want to hear a joke? What's the difference between the roads in the Free State and 20 Embassy Regal? There's more tar in 20 Embassy Regal! Having said that, it's been a real pleasure driving down some of those roads. You'll learn about it in my autobiography. No, you'll not! Things magic don't translate.

Friday 6 September
Our letters are fucking out of sequence and I'm getting some very late. You say your mood hasn't changed and I'm sorry to hear that. Given that I am so early into this sentence there is just no way we are going to see it through together. We just can't overcome the problems. My occupation – which was a constant strain anyway – got me put in jail, and it took its toll on you and *sin é*. You know what this teaches me? We would have broken up anyway. Look at the lies our lives forced us to tell. I still love you, with a passion with the drive of life behind it. However, I am a wee bit disillusioned with the so-called power of love! That's what I get for being a romantic.

Now, the problem, as I understand it, is that you can't, or haven't yet, found the courage to go through with your decision. You are going home. Do you understand that? It may not be for six months or a year but I need to start protecting myself, so I will be arguing on Tuesday that we start scaling things down very quickly. I don't have the emotional strength for a long goodbye and I'll want to start organising my back-up on the outside. I feel fairly drained yet strangely calm and collected.

Tuesday 10 September
This letter — if it is a letter: you may never see it — reminds me
of a suggestion made by Brendy Mead just after you left for
Toronto last July. He said I should write to you every day — that
is, put my thoughts down daily, addressed to you, but not post
it. Then, when you came back, you'd have about forty or fifty
pages to read! Well, I wrote to you quite regularly and posted
(let me check) nine letters. Maybe if you come back this time
I'll have sheaves for you!

    That was a very difficult visit and I hope that you are not
too distressed. It was a crazy visit: on the one hand, trying to
organise our lives along separate paths, separating our possessions,
and, on the other, telling each other truthfully how much we are
in love. I have a sickly feeling at the bottom of my stomach and
am heavy of heart. I can still smell your perfume on my hands.
I can still hear your shaking voice and see your tears. But it is
for the best. If you come up next Saturday your mind will remain
befuddled and I will have you back on insecure terms. Maybe
it is best if you don't come up. I write to fool myself into thinking
that I've still got you to write to or just so that I don't have to
face up to immediate desolation and the sentences will eventually
trail off. Right, I shall go and change out of my visit clothes.

Wednesday 11 September
Have thought about you all day, and my day began at 5 am when
I awoke and couldn't get back to sleep. I was out walking with
Sean Smyth and told him about us. He said he could never be
as cool and clinical as I was being. Oh God, my resolve turned
to jelly and I quivered and thought about the four o'clock post,
hoping you had written a letter. I then caught myself and

returned to my abiding principle that everything comes out good
in the end and if I don't hear from you it's for the best.

I am reading *Fabian* by Erich Kastner. It's about an advertising
copywriter in Berlin in the dying days of the Weimar Republic.
Fabian falls in love with a girl who eventually is forced to become
the whore of a film director. She has only recently arrived in this
Sodom and Gomorrah and she asks Fabian to take her back to
her apartment. You know the way someone's ghost lingers about
furniture and rooms which you've shared with them? Well,
Kastner, through the voice of this girl, brilliantly expresses the
sterility of unshared rooms when she says to Fabian: 'Would you
misunderstand me if I asked you to come in for half an hour?
I feel such a stranger in my room. There are no echoes of things
said, no memories of things done, for I have never spoken to
anyone in my room, and nothing has ever happened of which
it could remind me. And at night black trees sway to and fro
outside the window.'

I'll leave you, or rather leave my thoughts to you, now and
go bury my eyes in a book. Publicly I do not wear my heart on
my sleeve but, oh, I miss you badly.

Saturday 14 September
I picked up the *Andersonstown News* and said jokingly to myself,
'Let's see if she has put the house up for sale yet!' Did that
rebound! There was a photograph of the house. However, it was
next door that was up for sale. Still, I had a prescient feeling
of how depressed I will be.

Already I've been offered a pen pal. A thirty-one-year-old
travel agent from New Zealand, who says she is interested in
politics and classical music, wrote to Raymond McCartney after
she saw on TV Peter Taylor's documentary 'The Enemy Within'.
No, I'll stick to my books and if I never send this letter to you

I'll turn it into a diary.

Yesterday I got a letter from our Susan. I have written to her explaining what has happened and is happening. She asked for a visit and I said I'd arrange that. She had been talking to you since you came back and has rung a couple of times but no one answered the phone. Also got a letter from Roy down in the Crum' for his retrial.

My daddy, Kevin and Liam were up today. We got over one and a half hours. We all seemed to skirt around the subject of you but then I explained things. When I got back here one of the lads said, 'There's a letter for you. It's in your cell. A brown envelope.' You know what I thought, don't you! But it was a sympathy card I had asked the chaplain to get me.

Sunday 15 September

I have just finished letters to Pat Sheehan and Richard McAuley. I met Jackie McMullan on the visits yesterday and congratulated him on his marriage to Ella O'Dwyer in Durham Prison. No family guests were allowed and his 'best man' was a female Sri Lankan prisoner! Ella and Martina weren't even allowed a little party on the wing to celebrate.

Tuesday 17 September

Last night I went through several diametrically opposed moods, working up a dislike for you which kept collapsing! It was based on a range of thoughts, although self-pity was to the fore. I remembered you saying about one of the wives that she would never stick by her husband if he got big time, I mean big time, and I wondered whether it was actually transferred psychology. I thought about all the times you hadn't read my letters properly or hadn't responded to this or that detail. I was being really petty. At times I must seem a bit pedantic, always quoting from books, but that's because I am always attempting to express myself fully.

I quoted from a Julian Barnes book earlier this year (*A History of the World in Ten and a Half Chapters*) about the thoughts of a man lying in bed with his girlfriend as she snuggled up to him in her sleep. But there was another story in that book and it was about a fella who went to the South American rainforests to make a film. His girlfriend was in England and what we read is the sequence of letters he writes her. They start off confident, full of love and very romantic but as time passes and he fails to get a response the dark side of love begins to feature. All the things that the diplomacy of love had left dormant begin to be nastily aired and I think in his last letter hatred is in full flood. It made me think, could this happen to me?

I received a postcard from Jim Gibney, posted on the eleventh of September, and he said he would be back from Madrid in three weeks' time. Let's say the third of October. I thought, once she moves my clothes out then that is a definitive statement of intent. What I'll do then is write a cool note, thanking her for everything she has done to date but asking her to cancel my newspapers and stop doing my parcels because that leaves her in an ambiguous position.

Looking every day for a letter that never comes seems to point to weakness on my part and strength on yours. I think about all your difficulties and how hard you tried and all I want to do is make things easy and facilitate you, even to the point of helping you leave me.

Saturday 21 September
I had a good visit with Kevin and Liam. Some visits can be very draining and some can be very exhilarating and this one helped me a lot. We got our photographs taken. Kevin said he had been around with you last night and might see you again tonight. I

told him to tell you that I said 'I love you'. I also told him to take the Doctor Martens boots if they fitted him.

Monday 23 September
Spent all day finishing a book review for the *Andersonstown News*, a review of Ernie O'Malley's Civil War prison letters which I found very depressing.

Sunday 29 September
To David McKittrick
David, *a chara*. Thank you for your letter, which I received last Wednesday, and for the article which you enclosed. I had been collecting that series on 'The Art of Fiction' for the previous sixteen weeks and on that particular week the review section was missing from the paper.

You seemed very, very depressed. I can understand why. More deaths and funerals, tears, broken lives and endless tragedies. It takes its toll on everyone. You can report them in clichés if you are detached and don't really care. But if you are concerned then inevitably you get emotionally drawn in and question the point of it all and are left despairing. Sides mean nothing – everything's a mess.

Much of your analysis is very true except that we are dealing with human beings who are in trenches, whose rationale may often appear elusive or inexplicable but who feel they have no other choice. What options are open to the Republican Movement?

Calling it off would certainly not lead to reconciliation or a positive change in the unionist attitude, which would then be: 'It was close, but we hung on and beat the bastards in the end.' The British would hardly feel the need to accommodate republicans, and conceivably even their attitudes to the Dublin government and the SDLP would cool, though I doubt they would be that stupid. But do you remember the ending of the first hunger strike? The Brits – not just Thatcher – couldn't resist rubbing the prisoners' noses in it instead of resolving the issue.

The point is that people's pride and self-respect and all their past and present sacrifices and all the unrealised aspirations have a certain value and meaning and have to be taken on board. People would have to feel that a settlement was just and that their opponents were making compromises also. However, none of us trust each other. I don't trust the British. I simply don't believe in the façade of reasonableness which they are presenting and which you echoed in your analysis.

I am aware of all the realities, some of which you touched on: apathy in the twenty-six counties, the British not wanting to be seen to capitulate to the armed struggle and the present inability of the IRA to sap irreversibly London's commitment. So what does all this mean? Is there a meeting point between unionist and nationalist aspirations? I certainly hope so, and I hope it can be found. But the constitutionalists wouldn't agree, and that most certainly cannot be blamed on the IRA, can it?

Incidentally, I recognise the suzerain authority of the Brits and that the Free State does not constitute an alternative central authority. The Brits are a bit like the Syrians in Lebanon. And, by the way, no republican I know has the stomach for the Beirut scenario you suggested as being a possibility.

When Peter Brooke made his hundred days' statement he certainly bemused republicans and forced us to listen carefully to what he was saying. But he seems to have been in retreat from that position ever since. In Frank Millar's interview in Friday's *Irish Times* he seems to have given up on us! Sometimes it appears as if he is offering republicans an 'honourable surrender', which must be a classic oxymoron. My own opinion is that the Republican Movement remains in a strong position. I also believe, contrary to you, that time can exhaust the British. They will end up talking to us, and that's when our problems really begin!

When the time for talking does come and everybody's talking, republicans will have to address themselves to *realpolitik* – to the crucial issue of the unionists, their identity, their rights, their security, their fears and the institutions they would be prepared to support. That is a huge subject and, obviously, one for negotiation.

You know, I really hate fuckin' politics. In 1969–70 I dropped out of A-Level politics because it interfered with my reading *Wuthering Heights* and *Anna Karenina*. In here, I have plenty of time for reading. I also do a bit of writing – short stories, poems, some book reviews. I'll leave off here, David, and go read more about Mr Hemingway in Paris in the 1920s. You'll love this: Hemingway was a journalist before he became a novelist and once said that 'the best writers are liars'! Can't have seen him ever writing in the *Independent* or *An Phoblacht*!

Tuesday 1 October
Back again, Penelope. This morning I was moved to H-4, so here I am, settling in again. Bik, Pat Sheehan and Kevin McMahon are here. This looks like a good wing. When I was unpacking the brown bags in which I moved my gear I came across hard-boiled eggs, tomatoes, a malt loaf and about fifteen British tabloids, which those messers in H-3 had packed when my back was turned!

Friday 4 October
Both my windows are open and the rain is gurgling nicely outside; dripping and drizzling and splashing. I don't know why I am writing this because it depresses me rather than helping. I have spent the last few nights between half five and half eight with Bik, yarning and reminiscing. Being a Red Book prisoner

he is only here until Tuesday. But I come back fairly exhausted and have to rush to get my supper. It takes a little while to settle in and get to know everybody's names, etc.

As I said, I don't know why I am writing this. You being in Belfast still and us not being in contact is the same 'long goodbye' I thought I could have avoided by stopping visits and letters. Pat had a visit with Siobhan and he was saying that Hugh had phoned to see if you'd sell him the house. My moods have been up and down and I know that the cure is time and it seems to have been crawling on all fours since the tenth of September.

I have just looked over some of the things I have written and I now know that I will only send this letter should you decide to stay because otherwise it would hurt you and would seem like an act of vengeance.

Friday 11 October
Jim was up today and acquainted me with the facts – about how rough a time you've been having. He also said that he thought we'd made our decision too quickly. I gave him my account and obviously I was also pumping him for information about you as I've had no other real source for the past four or five weeks. Anyway, I'm sorry for what you have gone through. He also proposed that we have a visit. I had no plans to see anyone this coming week so there is a visit there. He says he doesn't think you will leave Ireland. I hope the same but I want your decision either way to be certain – that's been the sole reason for this break, hasn't it?

Monday 14 October
Susan and Liam were up on Saturday and she was telling me about her health problem and that she was speaking to you on the telephone last weekend and that you were upset. Both Jim and

Susan commented that you remarked that I had been very cool and calm on our last visit. But I behaved like that because I wanted to make it less painful for you, not to facilitate your leaving me!

Tuesday 15 October
I received Jim's card at about four with the succinct message, 'Our friend remains undecided. I'll be up on Friday morning.' Given that I hadn't invested any great hopes in our problem being resolved I wasn't hurt. In fact, I am glad that you are proving so strong. A visit – in fact, even a letter! – from you would only confuse things.

I got a nice letter from Kevin saying that he was glad I hadn't become emotional on our last visit and thanking us for the money. At the end of the letter he wrote, 'I love you, da', and that made me feel great. I hope he sticks at his new job in Corsica. He was telling me that he was embarrassed when his girlfriend burst into tears and ran upstairs in No. 37 over him going away. He hadn't realised how deeply she thought of him.

Two books that I had ordered from the library – biographies of Schubert and Mahler – arrived, so I shall be burying my head in them. I am also reading Ovid's *Love Poems*. He was born just outside Rome about 2,000 years ago. One of his poems is called 'The Cures of Love' and is full of advice about how to overcome heartbreak! He says you've to keep busy, burn her letters and pictures ('portraits'), stop thinking of the places you went and the things you shared, think of her shortcomings (even if you have to tell yourself lies), don't brood, pretend that you're not in love and mix with plenty of friends!

Ovid also says, 'Don't ask what she's doing, though you long to. Stand firm! To hold your tongue will profit you . . . You'll best get revenge by silence.'

Revenge by silence?

Well, honey, I'm going to send you these twenty pages

whether or not the decision is the right one. I'll not be writing again in the near future and I hope the decision to post this isn't wrong and that it helps you and doesn't make things more complicated. I am 100 per cent behind you. So please don't be worrying. You are a great person. Don't feel under any pressure for me or from me. What I am saying is that we both understand each other's positions.

Thursday 17 October
To Gerry Adams
Dear comrade

A little surprise from me! My views on the current situation! I know that this is not a great medium and I'll be as careful as possible getting this to you. Firstly, I don't know how healthy are our finances or what is the true state of resources so I'll be commenting from afar. Secondly, I am a bit concerned that some sort of discussion (which is being called a 'debate' here) has been initiated between Taoibh Amuigh and an unwieldy number of prisoners. I have been invited to contribute but it's so wide it's open to being misrepresented by the Brits. Is there a debate going on? If so, it should be conducted with extreme caution and discretion. A debate is a major mistake if it's in the absence of the leadership having made up its own mind.

I know how tiring and distressing is the work you all do. It's one long grind against a huge opposition. But I feel we are fairly strong, though the 'Ra would sometimes frustrate you with some of its counter-productive operations. I felt that we made two political mistakes this year. We misread the Brooke talks and our public statements showed that we were on edge and unsure of our position. We have an analysis of loyalism which has proved fairly correct to date. It might need adjusting now and again to allow for minor shifts but basically our analysis is sound.

However, we gave the impression that we were panicking, whereas I think a better position would have been not continually to bemoan our exclusion but to say, 'Good luck! We hope you can agree. We don't believe you can because of the Brits, loyalist veto, etc., but good luck!'

On the SDLP, I think we confuse our propaganda position and hostility with our analysis of them. There are certain things the SDLP will not settle for, otherwise the Brits could have co-opted them more forcefully against us years ago. If we view the SDLP more sympathetically, just as an exercise for a few moments, we can see that they are not totally craven, that they have some nationalism and that they reflect the middle-of-the-road views of thousands upon thousands of nationalists whose goodwill we seek. (Accept this as a belated acknowledgement of your wisdom in 1988 in initiating the SF-SDLP talks!) Depending on which way our struggle turns we will more than likely be in an alliance with them in the future. Our second mistake was the letter to the senior clerics. I can see the PR reasoning behind the invite but it appeared to me (unless I missed something) that it would be perceived as a stunt. The timing of the church leaders' rejection (reinforcing our isolation) was beautiful!

Unless we are saying something new about how to unravel the political stalemate we would be as well battening down the hatches and saying nothing. Otherwise, we only confuse our base, give the impression that we are indecisive and weaker than we are (and I don't believe we are weak) and give the opposition an opportunity to hammer us.

There is no doubt that Sinn Fein's *Scenario for Peace* (1987) sounds clichéd. But you can't dress it up in new clothes and expect to fool people. Just remember that no side has changed its position so neither need we – unless we are changing strategy and compromising – voluntarily, or because circumstances and resources are forcing us to. Incidentally, it is far wiser to anticipate such a change in circumstances and act accordingly than to act under duress (which could produce a split).

The world is changing in such a way that some of our ideas of sovereignty and nationhood are being overtaken by new concepts. Have you been reading up on the proposals for European union? Our opposition to the EC may be principled and proved correct in the long term (that is, in fifty to a hundred years' time) but in the long term we are all dead. The majority of people on this island (even among the unionist people) aren't that opposed to joining a federal Europe. Have we seriously examined the possibility of a compromise or interim settlement within the EC? We may have no choice anyway!

I recently read a book by a white member of the ANC, *The Soft Vengeance of a Freedom Fighter* by Albie Sachs, and he wrote something very interesting and appropriate to us. He said: 'We [the ANC] might find ourselves confronted with hard decisions, whether to hold out for generations if necessary, until we are finally able to overthrow and completely destroy the system of apartheid, or to accept major but incomplete breakthroughs now, transforming the terrain of struggle in a way which is advantageous to the achievement of our ultimate goals. In the end we have to find a way of consulting with the people to find out what they feel, and this means struggling for the opening of the jails and the return of the exiles and the creation of conditions of free discussion and consultation.'

Believe it or not I think we can fight on forever and can't be defeated. But, of course, that isn't the same as winning or showing something for all the sacrifices. I despair of the Free State and the contortions we've gone through attempting to build a base. I think we need to look again at our analysis of the Free State and consider the hitherto-unpalatable political realities. That is, the extent of their nationalism falls short of the people making any meaningful contribution to the struggle for reunification, though Dublin governments will take up certain demands of nationalists in the North (for reform, for an 'Anglo-Irish' framework, etc.).

I believe that the loyalists will remain fairly united whilst the armed struggle continues and until faced with the choice of 'an honourable compromise', let's call it, which Britain supports. Then they will split (between pragmatists and extremists) and be at their weakest. We could consider actively bringing about such a situation.

The Brits are dug in but it's hard to say how much bluster there is behind all their clichéd assertions of seeing the thing out. Sometimes I feel that they are a lot weaker and less sure than we suppose. When I'm in that mood I think, 'Blatter on!'

I would always prefer to deal with the Tories than with Labour and if Labour are elected to government their policy of 'reunification by consent' presents us with certain problems if they actively promote it.

In 1978 the new republican leadership issued its analysis and declared 'the long war'. There was much grumbling over this but at least everyone knew where they stood. There is a growing onus on the leadership to clear the air again. Too many questions are being left unanswered. There is too much speculation. We should take stock of our organisation and consider political realities, re-examine our demands (which are to be distinguished from our objectives) and honestly assess if they are realisable in just part or as a whole, adjust our expectations accordingly and publicly declare what are our intentions, even if it is to say that we expect the struggle to go on for at least another five, ten, fifteen or twenty years!

I've gone on too long and yet I could go on all night! Please don't be replying because I know how busy you are and I don't expect a written reply. Simply give my visitor some nice cigars for me. *Deja vu*! Take care. Regards to the missus.

  – Pennies

Wednesday 30 October

Hello my love. Like you I was shocked and saddened to learn of Derek Dunne's death. We got the *Irish News* here about half ten on Monday morning. I read the item and felt I had been in a bad dream and had to read it again. It has wrecked me. He was such a good guy. I was hoping someone would write and let me know what had happened and I am glad it was you. I keep wondering how he coped when he learnt that he had such a short time left on this earth with his family and I'm sure he faced up to it courageously. As you said, he was consistent in writing to me, giving me all the biz from down below and joking. He always had the ambition to write the biography of some old eccentric of a newspaper editor from Longford who was something of a local institution and used to invent front-page stories! I wonder did he ever get around to writing it or did he get finishing the biography of Joe Cahill he was working on.

It's good of you to take Liam to the fireworks display. He mentioned that you were organising a trip to the pictures but said that you and Susan were still talking on the phone at the time and he had to leave for somewhere and so it wasn't arranged.

I received a letter from Kevin complaining of homesickness and indicating that he would be coming back at Christmas. I wrote and said that if he wanted to come home he would be most welcome but that I thought it would be better if he at least stayed until Easter. There is no work here and he is too young to qualify for unemployment or housing benefit until next June.

Saturday 2 November

You were masterful in those opening seconds when you weren't aware that I was expecting you! I'm still in the heavens and all is peace within. It was good seeing you again and felt so right – even should we have to go through the same painful experience again! Not for nothing were the words to the song written, 'The best part of breaking up is when you're making up'! Anyway, I'll not forget Derek at Mass tomorrow for being an unwitting matchmaker, even though it turns out that you first felt like coming up last weekend, before his death, which triggered you to write.

I moved from a noisy cell to this one – Cell 15 – about two weeks ago. It's at the very end of the wing, is very quiet and suits me. These are the dark nights, okay. Winter seems to introduce an additional pigment into the blackness of these evenings. I don't normally close my curtains: just being able to look out – even into nothingness – gives a sense of freedom. In some of those cells in the Crum' the windows are made of frosted glass and are sealed, or else if there is a view it is a poor one.

My wrist wants to know what's going on – who am I writing to!

Monday 4 November

I went down to the big pitch this morning for the football. On one occasion I stopped the ball with my balls and that fairly took the wind out of me. Maybe my vas deferens have kissed and made up – it certainly felt like surgery. Brendy Mead asked me did I want a sweet and I said yes. He gave me a Tune, then disappeared. As I stood unwrapping the paper, he shouted from the other side of the field, 'Look at that greedy bollocks feeding his face!' Everybody looked at me and wanted a sweet!

The mail came in at half four and there was one letter for me. The handwriting looked like Rita's and the envelope was postmarked Dublin but it was from the editor of *An Phoblacht*, Micheal MacDonncha, asking me to write something regular for the paper. I can't give such an undertaking, given the OU course, but I'll offer to do the occasional book review.

I take it you are serious about moving house. A back garden for barbecues and a driveway for your Mini Metro! Not a very newsy letter but I'll 'punish' you with more letters soon.

Tuesday 5 November

Two letters from you! It's amazing how a letter can transform one's mood from pleasant to ebullient. I was glad of the extra bit of information on Derek and I will certainly write to his wife and mother. By the way, is his mother's name Leslie or Lolie – your handwriting wasn't clear. I hadn't thought much about what effect his writing the escape book would have had on his other journalistic work but I suppose he was bracketed as a crypto-Provo and suffered the sanctions without complaint, whilst, on the other hand, some republicans foolishly believed he was making a fortune!

Martin Meehan, the da, came over for a yarn tonight and we were talking about kids and families. His first wife, Mary, died of cancer in 1977 and about a year later he met Briege. He had three children from his first marriage and she had one from hers. They all moved under the one roof and everything was fine until after about six months he was arrested and jailed and his kids couldn't settle.

He can be very funny the way he tells a story. Do you remember him telling the story of his escape from the Crum' in 1971 in that film *Behind the Mask*? His father had been interned in the Forties and he himself had become interested in republican politics in his late teens, around about the time he got married. By 1968 he was doing quite well: he had a new job and he and his wife Mary had just bought a new house in Alliance Avenue. They had a car and a telephone. On the fifth of October there was a big civil rights march in Derry, the second in a series, though it was actually the first one in the public's mind because it was filmed by RTE. Martin went to the march with a busload of republicans and when the RUC began their baton charge in Duke Street, beside the Foyle Bridge, he fought to get to the front! He says that he saw a physically handicapped woman fall to the ground and he went to help her but both were trailed away and put in the back of an RUC tender along with a reporter from the *Derry Journal* and Erskine Holmes (then with the Northern Ireland Labour Party, now a bigwig in the Housing Executive, I think).

Martin noticed that they weren't locked in and tried to get back to the battlefront but was intercepted and booted back to the tender, to which he was then handcuffed. He spent until the early hours of the morning inside a police cell and was released after being charged with four or five offences. When he came out the republican bus had gone back to Belfast but there was a student bus waiting for the others to be released and he was invited on to it. He said that on the journey home they were planning marches, demonstrations and sit-ins for here, there and everywhere, and he was fascinated because they could all *talk* and seemed to know what they were doing! Paddy Devlin's daughter (who is now a playwright), Rory McShane (now a Newry solicitor) and Cyril Toman (later Sinn Fein) were all there.

When Martin got home his wife was distracted about him jeopardising their future and his good job but he assured her nobody would know about him being there. Then, in Monday's *News Letter*, there appeared a huge photo of him being trailed up the street by two RUC men!

Kevin Agnew represented all those prosecuted, and in court he threw all the charge sheets into the air to show his contempt for the RUC and the system. Eventually they were all given an amnesty (in a move which resulted in Paisley's release from the Crum') before it went to a full hearing. Martin claims that nobody from Derry – except the handicapped woman – was at the march and that all the men were at the Derry City v. Distillery football match in the Brandywell! For years afterwards he slagged Derrymen about that and also asked if anybody knew who the woman was. One day, walking around the yard in Long Kesh, he asked Charlie McSheffrey from Derry, who immediately recalled that his sister-in-law fitted the description and that she had been arrested on the fifth of October. In 1978, on the tenth anniversary of that march, Charlie reintroduced Martin to the woman!

There was an item in yesterday's *Independent* about a 106-year-old Chinaman who suffered a mild heart attack when his young wife told him that she was expecting his child. I wrote on the front page of the newspaper, 'Good News For Pat Sheehan, See p.12'! He admitted that he laughed when we were all found guilty so he deserves a tough slagging!

Thursday 7 November
It's a bit nippy tonight but I've a cup of hot drinking chocolate to keep me warm. We all had an extra blanket given to us today – the others must know something about winters here that I don't!

This morning I got up at half eight and after breakfast began to get washed and shaved but was interrupted by the warning cry: '*Sin na fir certach*!' That is, the search team were on the Block for their fortnightly duty. During a search we are locked up, though later we can go to the canteen or the yard. The morning passed ever so slowly. Everyone thought that this was a long day.

Cleaky was asked the time on one occasion and he said it was half seven. About twenty minutes later he was asked again and he said it was half six! And that's exactly how it felt – as if the sands of time were running back into the hourglass!

You mentioned the fact that Christy Moore played at Derek's funeral. That in itself is a fine tribute to his popularity. Speaking of Christy, a critic for a San Francisco newspaper went along to report on one of his concerts and wrote that when he came on stage she thought he was there to move the piano!

I ended up writing an article for *AP/RN* after all, despite my protestations about having no spare time. It was a radio review column which they may like to consider as a regular feature, though I'm half-hoping they turn down the idea.

Huck Finn on Mark Twain: 'There were things that he stretched, but mainly he told the truth'!

Monday 11 November
The cold would have cut the ears off you today. Some of the lads wear towels around their necks for protection against draughts when out walking. Today I borrowed Tom McAllister's DM boots and the joke was that I started walking like him. When the clouds sprint across the sky pursued by a gale and the air cuts like a blade and my eyes smart until tears roll down my cheeks, the wildness sets me free for a few precious moments and I love it.

That was good news from the courts about Pauline Quinn, Frankie Quinn's girlfriend, being acquitted. She was released today and will be up on a visit tomorrow, though I think they decided, in view of the time that he's doing, to break up. Nevertheless he was in great form tonight – he's so pleased for her.

Sunday 17 November

I got loads of letters yesterday and the day before and my first Christmas card. Rita wrote from her hospital bed explaining why she had been reluctant to write sooner. It was she who sent me *The Snapper* by Roddy Doyle. She is reading the poems of Philip Larkin, which she praised to the high heavens. He is the gentleman one of whose poems is titled 'They Fuck You Up' and is about your mum and dad, or rather about blaming your mum and dad for all your faults and problems.

David McKittrick wrote me a long letter, the second on his private thoughts about the political situation. What he writes is interesting and fairly provocative. The understanding is that he doesn't expect me necessarily to reply – because of the censor and NIO scrutiny. As I see it, in politics – and particularly the type in which we are engaged – the bigger the gap between one's public position and one's private position the bigger the hypocrisy! I don't have that much of a problem with replying.

That was a good article in today's *Independent on Sunday*. The leading item on Page 1 was about the generals saying that they couldn't defeat the IRA without reintroducing internment. I sat down and wrote a letter to the paper arguing that republicans did not want internment and that it was not the answer.

One of the warders here, Stan, arrived into the canteen at around four in his overcoat, which was drenched. He was bringing in our Sunday papers and I was joking with him, asking could they not finish reading our papers quicker and get them in to us earlier. There were about a dozen papers for our wing and only two or three for the other republican wing (though we share them). Stan wondered why there were so few for the other wing and I said it was because most of them were dyslexic. Quick as you like he quipped, 'Oh, they must all be in the 'Ra then.'

Tuesday 19 November

I'm sure you saw the oceans pour from the skies yesterday. Brendy Mead and I looked at one another and each could tell what the other was thinking and we said, 'Fuck the weather! Are you game? Then let's go!'

So, at about a quarter past two, when the rest of the wing were building arks, we came on to the 'centre court'! It was great craic. The ball came at you like a Catherine wheel spitting liquid blades and turned from a sponge into a rock when it was hit back. After a few minutes we were completely drenched but there was a perfect balance between the glow of physical play and the chilling rain. It had become so overcast and dark that some of the security lights were switched on. There is one image I shall never forget. Once, when serving, I threw the ball high into a falling chandelier of rain and as it fell in slow motion towards my poised racket I had time to focus on the top floor of the visits building in the background, where the windows were brightly lit, and focus my mind on you and all that you mean to me, and cheer inside myself, before I zoomed back into play. Everyone thought that we were mad but we came back in at about ten to four and jumped straight into hot showers. Brendy said that his girlfriend Lena is going to cook him a special meal of mince steak during his parole at Christmas.

I fell about laughing and he said, 'What do you think I said?'

'Mince steak,' I replied.

Then he roared with laughter and explained that he had said, 'Mint steak', at which I almost wet myself, never having heard of the poison.

Sunday 24 November

I have just listened to the news proper since first hearing about that frightening explosion inside Crumlin Road Jail which killed a prisoner and injured others. I had heard that things down there were pretty grim, with fighting regularly taking place right up to the door of the visiting area, but I didn't think it would come to this.

Wednesday 27 November
Ed Moloney was up this morning. I was called around eleven and it was the first time that he had seen the new visiting arrangements. I noticed he didn't smoke at all. He used to roll his own – perhaps he has given up smoking. Anyway, we had a good yarn on the overall political situation. I answered some of his criticisms and clarified other issues.

Pat Sheehan and his co-accused were all brought down to the Crum' today to be arraigned on the escape charges. He was talking to some of the remands and they said that the Crum' is wild – fighting is now taking place *inside* the visits! You'd love that – getting your hair wrecked! Actually, it's so serious that I expect the issue will be resolved this time. Let's just hope no one else is killed or seriously injured. The position of the administration is so untenable given the fact that we are segregated up here. They had a similar attitude of course during the blanket protest, when there were prisoners with political status in another part of the jail. They lost that battle and are going to lose this one as well.

Wednesday 4 December
I received a letter from Gerry Hanratty. He and Gerry McGeough's court hearing is continuing in West Germany. Last month a senior Dutch detective was called to give evidence and he produced a copy of a letter which Gerry had sent. The letter began, '*A Chairde*' and the detective explained that this is a term used by IRA personnel and in translation means, 'Weapons

brother'! A few days later he was recalled to the stand and was shown part of another letter (most of which was covered up) which began, 'Sean, *a chara*,' and had liberal references throughout to '*cairde*'. He was asked again for his opinion and he said that he had checked with the RUC and '*A Chairde*' means 'Weapons brother'! Gerry's lawyer then showed that the letter had been sent from the German ambassador in their embassy in Dublin! The expert had to be helped from the stand!

The evidence against Gerry McGeough for allegedly bombing a British army barracks in West Germany has also been rubbished. He had been charged on the basis that a Dutch witness statement read, 'That's the man that bought the car' (the one which was used in the attack). The witness showed up and said that he never said that. The DPP told the court that the witness must have been got at by the IRA to retract. An interpreter checked his statement and it was then found to read: 'He [McGeough] looks a little like the man who bought the car but it's not him.' So it looks like they'll be facing extradition proceedings in early spring as the time they have served on remand will probably be equivalent to the sentence they eventually get for possession of weapons.

Bobby Storey, who is the longest-serving prisoner on a Red Book (eight years), came on to the other wing last week. When I was in Cage 2 he came into Cage 3, interned at the age of seventeen. He has been in jail more or less since then, apart from brief periods of freedom. For example, he was on remand in Brixton from 1979 until April 1981, was then released, was arrested again in August 1981 and has been in jail ever since.

Phew! There's just been a huge rumble of an explosion. It's five to ten.

Saturday 7 December
I had a weird dream last night. I was released on parole and came
out to see you. You were living in Divis Flats! I came into the
room – which resembled our old house – and sat talking to you.
Your hair was exactly the same and your face was almost the
same. But this person's personality was dead – she had no
humour or animation, though she loved me. Suddenly I realised
that it wasn't you! I made an excuse to leave the room and as
soon as I got outside I ran down the landing and the stairs. There
was someone chasing me and he caught up with me just as I
reached the street. It was Frankie Quinn, and he wanted to know
where I thought I was going, that my girl was sitting upstairs
waiting for me. I told him that it wasn't you, it wasn't you, and
he said it couldn't be helped, that's the way things turn out and
I better go back. I said I couldn't go back and I remember
running up a street covered in broken glass. Then I awoke!

Saturday 21 December
It's just after ten o'clock and I felt the urge to speak to you in
the silent words of a letter. The Christmas train is on full steam
now, though when I finish this letter in a week's time it – and
1991 – will be buried. I hope you are having a good time with
your family in Toronto. The world has been very kind. To begin
with yourself: your cards and letters have been the sweetest ones
you have ever written and have filled me with elation and sheer
joy. Last year some of the lads joked with me about the number
of cards decreasing with each Christmas that you are in jail but
I can't say that has been the case because I've received almost
150 so far.

Kevin brought me up a big King Edward cigar today and I've
still got half the small ones you sent in. I'm in clover! To top
it all, *It's a Wonderful Life* was on the TV today and the eyes were

dabbed throughout! Ned Flynn confessed he was close to a waterfall at the end! Yes, girlfriend and life partner, it is a wonderful life.

I haven't heard this myself but it was on the radio yesterday and Danny Caldwell confirmed it today out on the visits that we shall be up on the ninth of March for our appeal. I am sending you out a visit pass for the eleventh of January.

Tuesday 24 December

Yesterday morning there was a great atmosphere in the wing as the parolees left. Some of them were ashen-faced, like children facing a vaccination for the first time, but some were also a bit depressed because of the situation outside and the killings over the weekend. After they left there was a great atmosphere among those of us still here! I shouted, 'Let's revert to individualism!' and there was a cheer. Nobody washed the toilets last night or tonight! It was the novelty of rebellion and it has only lasted a short time, as the culture of sharing is fairly ingrained. Tomorrow morning everyone bar Pat Sheehan, Ned Flynn and myself are having a lie-in and we will be serving them their breakfasts in bed!

Last night the IRA once again declared a three-day ceasefire. On Saturday a nineteen-year-old student was shot dead in his father's gunsmith shop in Moy. The student died trying to shield his father from the gunman. His father was a former member of the RUC. The gunman was overpowered and was himself held at gunpoint. According to Downtown Radio he begged his guards not to shoot him. Whether it's true or not, it made a good story for the media because it made the killer sound like a coward. The INLA are believed to have been involved. On Saturday night gunmen burst into the Donegall Arms at the loyalist end of Roden Street and opened fire, killing two men and injuring three others. The IPLO has been blamed but so far they have made no comment. That night a Catholic man who had moved in with his Protestant girlfriend in the same area was shot dead. On Sunday afternoon loyalist gunmen entered the Devenish Arms on Finaghy Road North, Andersonstown, and opened fire, killing one man, seriously injuring an eight-year-old boy who was playing snooker with his father and wounding two others. So all these incidents made 'outside' a bleak and forbidding place, especially to those parolees who were going out for the first time and who would be 'fair game' for the loyalists.

Wednesday 25 December
To Tim O'Grady
Dear Tim

It's Christmas night here, half past eight, and the cell door has just been locked. It's nice and peaceful. I'm sorry for the delay in writing to you. I should have written after our visit in August but the passage of time in prison is very deceiving. I got your letter and the book *Once in Europa*. The stories are well-paced and I liked Berger's measured style. I don't think I like his method of annotating – or rather not annotating – dialogue, though. In order for sense and context to prevail, such a style probably forces him to compromise on prose. But he's in good company: Joyce refused to use what he called 'perverted commas'. Berger's consummate use of 'facts' occasionally comes across in a Robert Fisk style of reportage, which enhances his authority and makes everything that bit more believable. However, I would have liked the stories more had he gone deeper into the psychology of the characters.

My cell is at the very end of the wing, where there is the least noise. It also catches the sun – when the sun penetrates this cloudy country. The rail line between Belfast and Dublin is close to the camp and when the wind is in the right direction we can hear the train speeding by or hear the whistle when it blows approaching a nearby level crossing. When the sky is clear we can see many of the flights from Aldergrove, which is about six miles north of here.

You were asking what writing was I doing. Well, about seven weeks ago I began a weekly column for *AP/RN* called 'Radio Times'. It allows me to wax lyrical and mix satire with reviews and political commentary. I think I told you that the BBC accepted a short story from me. It's scheduled to be broadcast on the twelfth of March and the reader will possibly be Stephen Rea. I've also written a few poems and have lots of ideas for first chapters which end right there! In five weeks' time I start at the Open University and on the ninth of March we've to go back down to the Crum' for our appeal. The OU course is really going to put a stop to my reading and already I'm half-regretting it, so I think I'll just do the one year at the OU and firmly commit myself to writing a novel in my last two years here.

Besides classical music I love listening to golden oldies. There's a show on BBC Radio 1 every Sunday called *Pick of the Pops,* presented by Alan Freeman. On Sunday week he was playing hits from December 1971, and some of the songs suddenly made me think of where I was back then. I had gone to Yorkshire for a few days to attend the wedding of my sister Margaret, who was marrying Greg, a soldier from the Green Howards. His regiment had been stationed in Ardoyne during the summer and had had a reputation for being fairly brutal, though they got their come-uppance during internment week in August, when many of them were killed or seriously wounded. I hadn't intended going to the wedding, though I knew my future brother-in-law and did not dislike him. The family were already over there so on the spur of the moment I decided to join them. I arrived the day before the wedding and went out to help Greg wash his car. Of course, it wasn't too long before the conversation turned to politics and Ireland.

Greg was furious because about a week earlier Martin Meehan from Ardoyne had escaped from the Crum' only weeks after his capture by the Green Howards. Greg said: 'That bastard shot nine of my mates. It took ages to catch him and then they let him escape . . . '

Well, I waded in with 'You shouldn't be in my country!' etc. The atmosphere was very sour but we cooled down and made peace for the sake of the wedding. I was telling Martin Meehan about this a few weeks ago and we had a good laugh and he said – quite genuinely – 'Tell Greg to drop me a line. Sure, we should all be friends now.'

When Martin was arrested they cracked open his skull in two places with their rifle butts and his arrest was witnessed by his kids. One of those kids, Martin Junior, is now in here serving twelve years. So, when Alan Freeman played the charts from December 1971 I remembered that it was Margaret and Greg's wedding anniversary and that I had forgotten to send a card. I wrote them a wee letter wishing them well and told Greg that Martin Meehan said, 'We should all be friends now.' I can tell you an almost certain truth about here that you'll find in the pages of books like *Bury My Heart at Wounded Knee*: there is less bitterness amongst the oppressed. I hope I am wrong in that but I can imagine Greg reading those lines (that is, if my sister judges that he should see the letter!) and remaining bitter, whereas Meehan could justly lay more claim to being the injured party. Some of his comrades have been killed, he's been in and out of jail over the past twenty years and now his son is in jail with him.

1992

Thursday 2 January

Happy New Year my love. At present I am doubled up with Kevin McMahon. On our first night together we talked until about four in the morning. Our parolees all returned, some in several pieces, with their tales of days stretching to twenty-five hours without sleep and of friends and relatives thinking they owned them, much to the consternation of wives. One lifer got engaged and still doesn't know how it happened. Three or four came back with heavy colds. On New Year's Eve we had a party. It was officially over at half eight but mine continued into the early hours and at midnight I bellowed greetings out the door. One lad was telling me that he fell asleep at nine, woke up and switched on his radio, only to hear the presenter declare that in five minutes' time it would be the New Year. Oh God, he thought, it's still 1991! He put the pillow over his head and buried his face in his mattress.

Saturday 4 January

Hello honey! Got my first birthday card today – from you! I had Chrissie up seeing me yesterday. Richard couldn't make it. He was loaded with the flu. Chrissie had me laughing the whole time.

There was bad news last night. In Moy, UVF gunmen went into McKearney's butcher's shop and shot dead Kevin, critically wounded his uncle and grazed a young girl in a car parked outside. God help Mr and Mrs McKearny. That's three sons have been killed in the Troubles and Tommy is in Maghaberry serving life. How could you cope, face the future or even take a breath without your heart being crushed?

I have written to Theresa Burt, thanking her for looking after my parcels while you were away. I really missed you. I hope that your leaving your family wasn't as traumatic for you this time as it was in August. Looking forward to seeing you in a few days' time.

Tuesday 7 January
To David McKittrick
Firstly, belated Christmas and New Year greetings to you and your family. I received your letter of the twelfth of November, and my apologies for not replying sooner, though even this is not a reply as I am still mulling over your questions. The issues you raised (that the IRA campaign is futile and that that outweighs all other arguments) have actually helped me formulate my own ideas and I've tried to tackle some of these issues in the weekly column I write for *AP/RN*.

I have also thought a lot about the circumstances in which the IRA could call a ceasefire. I cannot see a weak IRA ever being able to halt the campaign, paradoxical though it sounds, and I can only see a strong IRA calling a halt provided what is on offer (and you can probably forget about a ceasefire unless *something* is on offer) appears capable of transforming the situation and creating real justice and a lasting peace.

If that appears to be the case or the republican leadership believes that such a settlement can be achieved by a change of strategy, then a republican consensus is likely to be established, and therein lies the key to flexibility and compromise.

However, at the moment (and for the foreseeable future I should think) the IRA presumably feels itself strong and believes that Britain is even more vulnerable than ever and that time is again on the IRA's side rather than counting against it (as in the 'war weariness' theories in the media in 1989).

The IRA keeps challenging the authorities (bombs in the city centre, for example) and the British government cannot stop it in Ireland or even in Britain. The British public has to come into play at some stage with the question: 'What the hell are we doing over there! You've had your chance: it's now time to get out.' The possible variable in the situation is a change in or a modification of the British government's attitude – and that has to be to the advantage of republicans.

Now, I acknowledge that that doesn't answer the question of the unionist people and their rights and fears, but the republican analysis is that unionist intransigence stems in part from the veto which Britain underwrites. If, as you say, there is a mellowing within a large swathe of unionist opinion on an issue such as fair employment (though it hasn't translated into support for power-sharing), then the people to whom you refer will also probably be inclined to accept a compromise settlement which takes into consideration our sensibilities.

You see, the settlement cannot be based on political superiority as a consequence of one's numbers (the majority/minority definition changes according to perspective) but on the basis of equality. A six-county British state will always make me feel like the vanquished party. Nor am I so stupid as to believe that republicans can win at the negotiating table what they haven't won on the battlefield. Nor am I so stupid – even if it were possible to achieve a triumphalist outcome – as to want an all-Ireland state from which a quarter of the population felt alienated. We have to find a settlement which takes into account all the contradictory objectives.

The revisionist movement in the Free State is continually berating us republicans about the unionist tradition. My God, there was even an editorial in the *Irish Times* last week sympathising with unionist difficulties in talking to Sinn Fein because of all the deaths, as if republicans felt no resentment or knew nothing about suffering. Few unionists attempt to empathise with the small-'r' republicans whose lives are filled with stories of discrimination and experiences of harassment and repression.

Nevertheless, regardless of our complaints I appreciate that we still have to try to understand the unionists and envisage settlements to this crisis which take them into full account, without of course doing injustice to our own sacrifices. I can assure you that when I'm lying in bed at night, staring at the ceiling, I think as constantly about this problem as I do about my love!

Saturday 11 January
At long last! The cell door has been shut and I can imagine that I am at home. It was great seeing you today – a feast for famished eyes. I feel quite elated. I was a little bit worried about you and whether it would be August all over again, though I didn't believe it could ever be as sharp as that again. I just want you to be happy. I got the parcel and the Brian Moore book, *Black Robe*, which I have actually read before.

Screwed into my wall is a small bookcase which holds about two dozen books but into which I have squeezed about forty. On top of my bookcase is my radio, which is tuned into a foreign station playing pop music. The signal fades in and out, eaten up somewhere in the stratosphere. Then another station comes in and the combined effect is quite hallucinogenic!

Sometimes at nights, before lock-up, Cleaky gives me soup, which he is on as part of his diet. But tonight I had no appetite so he offered it to another prisoner who has only recently come on the Block. The fella hesitated taking the soup bowl off Cleaky and quick as a shot Cleaky said, 'It's only cancer I have, not fuckin' leprosy!' The guy was skundered until Cleaky and I burst out laughing.

It is almost ten o'clock and somebody down the wing is

A Prison Journal

playing 'Fur Elise' on the mandolin! Several loud sneezes have also echoed down the landing so I suspect the flu is taking hold.

Saturday 18 January
My pen is almost done. They say that a Biro can write for several miles! Most of this distance has been travelled to you.

Eugene McKee came on the wing on Wednesday. He looks well and his spirits are high even though he got twenty years. Regina was shattered – she thought he was getting out. I got the parcel and the books. *Jiving at the Crossroads* got a good review in *AP/RN* and Eugene borrowed the book on the strength of it.

In an attempt to squeeze another hour out of the day I've decided to rise at seven. I arranged to have my light switched on at that time, and this morning by ten past seven I was at my table. It was so peaceful and quiet and the birds were chirping away in anticipation of dawn.

Tomorrow night I'll be taken to the boards and then to Belfast for my court case concerning the diaries the RUC stole from my da's. The ones they didn't return cover internment in 1971, all of 1972 and my prison diary from Long Kesh in 1973.

Monday 20 January
It was foggy and the window of the compartment in the 'horse-box' into which I was locked was covered over so much that my view of the outside was through a pinprick. Even so, I managed to see some of Belfast and the still waters of the Lagan as we crossed the Albert Bridge after having come down the Ravenhill Road 'for security reasons'. My cell in Townhall Street was absolutely freezing. The RUC didn't show up for the case. Neither did the Crown lawyer. My barrister, Kevin O'Hare, is the son of Pascal O'Hare, a former SDLP representative. He eventually tracked down the opposition, who claimed that the

recent IRA bomb in Victoria Street had blown papers and files everywhere and that they had lost their notification. However, a court clerk privately told him that they knew about the case last week. Anyway, it has been postponed for a month or two.

On my return journey I was in a different compartment; its window let in more light and I saw a great deal of the city centre from High Street, down Donegall Place, around the City Hall and down Bedford Street. I saw all the windows that had been boarded up because of the bombs and thousands of people going about their ordinary lives. The prison van hardly stopped at any traffic lights. The van had a big escort of RUC and British Army jeeps and occasionally the lead jeep used its siren to make way for us!

Tuesday 21 January
Would you stop thinking about your age! A quick reflection on your family suggests that there's a good fifty years of life in you, so shut your face, take up a hobby, go out more, shrug off the lassitude, take a good sup of wine more often and think of the future. And remember – you'd be thirty-six if you were in New York, New Mexico or the New Lodge! You'd be thirty-six no matter where – or with whom – you lived! Do you know that my mother used to fib about her age! Any time I asked her what year she was born she would say 1928. But one day while I was looking through old papers and documents I came across her birth certificate, which was for 1924. She was twenty-four when she married me da, who was twenty-two, and she was forty-four when she had Ciaran.

Wednesday 22 January
I've been reading an OU course book on mid-Victorian Britain over the past three dark dawns and I've only got as far as page 50! Our library here is full of great books which I haven't the

time to read – which annoys me. The American novelist John Updike wrote that 'most of writing is reading', and that is so true.

Cleaky got moved today to H-5. He was a good laugh and I'll miss him. Before he left, another prisoner came up to him and solemnly shook his hand in case he never saw him again. 'Fuck, thanks,' said Cleaky in that droll manner of his.

Thursday 23 January
I see yesterday's *Guardian* quoted from my *AP/RN* column of two weeks ago as an indication of Sinn Fein flexibility and preparedness to talk. Their feature article argued that there could be no peace until Sinn Fein and the IRA were also at the negotiating table.

There's a train just after blowing its horn and it's hurtling past the camp now. You can hear the rolling sound of the wheels on the tracks for about thirty seconds. It's just like being on a station platform.

I played tennis this afternoon, although it was cold and we had to scatter salt on the icy patches. I played Alex Murphy and we had a good game. Tonight I did some writing, then my washing, but rarely was I in jail when engaged in these acts. As I said to you recently I have a number of lives running simultaneously. I feel really blessed with my existence and I am sorry – for all sorts of reasons – that you get down so often. I turn clouds into dreams, gamble over water dripping off a shirt I've just hung, see stained glass in a bit of sunlight and hear the dead inside my head. It all feels so incredible – partly miraculous. How could you marry someone so insane!

Tuesday 28 January
Ned Flynn and I walked around an empty yard this morning. Many of the lads had gone to football in the big pitch and the

rest of the lads stayed inside, assuming that the cold spell was still with us, which it wasn't. Ned and I were talking about people's oddities. He says that when he first comes on a wing he eyes a sink (we have seven) and thereafter can only wash and shave out of that particular one. I said that I can only fall asleep on my right-hand side – which isn't completely true but is true enough for a conversation! He claimed he could fall asleep on his left or right after tossing and turning for about fifteen minutes. I said, surely it related to which side of the conjugal bed he slept in but he said he and his wife (ex-wife, now) had no preference. That I found hard to believe. I thought everyone had a preference.

Tuesday 4 February

I've been glued to the radio since hearing the newsflash about the shooting at the Sinn Fein offices on the Falls. I still don't know whether the gunmen opened fire on the advice centre, where a lot of fellas come in and eat their lunch, or whether the deaths occurred in the room where relatives wait for prison transport. People here who are expecting visits today are extremely anxious.

4.30 pm

There's something very bizarre about this shooting at the centre. The news is saying that a man believed to have carried out the attack drove to Ballinderry beside the shores of Lough Neagh and killed himself. I wonder was he related to someone whom the IRA killed and did this make him flip? Rab Kerr was supposed to be visited by Jennifer this afternoon but she didn't show up. One woman was shot at the centre but fortunately was not seriously injured.

9 pm

Well, the news is a bit more clear, though why the dead RUC man who carried out the killings was so close to his colleague, who was killed by the IRA last year, remains a mystery. Those returning from visits say that two of the dead are Paddy Loughran, who does the doorman in the centre, and Paddy McBride, who runs the advice centre.

Wednesday 5 February
We were out in the yard when the news came through about the gun attack on Sean Graham's bookies on the Ormeau Road. Kevin McMahon was agitated because his wife moved over there when she stopped visiting. A few months ago the taxi driver who takes their kids to school was shot and wounded by loyalist gunmen on a motorbike.

These loyalist shootings suit the RUC and the British Army, who have been arguing for some time that we are in the middle stages of a complete breakdown and that their powers are inadequate. They are hoping that nationalists, exasperated at their helplessness in the face of such attacks, would support internment. I'm sorry I am not at home to hug and comfort you at this grim time. You'd be as well getting out of here. Things can only get worse. The irony, of course, is that when there's the least respite this place is a great place to live.

Wednesday 12 February
It's a beautiful evening outside. There are a couple of wagtails chirping away on the wire fence which is about six feet away from my cell. I can hear distant traffic. It all creates a little ache – a longing to do something ordinary instead of at half five traipsing down to the sluice to empty the pisspot. It's so hard to know what life is all about. Do we just enjoy ourselves and ignore the state of the world or do we do our little share for humanity to square our conscience? I am always restless and at times I think I know absolutely nothing.

And now it's half five so I'll leave you and be back here in three hours' time – or three seconds, which is the time it takes you to turn over this page and read on.

9 pm

Although the skies were blue and the sun glazed everything this afternoon, this morning's weather was incredibly stormy. The rain poured down from every direction, criss-crossing and falling in tongues. I looked out my window and was haunted by all the rain I'd ever experienced. As a child, far away from my Corby Way home, caught in a downpour without a coat. The smell of rain in my hair. Steam rising from a tarmac footpath when the sun came out after a shower. Sheltering under a beech tree just outside Newcastle one summer and afraid that we'd be struck by lightning. Giving my jacket to a girl I once left home so that she could keep dry. Dancing with you up Cavendish Street at half one in the morning. Kissing you in the sea at Iniscrone. Walking around the yard on my own in H-7 last August when you returned from Toronto. Walking in the bleakest of moods. So much of one's life consists of turning over the past, the only part of our lives that is certain.

Eugene McKee came into the canteen and joined with everyone else laughing at the big – and I mean big! – Valentine card on display on top of the TV until he was told it was for him!

I shall be leaving out my excess mail for you to collect next Saturday. Reading through your letters again reminds me of how involved we are with each other and how steadfast you have been, writing almost every night. Oh, the rewards that are in store for you! You'll never again have to cook, wash a dish or light a fire!

Sunday 23 February

Inside Politics on Radio Ulster yesterday was about Sinn Fein, and Gerry was interviewed – an actor's voice substituting for his.

He denied that Sinn Fein had an armalite and ballot box strategy and then said, 'and Danny is a good friend of mine'! He explained my 1981 statement in terms of an appeal to republicans, for whom physical force was sacrosanct, to appreciate that we should be involved in electoral politics. I had given a similar explanation (which is actually the correct explanation) to the court during my trial. Of course, there was an element of me playing to the gallery in 1981: we needed to win that vote, for had we not we would never have become involved in politics proper.

I was slagged a lot after Gerry's interview: 'Fuck, did he drop you like a hot potato!'

Sunday 1 March
Father John Murphy said Mass this morning. He had been away from us since last September after suffering from a rupture. He thought he would only be away for six weeks. After the Gospel he delivers a sermon which can become a marathon unless he is stopped! I've seen men pointing to imaginary wristwatches to let him know that he is ripping the arse right out of it! But he's dead fly and won't look at the congregation but talks to the ceiling or the bit of sky visible through the window. Then you have to harrumph or shuffle in your seat and he stops, smiles beatifically yet impishly and says, 'Okay, okay, I'm going on too much.'

Late yesterday afternoon and last night I was racking my brains to think of a subject for this week's *AP/RN*. But when I got up early this morning and the light of dawn streamed into my cell I started to describe the scene. Then, thinking of what you had said, what had happened yesterday on the visits when another wife left her husband for good and what Mary Jane Rossa had written in her letters to her husband, I realised I had a theme about the difficulties of 'Love and Jail'. But relax. There is nothing autobiographical in it! Here it is:

LOVE AND JAIL

The first of March. The creamy light of dawn streams through the oblong spaces between the slatted concrete bars of my window, and the cawing of the restless crows trails off as they at last take to the sky. At night they rest in clusters of trees beyond the perimeter. But they dominate the landscape so much, wheeling through the heavens until they fall squabbling on carrion, that it comes as no surprise that they featured as recurrent dark symbols in Bobby Sands's writings.

Early morning builds up its own profile in noises, and the distant sound of traffic, faint but unmistakable, often breaks over the horizon. Some drivers won't even notice this jail, which for half a mile runs parallel with the M1. Others will feel that bit safer as they glance with satisfaction at the long wall, the observation posts and security lights. And those who know what jail means to the imprisoned and their families will sigh and feel sore. Twenty-one years ago this camp was opened as a temporary measure.

When I first came here last May my mate Brendy told me that his brother sounds the foghorn on his articulated lorry in solidarity each time he passes the jail. I still don't know whether he was pulling my leg but on one or two very quiet nights I counted four brothers for Brendy .

Outside the jail there are hundreds of wives, girlfriends, husbands and boyfriends doing time with the prisoners. And they don't all finish the sentence, nor are they necessarily set free when the ink in love letters runs dry or when they stop coming up on visits or if, as is often the case, they find someone else to take the edge off their loneliness. Yes, just to the side of the struggle, out of sight, lie the corpses of marriages and broken relationships shed by the despairing, who simply couldn't take any more.

It is a very delicate subject.

There are no guidelines for coping. Each situation has its own set of unique circumstances. No help is available and advice is less than useless. For someone struggling desperately to hold on to love, no appeal to the happiness of the past or to the promised rosiness of the future can allay for the other person the pain and desolation of the present.

I was reminded of such predicaments whilst reviewing for the *Andersonstown News* O'Donovan Rossa's account of his time in English jails, *Irish Rebels in English Prisons*.

Married with five sons, his wife pregnant with their sixth child, Rossa was running up and down the country from the day after his wedding organising the Fenian Brotherhood and visiting America, Scotland and England on republican business in between managing the *Irish People*.

Mary Jane was not amused.

Then, in September 1865, her husband was arrested for high treason and was sentenced to penal servitude for the term of his natural life. He was sent to jail in England, where visits were a rarity. However, he was legally entitled to one letter every six months, but for over three years these were suppressed because he insisted on including details about his maltreatment. Rossa, to his credit, later published this correspondence between his wife and himself, allowing us an insight into the tension in their relationship.

He scolded her for writing short letters and not giving him enough news from home. In her letters she expressed anger at his jail protests (he was fighting for political recognition), which only added to the difficulty of their trying to maintain a marriage: 'What is the use of bringing so many successive punishments on yourself, by defiance of a rule that holds you in its grasp?' she wrote. 'You make no effort to win the goodwill of your jailers.'

She accused him of selfishness for considering his 'Fenian business' and his talk of 'prisoners and battlefields' more important than her and the children. (Though she didn't know it, Rossa at this time had sent out word to the leadership not to be deterred in its actions by any considerations for the prisoners!)

Poverty eventually forced Mary Jane to leave her children in Ireland – a decision which made her bitter as well as broken-hearted – and emigrate to the USA for work. From there she wrote: 'Need I remind you that you have a wife whom you took, in her ignorance and inexperience, whom you afterwards left unprovided for . . . Ah, Rossa, Rossa – think of these things, think which has most trouble: you who took it on yourself and drew it on me, or I, who depending on your love to do that which was just to me, find myself a married woman without a husband . . .

'I solemnly tell you that if you escaped tomorrow, I would not live with you unless you atoned to me for the past by minding your family and your own affairs in the future.'

She sent no letters for eighteen months, and then she suddenly wrote, telling him, 'There's no man living, if I were free to choose, I could love better.'

And so it went. Ups and downs, even as his release approached. Letters of hope, followed by words of despair: enough to test anyone's sanity. She returned from America and visited him, and he was troubled that she was going to put him under pressure to compromise his principles because at this time the government was making overtures about a conditional amnesty. Eventually a deal was struck and the Fenian prisoners were released on condition that they leave Ireland for twenty years and would forfeit the pardon if they should return without permission. Rossa agreed to the pardon on the basis that he was not promising not to return.

In January 1871 Rossa was released and he and his family settled in the United States. Mary Jane was still with him, but so was the Fenian Brotherhood. Rossa was now its secretary!

Certainly a happy ending and a true one: the sort of story it is in the best interests of a liberation movement to promulgate, but not the full story. Perhaps not even half or three-quarters of the story. I would be afraid to count.

So, with this in mind, solidarity goes to those whose love lives became a casualty of their republicanism and selflessness and whose imprisonment (let's not forget the Brits) has changed their lives forever. With this in mind, acknowledgement also of what they have given – and what they have lost . . .

Monday 2 March
Did you read the statement made in Leinster House by David Andrews? (I almost wrote Eamonn Andrews!) Prompted by another deputy he urged people in west Belfast to vote for Joe Hendron and against Gerry Adams! What a gobshite. During Bobby Sands's election campaign Don Concannon issued a statement on polling day urging people not to vote for Sands. I think he made the statement from the House of Commons. But on polling day it is an offence under the Representation of the People Act for the media to carry statements favouring one candidate over another. However, that didn't matter and Concannon got widespread coverage.

Thursday 5 March
Got your 'perky' letter just now. Um, we do seem a bit bristly! Yes, I do try to be tactful because what is the point of telling you how

exasperating you can sometimes be when in the next hour or next visit you'll softly punch me on the shoulder and tell me I should know not to listen to you or take you seriously! At which stage my heart glows and happiness turns my legs to jelly!

Saturday 7 March

That was a wonderful visit today. Put me in really good form and I sort of danced my way through this week's article for *AP/ RN*. I got a short letter from Pam Brighton at the BBC. Surprise, surprise – the broadcasting of my short story has been 'postponed'. Joe McCarthy lives on. That's the only explanation I can come up with, for she writes: 'I talked to Barra about it this week and explained everything so the next time he comes in to see you he'll pass on the facts of the situation.' If she can't give me the explanation in a letter it must be because there is skulduggery afoot. Perhaps you can find out from Barra and let me know on Saturday. I just hope she hasn't stuck her neck out for me. But I signed a contract and I hope I get the fee!

I've been listening to Albert Reynolds's address to the Fianna Fail *ard fheis*. He says that everything should be up for discussion and has linked Articles 2 and 3 with Section 75 of the Government of Ireland Act, which is a very interesting move. I wasn't too impressed when I saw him on TV during a live debate from Leinster House. Perhaps he'll surprise us.

Sunday 8 March

What a beautiful afternoon. The sun is filling my cell and laving my face with little bubbles of warmth. I've had two showers already today! One, at half nine, before Mass; then, after I finished a game of tennis, at five to twelve. I love the glow of cleanliness it leaves in you – that mellow, languorous feeling.

Happy International Women's Day, sister! There's a programme on Radio 1 tonight which examines how women view themselves and their bodies. I read also that in the Pacific island of Tonga 'male loins don't stir for any woman under sixteen stone'! Beauty is in the eye of the beholder. Or, as W. B. Yeats said, 'Beauty is an accusation'!

Could you do me a favour? I was thinking of writing an article about an orderly in the Crum' called Shorty who used to sing Sinead O'Connor to us and who after his release was beaten to death. Could you put your hand on a letter I wrote to you around November and tell me what I said about him and his sentence. I think I said he was given nine months for stealing six pairs of Wrangler jeans and I compared it with a sentence which a loyalist or a soldier received around the same time.

Thursday 12 March

I didn't see that programme on Nicaragua you referred to but I appreciate the tragedy for those who struggled, suffered, saw a lot of death and have little to show for their revolution. In our case, because we have a considerable amount of negotiating power (but which falls short of tipping the balance) I think we will have the ability – should we so wish – to cash in the chips in return for substantial changes. That's why I remain optimistic.

There is a big lad called Conor Gilmore who sits at our table. He's very young (about twenty-two) and was sentenced to fifteen years just before Christmas. He's keen on politics and also attends a feminist class. Well, didn't he make the mistake of his life at dinner today! Most of us talk rubbish and use as much hyperbole and ultra-leftist language as possible to satirise those whom we consider much too serious. Conor, very genuinely, remarked that he always had a healthy attitude to women and, in fact, girls, and reckoned that he was a feminist since about the age of five! Well, fuck, did he get slagged over that! 'Ask Ms Gilmore to pass the salt, comrade, please.' He was sorry he spoke.

An English fella, Steve Burn, who is a republican supporter, writes to me about once a fortnight, though I don't write back often. He has just started work again, tarring roads after months of unemployment. The foreman who got him the start agreed to meet him for a pint but insisted they meet in the local Conservative club! He said he stood across the street from the club in pouring rain for twenty-five minutes trying to catch the foreman going in. Eventually, he went in and discovered that the foreman and several committee members, who knew he was a republican supporter, had been watching him through the curtains wrestling with his conscience! He was having a drink when a member of the club said to him on the side, 'Don't feel so bad with yourself, Steve. I've been coming here for all of ten years and never voted for the bastards once!'

Sunday 22 March

I see that the counts for the Belfast constituencies in the general election are scheduled to begin a few hours after the polling stations close. The judgement in our appeal will also have been delivered that day, so by the eleventh of April I'll be into the second day of either a severe depression or sheer elation. In either case I'll be badly needing to hold your hand! I remember how I felt after the Sandinistas lost the election in Nicaragua two years ago. I remember how you felt! I think you mentioned it in a letter and then went on to 'put it into context' (those famous words)!

Wednesday 25 March

You'll never guess what I did this morning. I got up at seven and rewrote my bloody essay on Dickens's *Hard Times*. Having slept on it – as the expression goes – I was dissatisfied, but I am now fairly pleased with it. Writing conditions here are not the best! From one cell comes the sound of someone learning the *bodhrán*; from another the tin whistle; from yet another the radio commentary of the England v. Pakistan cricket final of the fifth World Cup; from the landing, Geordie Hagans, Ballymurphy, trying to lose his belly so that his kids will recognise him upon release; and from the yard, the sound of timbers between our yard and the yard of A-Wing being taken down by tradesmen.

Ned Flynn actually got the night guard to wake him at 4 am for the start of that cricket match!

Another noise is made by a couple of prisoners who sit in the yard breaking up tiny stones which they then wash and clean (by steeping in Steradent tablets) before sticking the pebbles on a cardboard-shaped, three-dimensional Celtic cross. They turn out to be brilliant handicrafts! One of the warders here, Stan, said, 'Youse are fly bastards. Youse are digging tunnels and then making crosses with the waste!'

Then there is Brendy McIlkenny, from the Falls, who is due for release next Tuesday. He is up to a million and is like a cat on a hot tin roof and is in such a good mood that he is beginning to get on everybody's nerves! He brought me into his cell to show me a jewellery box he has made for his girlfriend. I lifted the lid and then said, 'Why doesn't it play music?'

'Don't be stupid,' he said 'Open the drawer.'

So I opened the drawer and the chime proceeds to play the theme tune from *The Sting*, Scott Joplin's 'The Entertainer', 'Deededeededeede . . . *dee!*'

'That's brilliant,' I said. 'But shouldn't it be something romantic, like from *Doctor Zhivago*? You know, "Somewhere my love, we'll meet again somehow . . . "'

'Why, is that not it?' he asked, as I placed my fatherly hand on his shoulder and wondered could I wangle the jewellery box off him!

Your letter arrived at half four but I couldn't get reading it because a friend approached me and asked could we lock up together. So I went into his cell and he showed me a solicitor's letter which arrived out of the blue stating that his wife is seeking a divorce. She stopped coming up to see him about fourteen months ago and is living with someone else but wants him to sign a form agreeing that they have been separated for two years. Up until now he was, I think, always hoping for a reconciliation but is now very, very angry. We had a good long talk. The world continues to fall apart. Or, as Yeats put it, 'The centre cannot hold.' (Not a bad line for a French refuse-collector snuggling beneath Ben Bulben.)

Sunday 29 March
I am writing from H-Block 7 and we have just been locked up. I am fucked. I spent last night and most of today yarning with Bik, who is an inveterate conversationalist. Then, tonight, both wings gathered in our canteen while I made a speech and presentation to Brendy Mac, who gets out on Tuesday and who says he'll be down in the High Court to see me on Wednesday. After that, Bik and I went into the cell of Geordie Hagans, where we had a sing-song, with me doing most of the singing! I've discovered that I like singing! What a strange discovery after so many years!

Bik is brilliant on guitar. We did numbers by the Eagles, Bread, Simon and Garfunkel, the Beatles, Gordon Lightfoot, Labi Siffre, Fleetwood Mac and the Everly Brothers! By eight o'clock – I had packed my belongings for the Crum' earlier – Geordie Hagans's cell was full and I was being called out to leave the wing – prison transport was waiting. That bastard Bik then began to sing 'Homeward Bound' and I was embarrassed! Then I was put on a hospital trolley with my brown bag, I shook hands with everyone and I was pushed at high speed down the landing!

Everybody was cheering and clapping and I kept trying to tell them that I would be back!

My minibus stopped at H-Block 5 to pick up Gerard Hodgins, and when we got here, H-7, he told me that he feels worse than he did before his trial. Anto then arrived, carrying a big bag, and said that he had been told we could be down in the Crum' for a week!

Monday 30 March
Hello love

Talk about one disappointment after another. Firstly, we lost the right to a separate trial. Then Sandy Lynch shows up at our preliminary enquiry. Then we get Hutton as the trial judge. And now, as a result of political manoeuvrings, Judge Higgins is removed from our trial panel and we have Judge McCollum. My barrister, Desmond Boal, was happy with the original appeal panel. It was believed that Higgins, because of some knowledge of the nationalist community, could understand why someone like myself would run off when he saw a raiding party. Higgins is also a keen lawyer and would judge the points of law without political prejudice.

Last Friday Boal met Judge Murray in court and Murray said, 'I believe you and I might be involved in an appeal.' Boal asked him what he meant and he said that he had been given our trial papers to read and that he was being asked to postpone a loyalist murder trial on which he was presently sitting and replace Higgins on our panel today. Then, late on Friday afternoon, Murray told Boal that he wouldn't be adjourning his trial after all and that our original panel would be hearing the appeal.

Then, over the weekend, Creaney phoned Boal but Boal was not at home. It was not until Sunday that it emerged that this morning the appeal would not be going ahead and that the court was going to reconstitute itself. We weren't even in court for the announcement. So our appeal judges are Kelly, McDermott and McCollum.

The appeal is being heard in Chichester Street, Belfast. We'll be there on Wednesday and Thursday. McCollum says that he is busy on Friday (probably has a golf appointment) so we will not be back down again until Monday. Boal is great the way he can put you in fighting form! He says that he will be taking the floor on Thursday afternoon, all day Monday and Tuesday. Creaney sums up on Wednesday morning. Both Boal and Creaney have appointments outside the country next week but it will probably be over by then.

Wednesday 1 April

It's not quite nine but both Anto and Hodgies are in bed already. We are all totally exhausted between the disruption, the discomfiture, the mode of travel and the tension.

Kelly, one of the judges, said that he wanted to begin at half nine this morning, so we were up at the crack of dawn, sped into Belfast with sirens wailing, and yet the hearing didn't start until eleven. Weir, the barrister, put forward a very strong case for Hodgies which actually revealed lots of weaknesses in the quality of the prosecution case. On Anto he was very, very good. Kelly's interruptions haven't been too bad and McDermott's have all been on points of law and have been pretty justified. But McCollum is pig-headed and constantly interrupts to make frivolous objections and posit alternative, sinister scenarios, which even Hutton, in the original trial, rejected. He has let slip a few comments which reveal or seem to reveal that in my case (though I should say that my case hasn't been put yet) he accepts that there was going to be a press conference. (Hutton had said we 'may' have been there to kill Lynch but that the proof wasn't strong enough to prove conspiracy to murder.)

I spoke to my lawyer and he said that you can see how hostile they are. He was scathing of McCollum's legal brain and said that he was going to hit them solidly with the law, and then he smiled at me reassuringly. I am not optimistic but how are you supposed to feel when your lawyer is so full of pluck! I am really looking forward to his submissions. Tomorrow morning Seamus Tracey finishes his submissions on the right to silence as it applied to Anto and Hodgies upon arrest. Then Dessie Boal takes the floor. Mrs Hodgins and Lucy Murray have been here throughout.

My other barrister, Kevin O'Hare, called in to see me. The RUC phoned him. My two diaries have 'miraculously' turned up! They had been 'mislaid' in some barracks! I've told Barra to get them and put them in his safe. We drove past your workplace at a quarter to five, sirens wailing!

Thursday 2 April
What a strange day it was. Poor Seamus Tracy, the barrister, was given a very rough time by McCollum and Kelly. I thought Tracy did well but he looked angry, if not demoralised, and subsequently said to Lucy that he didn't think it was even worthwhile asking for a reduction in sentence for Anto and Gerard.

Boal took to his feet at about ten past eleven and spent an hour outlining the bones of the legal arguments he would be submitting. His delivery and his grasp of the law was breathtaking – and clearly far superior to that of the judges. He is quoting from fifteen separate law books and has got through about six examples so far in great detail. He has quoted numerous other cases just to demonstrate a point here or there. McCollum was the most quarrelsome, initially. Amazingly – and ironically – McCollum by late afternoon had moved towards substantially

agreeing with Boal! It was simply incredible seeing the transformation. At ten past four Boal said to me, 'Right, they've got three
days to look up all the law books in Britain but they'll not come
up with one example – not one! – to contradict me. Let's see
if they have the balls to admit that the Chief Justice made a
haimes of it.'

Anyway, we are points in front but you and I know that that
is not the decisive factor. This morning when Boal was explaining
the difference between the states of mind of various accused
people I was on the edge of my seat. For the purpose of argument
he made the point that I couldn't be held responsible for anyone
else's actions – this was a direct reference to Anto, whom he then
named, but he made it clear it was a theoretical supposition.
Both Anto and I were anxious and I spoke to the junior barrister,
Charlie Adair, who saw Boal, and Anto spoke to his solicitor.
But it was cleared up. Although it's a perfectly legitimate device,
it's a form of argument that a layperson can easily misinterpret.

Lucy, Anto Junior, Mrs Hodgins and Paddy McManus from
Sinn Fein were in court all day. Sandra and Liam were in all
afternoon. I am sure Liam was bored to tears and hadn't got a
clue what was happening. Thank God we have a break until
Monday: I need the rest.

I got a nice letter from Tim O'Grady. He has been awarded
a fellowship by the American equivalent of the Arts Council.
He's working on a project about Yeats, is researching a book on
the theme of 'memory and Ireland' and is going to six states in
the USA in May to do a project for BBC radio on young
American fiction writers. So things are looking up for him.

Saturday 4 April
What about Cardinal Daly! He was attending a Confirmation
service in Beragh, Tyrone, and gave a homily – to ten-year-olds,

or, rather, their parents! – on the election. He urged 'Northern Ireland voters to quiz candidates about their attitudes to paramilitary violence. People should use this election to demonstrate their will for peace,' he said. Last week, when pressed by journalists on whether he was encouraging people to vote for the SDLP he said that the Church couldn't take sides but that people should vote for constitutional parties! But in an interview on Radio 4 on Wednesday night I heard him call upon people not to vote for Sinn Fein because before an election Sinn Fein claims a vote for it is not a vote for the IRA, but then after the election it claims its vote *is* one for the IRA. What a fucking barefaced lie! The only people who claim that a vote for Sinn Fein is a vote for the IRA are Daly and the unionists. Even the Brits don't make that stupid claim.

There's a lad here from Portglenone – or 'Port Glen One', as the English pronounce it. I was singing as I was going up the landing and he said to me, "The lands still in bread.' I stopped and asked him what was he saying and could he repeat it. 'The lands still in bread.' Bingo! I knew what he was saying. He was indicating that I should keep the singing down because the lads are still in bed.

Monday 6 April

Well, I could scream at today's shenanigans. Boal is about a thousand miles in front but they refuse to accept the legalities. The morning started out with the three judges attacking him – obviously the strategy that they had decided upon over the weekend. But he laid to rest every petty point. By the afternoon the atmosphere was electric. Boal won hands down but I felt pessimistic. This is more or less what they were saying: 'Morrison is a republican and supports the IRA, so he must be guilty.' And that amounts to their case.

Boal quoted Lord Diplock, who said that a trial judge in a non-jury court had to give the reasons why he reached a certain verdict. They squirmed at that. The prejudice is incredible. Boal continues tomorrow. I am unstinting in my praise of him. His eloquence is stunning and he takes no nonsense from the panel.

Tuesday 7 April

I felt that we did very well today, especially this morning. Boal was supposed to begin arguing 'the facts' of the case but the judges returned to the issues of the law on aiding and abetting. They must have been up all night because they introduced a decision of Lord Lowry in a non-jury case in Mauritius, Africa, where he stated that a trial judge didn't have to cross every 't' and dot every 'i' when addressing the issue of defence submissions. Boal drove through it in about five minutes and again quoted from Diplock, who said that the judge had got to give his reasons for reaching a verdict. So they withdrew that example. Boal finished at three and Creaney the prosecutor was on his feet until after four, when we broke up for the day. God, is he getting a sympathetic hearing! It's all 'yes, yes', jokes and smiles and no interjections. So it can easily go either way. My da was in court for the morning, God bless him.

Wednesday 8 April

Creaney's submissions have been sprawling and all over the place but have mostly concentrated on my witness-box testimony, from which he is extracting bits and pieces to try and give substance to Hutton's findings. At one stage something that Kelly said made me sit up and take note. He seemed to be suggesting that in dropping the charge of unlawful imprisonment and finding us guilty of aiding and abetting the judge had created problems for himself (because he couldn't find all the ingredients necessary to support the lesser charge). Those problems, Kelly intimated, wouldn't have arisen had he found us guilty of the original charge! I couldn't believe it! For what it's worth, Charlie Adair said such a move would be too blatant.

You may prepare yourself. Our appeal is going to be thrown out. There is no such thing as law.

Thursday 9 April

I got your letter when I returned from court and was glad to read that you had abandoned hope even before they gave the verdict this afternoon. Thank God it's over and we can get on with our lives knowing something of the map ahead. The judges made not even the slightest pretence at going into a grand session to consider matters. I suppose they couldn't resist the opportunity to announce a 'Sinn Fein defeat' a few hours into polling!

Saturday 11 April

That was a great visit this afternoon. You are a wonderful person and I love you so much.

It's late, almost half eleven, and I've been trying to write that article I mentioned to you about the Movement and where it's at after Gerry Adams's defeat in West Belfast. Maybe I'll have another stab at it now before finally hitting the sack.

Sunday 12 April

I have finished my article and it is a bit depressing. I've tried to squeeze the real meaning between the lines but it keeps spilling out. David McKittrick's piece in yesterday's *Independent* was short but accurate. He wrote: 'While the party has never wavered in its support for the IRA campaign of violence, some observers have believed that its foothold in politics was useful because it tended to inhibit the IRA. One theory now is that the arguments of the pure militarists will be strengthened, leading to more emphasis on violence with less reference to politics.'

That's the sort of thing I am arguing against, though I go even further and state that some day we will be faced with different choices and hint that the correct one won't be so hard to swallow! Now, if I was the editor of *An Phoblacht* I'd probably not print such an article and would be justified in one respect – that the thinking of a prisoner is usually warped.

10.15 pm

I've just finished rewriting and retyping my article. I'll be surprised if it is published even though this version is much milder than the first draft!

I love you dearly. Go through this week knowing that there is not a minute passing when I am not thinking of you.

I've enclosed a carbon copy of my article for *An Phoblacht*.

A Bitter Pill

In the canteen, as the last of the results bore heavily down on us, we sang 'Always Look on the Bright Side of Life' and resumed our patient wait for an 800-year break in misfortune. In the wing across the yard a loyalist prisoner with a sense of humour had hung a poster from his window which read, 'Adams Out! Danny In!'

In an article such as the one I am writing what do I do? Point out how relatively 'well' Sinn Fein did across the North despite all that was stacked against it? Which is true. Emphasise the fact that the nationalist people of West Belfast are quite justified in being angry at losing the seat to Hendron and the UFF? Which is very true. I should also repeat that there are lessons to be drawn from these defeats. However, I wouldn't be that confident that the lessons, if grasped, will be acted upon. The thrust of this article is that if the IRA does not raise the quality of its campaign the struggle could go on forever, and if it cannot raise the quality of its campaign it should consider the alternative.

I am not one for doom and gloom, for defeatism or surrender, but the election results were very bad for Sinn Fein, for the IRA and for the struggle, in whatever order you prefer. The trend is going in the direction of our vote in the twenty-six-counties – downwards – and I hope that no one will have the temerity to claim the opposite or accuse me of overreacting. Some good can come out of this defeat if it causes us to take stock and analyse what the decline in the Sinn Fein vote should tell the Republican Movement about either the perceived quality of the armed struggle or the popularity of constitutional nationalism.

The armed struggle in the North is fairly unique in that it doesn't fall into any classical category (though later I shall be using an analogy with the Sandinistas). The liberated territory is in the hearts and minds of a section of the nationalist people. The IRA will never overthrow the government or drive out Crown Forces. The landscape of the struggle is a West European consumer society with sectarian divisions and vestiges of social democracy. And our starting position was the demand for civil rights and reform.

Where did the 'armalite/ballot box' strategy come from?

Well, the whole purpose of opening up a political front in the first place was because of the acknowledgement that the purely military struggle was being isolated and marginalised and could not on its own win. We needed to muster the full potential of the community and bring everyone into the struggle. We had to join other struggles.

I hope republicans can remember realising this.

It came in several stages: Jimmy Drumm's speech at

Bodenstown in 1977, the declaration of the long war (and what it meant) in 1978 and the H-Block/Armagh political-status campaign in support of the prisoners, 1979–81. Later, there came the ending of abstentionism in the Free State.

Bobby Sands's election campaign was principally about resolving the hunger strike but provided a massive, collateral boost to the case for electoral intervention, otherwise electoralism would have met with considerable resistance and scepticism from a movement historically suspicious of politics. Politics usually equals compromise. The in-built weakness of the electoral strategy was that activists were vulnerable to disenchantment when it didn't keep producing successes.

Perhaps some of the 43 per cent of the nationalists who voted for Sinn Fein in 1983 when our vote was still rising had different expectations and felt that Sinn Fein would get the IRA to introduce a ceasefire.

Perhaps the fact that the IRA never really refined its activities was the biggest factor in the slow decline of the vote. Whatever the case, disenchantment amongst republicans cuts both ways – either a reaction against politics or dismay at the failures of armed struggle.

There may now be a big temptation, because of frustration and alienation, for many republicans to abandon even their limited faith in politics and place all their trust in armed struggle. That emotional reaction should be resisted. It is no guarantee of success. It is to go in the wrong direction.

The IRA has to resist the temptation to allow military considerations to predominate even if that is the direction in which it is being pushed. It would be a gross mistake. If such circumstances were to come to pass what is Sinn Fein to do? Further distance itself from IRA actions and leave itself with no republican credibility – and indeed no public credibility (because

Sinn Fein's recently adopted stance of having nothing to say about IRA actions is, in my opinion, proving an untenable one)? Or is Sinn Fein to ally itself with the IRA out of a sense of loyalty, whatever the outcome or cost? The fortunes of Sinn Fein and the IRA are inextricably linked: they have the same cause and ultimate objectives and their memberships are drawn from the same pool of support.

The decrease in the Sinn Fein vote has to be a cause of serious concern to the IRA. It is a situation out of which it cannot simply bomb its way.

I am being necessarily alarmist because 'indifference to setbacks' seems to be our middle name.

A republican consensus on which of our objectives and demands are realisable is difficult to arrive at because such discussion by its very nature tends to undermine morale and resolve. Yet silence can create group deception.

When the Sandinistas lost the election in Nicaragua two years ago they were under big pressure to go back into the mountains and melt back into the barrios and resume armed struggle. But they stood their ground, swallowed the bitter pill and went into opposition because they realised that with their still considerable support they could fight a popular rearguard action. They realised that people, their lives and their livelihoods were the things that really mattered. Indeed, in the future they will probably retrieve the support of many of those who, because of war-weariness and the fact that they were impoverished by the USA's embargo, voted for the UNO coalition, clearly signalling that they wanted compromise. The Sandinistas had to come to terms with reality. The pragmatism of the head had to take precedence over the principle of the heart.

Some day we shall be faced with the same choice.

We should never allow the situation to decline to the

extent that we face such a decision from the depths of an unpopular, unseemly, impossible-to-end armed struggle or from the point of brave exhaustion – another one of the 'glorious defeats' with which our past is littered.

We should only face such a choice from a position of relative strength, when we still abound in energy, taking stock like the Sandinistas, finding other vulnerabilities in the armour of our enemies, seizing the moral high ground and using the ingenuity for which we are renowned – the ingenuity which has ensured our survival.

Sunday 19 April

Well, I see *An Phoblacht* banged my piece! Not surprising – but I was still annoyed. I told Micheal, the editor, when I began writing the column late last year that it was only for six months because I had to concentrate on my OU course. Now is as good a time as any to stop. I am supposed to have my third essay in on Friday and there is no chance I'll have it done in time. I have to write 1,000 words analysing the minuet of Mozart's Symphony No. 39.

Thursday 23 April

All afternoon lads were washing and ironing their best clothes, putting on clean socks and underwear. Everyone was fighting for a place in the wash-house. Some men showered and shaved twice! Yes, the photographer was on his way in!

Both wings posed together for a group shot, then into separate wings: lifers; the over-thirties; the under-thirties; Belfast; north, south and west Belfast; Derry; Tyrone without Strabane; Strabane; musicians; and then special requests. Bik and Pat Sheehan insisted on choosing my clothes so as not to clash with Bik's top and Pat's silk shirt!

Tuesday 28 April
Got a letter from Micheal MacD., editor of *An Phoblacht*. He
apologised about the article not being published. He said he
agreed with 99 per cent of it but that it would have been seized
upon by our opponents. He said he would be very disappointed
if I stopped writing. Well, I'm very sorry about people's
expectations but I haven't got time because of my OU course.
Also, I'm not in the mood to write and if a second article was
spiked I'd be angry and frustrated. I used to write a satirical
column for *AP/RN* called the 'Liam Óg' column. I began it after
Mick Timothy, the paper's former editor, died in February 1985.
He had written a column called 'Burke at the Back' so I picked
up his mantle. But I stopped writing it after about eighteen months
and then began *West Belfast*. After I finish the OU course in October
I'm going to begin that book I mentioned to you before, about a
young man who slowly realises he is gay and is then persecuted by
society. I've already written the part where he goes to jail!

Thursday 30 April
Bik and I walked around the yard and continued our conversation
from the night before about the sixties and schooling. We were
reminiscing about where we were when Peter Green of Fleetwood
Mac sang 'Man of the World' on *Top of the Pops* in June 1969.
Bik was in a seminary and dinner had just finished. He and
others begged the superior to let them watch *TOTP* and he
relented. At the time, I was revising English Literature because
I had a GCE examination to sit the next day but I still took time
out to watch my favourite programme.

I was talking about my old music teacher Tommy Cooney,
who died last year I think. As it turned out he was a friend of
Bik's family and also taught his nephew or niece the piano – and
only charged about fifty pence a lesson because he was just so

glad to promote music. Tommy had played in the Northern Ireland Symphony Orchestra from the age of sixteen and had met Elgar, Hamilton Harty and Henry Wood. He knew my mother's brother, my uncle Jack, who played the saxophone in one of the big bands, and he took a shine to me. Tommy had no authority in class so everybody took advantage of him. When I moved from Glen Road CBS to St Mary's Grammar School to do my A-Levels Tommy Cooney had also moved to there as the new music teacher. Very few of the pupils were interested in the classical music he used to play us and analyse.

Then, one day in late November 1969, whilst everyone was misbehaving, smoking dope or flying paper aeroplanes (and piloting them!), Tommy said, 'I want you to listen to a piece of music . . . '

'Ach, fuck off Chanter and give our heads peace,' was the type of comment you would hear from the back.

He put on an LP. Crisp sunshine. Blue skies. 'Dee, de, dee, deee, I feel that ice is slowly melting.' It was 'Here Comes the Sun' from the Beatles' *Abbey Road*, which had just been released. Everyone went quiet. Tommy lifted the stylus and played it again, analysing the melody and harmony, praising the way it had been composed. He then went on to compare 'Because' with, I think, the second movement of Vivaldi's 'Autumn'. We were all spellbound. We all thought he was great! He was an innocent man and at the end of the class he had the biggest smile on his face that I had ever seen in the five years he had been teaching us.

Sunday 3 May
Have just finished a great biography of Gustav Mahler. It's called *Mahler – His Life, Work and World* and is by Blau Kopf and Herta Blaukopf.

His fiancée, Alma, was eighteen years his junior and a

composer in her own right. But when they got engaged he forbade her to compose any more! He wrote: 'But from now on you have just one profession: to make me happy! Do you understand, Alma? Of course I know you have to be happy yourself (through me) if you are to be able to make me happy . . . the role of the 'composer', of 'working', falls to me – and to you the role of loving companion, the understanding comrade!'

Anyway, in later years he became so obsessed with composing that he neglected his wife's needs and discovered that she had taken a lover! He confronted them both and called upon her to choose which one she would stay with. They got back together.

Jealousy is probably the worst emotion of the lot! That claw in your gut which rises in waves to choke your heart and make you want to die – or, in some cases, kill. It makes me shudder just to think of it. Mahler died at the age of fifty of heart disease. Earlier, he had set a poem 'Ich atmet' einen linden duft' ('I breathed a soft fragrance') to music. I loved his description of it: 'It contains something of a contented, happy feeling such as one feels in the company of a dear person of whom one is completely sure without a single word needing to pass.'

I put into my notebook all the quotes I had marked with a pencil whilst reading the Mahler book. I cannot read a book innocently, and I always take notes. Sometimes they take hours to copy but they will come in handy in the years ahead, especially for reference purposes when reviewing books.

Thursday 7 May
I have been given permission to receive a new hardback dictionary. Great! My old Chambers dates from 1973 and was bought by our Geraldine and sent into Cage 2. It is of some sentimental value but Roy really liked it and often used to thumb his way through its pages. I am going to send it to him because he'll

appreciate it – and he will be here for quite a few years yet.

Bik's six weeks are up tomorrow and he will be moved to another block. I hope the rain stays off tonight because we'll be walking for a few hours. He told me that occasionally – perhaps every three weeks or so – you just feel completely pissed off with jail and all the restrictions. Maybe that's what I sometimes go through, though I am usually perky.

Thursday 14 May

So, you've had your first real prospective buyers around. I was surprised at how composed I was as I read that in your letter. 'Home' will always be a house with you in it, not the house itself. I saw our house in the property section of the *Andersonstown News* and it was strange looking at it. It made me think of all the great times we had. From your letter it seems that I didn't make my meaning clear a few days ago. I meant that I had been thinking too much about myself. I've been selfish in resisting your plans. Your plans are what you need to do to survive this so they are for the best. I am now used to the idea and accept the fact of you going away for two, perhaps even three years. And I deserve a good kick up the behind for not having faith.

That's a good idea, you getting birthday cards for Kevin and Liam. I can't believe Liam will be thirteen next month! My mammy forgot my birthday once, when I was a child (or maybe just turning twelve or thirteen) and she almost died with shame when she remembered, very late that day. Of course, I had died much earlier. Several times, in fact. At breakfast, lunch, and after school when no cards materialised! Toughens you up!

Wednesday 20 May

You said that you gave the estate agents a key. I presume someone from that office accompanies potential buyers? What a strange woman you are! You are more indecisive than Geraldine – and that's saying something! You now say you are on the lookout for a new house. Well, I'll not be building up any hopes.

Wasn't that some news about your sister Wendy and Terry getting married unannounced. I don't think it was 'crazy': I find it really romantic.

I haven't heard from Barra McGrory about what action he is taking with the BBC over the fee they refused to pay me. Hint: my money is running low. I am thirty-nine years of age and I've only seven pounds to my name! Could you leave me in some money next week and I promise to make you a millionaire by the time you're forty-nine!

By the way, I got eighty-eight in my music essay, which was okay given how distracted I was over it. I wonder how many marks I'll get for the art essay. Because of my colour-blindness I didn't go into great detail about the use of colour but instead concentrated on the 'meaning' of the paintings! The OU course certainly helps you discipline yourself but it is not going to help me in terms of what I want to do, which is to write professionally. I know you've been pressing me to stay at the OU but I'd rather use the time to study the different writing styles of various authors (and that means reading and reading) and to practise my own writing (which means writing and writing). Even these letters to you help me a lot because I try to express myself coherently. Or hadn't you noticed!

Saturday 30 May

Thank you for sending me Jimmy Quigley's 'In Memoriam' card. Jimmy looks very like his brother Frank, don't you think? For years I had it in my mind that Jimmy was seventeen when he died, not eighteen, and in fact that's what I used to put in his anniversary insertions in *An Phoblacht*. That photo in the card must be from Frank's wedding in 1971. Today, you were bemoaning the passing without trace of the last twenty years. Time isn't important. What is important is the quality (and I don't mean material quality) and depth of your life – what you have brought to it. Whether you saw through the trumpery and voiced the truth. In his way that's what Jimmy did, and it is a trick I suppose of my existence that I think of him as growing old with me. Often, a genuine moment from the past will sweep through my mind with the authenticity of re-experience, closing that twenty-year gap and making life eternal. It allows for continuity. Don't worry about time. Make plans. Build. Have ideas. Water hope. From that draw satisfaction.

Have you seen Theresa Burt recently? I presume we will be relying on Theresa to do my parcels while you are in Toronto. However, I can go without. We always seem to spend about two months discussing your going away and then you're back before we know it!

Monday 1 June
I was asking you in yesterday's letter how you store my letters. I keep yours in the first large brown envelope of the month that you send me. As I receive a letter I mark on the envelope the day and date of receipt and as the column lengthens it advertises your dedication as well as the march of time. The envelope juts out from my book shelf. Bik once spotted it and couldn't believe how often we write!

I wonder what Laurence McKeown and Deirdre McManus will do with their lives now that his life in jail is over shortly. He's one lucky man, having survived over seventy days on hunger strike. Will they marry, do you think? Brendan Lillis, another lifer who is on his way out, gave me a jumper, three bars of soap and a tape of Marvin Gaye's greatest hits. I'm now into my ninth month here in H-4 and I wouldn't mind a shift – for new company, new stories and conversations. Roy and Hodgies are in H-7. I'd love to get a swap to H-7. It was nine months ago that we stopped writing for a time! And I loved you when you appeared on that Saturday afternoon on the second of November. It was wonderful.

Which day in the week that you go away do you want me to book the visit we spoke about? If you are returning on the seventh of August (Friday) would you be ready (diplomatic, or what?) for a visit on the eighth of August or shall we leave it until the week commencing the eleventh.

Thursday 4 June

Once again it is time for the last letter of the week. There are a few swallows in the sky. They come here from South Africa to breed and then fly the whole way back again at the end of the summer, climbing very high into the sky and able to sleep on the wing.

Got a letter from Pam Brighton. She is trying to sort out the question of the cheque. She has passed on my letter to the BBC's Head of Programmes asking for an explanation for my story being dropped. The other letter was from the Home Office in London, informing me that my exclusion order (dating from December 1982) was up for renewal on the seventh of January next and do I wish to appeal.

I was very impressed that you were familiar with the writings of Jerzy Kosinski! And there was I berating you for being a philistine! Can you get me *The Painted Bird* while you are in Toronto? And you were right about the fact that he was supposed to be in Roman Polanski's house the night that Charles Manson attacked. Kosinski was flying from Paris to Beverly Hills when his luggage was unloaded by mistake in New York. Unable to catch the connecting flight to Los Angeles, he reluctantly stayed overnight in New York.

Tuesday 9 June

Finished *A Writer's Diary* by Virginia Woolf. I picked up some tips. She was very successful and yet constantly lacking in confidence. But the thing is always to plough on. She was also a voracious reader. I then began *Immortality* by Milan Kundera, whom Joelle admires.

I got 95 out of 100 for my art essay. Still doesn't beat my 100 for Dickens's *Hard Times*. My tutor is an American, Chris Agee, who lives in Belfast and is also an accomplished poet. One of his other students is an RUC officer and he likes to compare our work! One of his criticisms is that I write 'too well' and by that he said he meant I could be 'too literary'. I know it's true but sometimes I can't help but aim at precision.

One of my mates here, Geordie Hagans from Ballymurphy, is making a drawing of your sister Wendy (as a baby, taken from one of the photos I have) and her son Peter, sitting together as babies the same age. Actually, I really wanted it for her fortieth birthday, as a small token.

Did you see *Panorama* on BBC last night? I had a big fallout with its presenter, John Ware, many years ago, but this programme was thorough. One of the most revealing points about British involvement in loyalist assassination squads was the British intelligence officer on the phone to their agent Brian Nelson confirming that the car parked outside the Gregory Hotel on the Antrim Road belonged to Sinn Fein's Alex Maskey! If a scandal of this nature were taking place in any other European country, the USA, Canada or Australia, it would be enough to topple a government. But the British are so smug because nine hundred and ninety-nine times out of a thousand they cover their tracks so well. And when they are caught out somebody simply claims that they were not familiar with the Home Office guidelines on agents! There is more to come out – and it will come out!

I hope that that deal on the house comes through very quickly. It is very exciting news and would give you a strong focus on the time until we are back together. By that I mean you could be improving the house and furnishing it and you would be so preoccupied that you would panic when you realised that I'd be out the next month and you hadn't met all your objectives! I'm sure your cat Gemma is very excited about the possibility of moving house and having a big back garden full of succulent robins and tasty sparrows! (I know such murderous talk drives you crazy!)

Thursday 18 June
Well, congratulations!

Now you have a brother-in-law! You had told me in a letter that Wendy and Terry were thinking of getting married but I thought it was to happen towards the end of the month. You said that had you been there you would have cried. I bet you have had a wee cry since!

I look at all the blank lines before me and think, what was there about my life today that I can tell her and that would be interesting? I loved you all day. I said a prayer for you at Mass. I was thinking of you tonight when I scored an ace at tennis.

I see from your letter that already you are making renovation plans to the new house and you haven't even done a deal yet! Keep shopping around because you might miss a better house that comes on the market.

Monday 22 June
Jim Gibney's speech at Bodenstown has fairly grabbed the headlines. His talk of the unionists not being able to hear the republican message above the sound of gunfire and explosions was very vivid. I am looking forward to reading it in full. However, I don't know what to make of what he is saying.

Sinn Fein complains too much about its exclusion from the so-called peace process – as if its presence would make any difference to the situation. It is in grave danger of sending a signal of weakness much greater than its true state of difficulty. I'm hoping that the interparty talks continue because the Brits will be forced to reveal that they are not 'neutral' (which is the SDLP's analysis) once they comment on the SDLP proposals and side with the unionists. However, if a British government pushes the unionists towards a settlement which nationalists generally perceive to be just or fair-minded then the Republican Movement needs to respond positively. It all really hinges on whether the British government is genuinely interested in peace and a long-term settlement.

Tuesday 23 June
That was very kind of you taking Kevin and Liam out separately for meals. Kevin certainly loves his food and Liam's tastes are simple and usually easily gratified. He used to love swimming on Sundays or going out for a hamburger on Saturdays, when I had them at my da's. Since jail my influence has been reduced to an hour a week – or a fortnight – and the worst type of visits are those when there's discord and I'm lecturing or hectoring them continually about their behaviour. Liam did poorly in his school exams. He has no interest in schoolwork, whereas Kevin always grasped concepts pretty quickly. Albert Einstein developed so slowly that his mother thought he would never learn to speak.

At school one of his teachers told him that he would never amount to much. At twenty-six he wrote the theory of relativity!

Wednesday 24 June
I received another mad letter from Hodgies. He's a scream. He is corresponding with an English girl called Kathy who wrote to him out of pity after I 'interviewed' him on my 'Desert Island Discs' for *An Phoblacht*. They write erotic letters to each other! If this isn't the craziest struggle on earth, I don't know! At the moment she is composing a poem for him. And she is shocked at the horrible conditions we live under, so God only knows what he has told her! He's in H-7, where they have washing machines!

I got my philosophy essay back. I got ninety-five, so am feeling smug. And, of course, I received your letter: it's the best, the highlight of the day. I see the flourishes of your handwriting on an envelope and I smile. Sometimes when we talk about what life would be like for you were you to return to Toronto you quote the wasteland-like lives of your friends. I often wonder whether it is really that different from here. But here we have a wonderful community. I don't experience any sense of *schadenfreude* from the poor social and love lives of your friends over there even though their dire stories provide grounds for you staying here where there will be happiness and somebody wonderful who loves you! (I always get defensive before you go away, don't I?)

I should send out a pass to Ed Moloney – though his pessimism is depressing. Fionnuala O'Connor is writing a book about Northern nationalism and wants to see me. Or maybe when you are away I should see Anne Cadwallader, my possible new neighbour! Never did hear any more about that house in her street, news of which filled three letters!

Wednesday 1 July

A little bird has just flown onto the very narrow ledge of my window, balanced delicately for a few seconds, stared at me cheekily and then flown off! It's well past its bedtime. But these nights they sing until late. Birds remind me of gardens and that takes me to the subject of the new house in Norfolk Gardens. I thought I detected in your weekend letter that you felt under pressure about buying it, and I see from today's letter that you are due to get the builder's report soon. Don't feel under pressure and don't take on a debt you are not comfortable with. You don't have to buy! You don't have to move! (You don't have to stay! Regardless of how I may get on at times I'll support you in whatever decision you take and you know that.)

Tuesday 7 July

What a hectic day at court. I'm absolutely exhausted. It took Kelly two and three-quarter hours to read out the judgement – which was, as expected, a full endorsement of Hutton's ruling. Afterwards, a barrister said to me that it pushed back the boundaries even further with regard to an appeal court smoothing out the legal errors committed by a trial judge. Going to and coming from the court the horsebox drove across country via the back of the mountain and Ligoneil. It was nice seeing fields of green grass and full-leaved trees. I even caught a glimpse of Lough Neagh floating in a haze on the horizon.

Thursday 9 July

My last few words to you before you go on your holiday! I just want to say that I love you and shall miss you. Find enclosed a sonnet by Shakespeare:

Sonnet 30

When to the sessions of sweet silent thought
I summon up remembrance of things past,
I sigh the lack of many a thing I sought,
And with old woes new wail my dear times waste:
Then can I drown an eye, unus'd to flow,
For precious friends hid in death's dateless night,
And weep afresh love's long since cancelled woe,
And moan the expense of many a vanished sight:
Then can I grieve at grievances foregone,
And heavily from woe to woe tell o'er
The sad account of fore-bemoaned moan,
Which I new pay as if not paid before.
But if the while I think on thee, dear friend,
All losses are restored and sorrows end.

Friday 24 July
To Tim O'Grady
Dear Tim

Got your letter back in March okay but don't worry about the delays in replying. My own relationship with time is continually being put into context. A friend of mine, thirty-six-year-old Micky Hillen from Newry, was sentenced today to twenty-one years, two-thirds of which he has to serve. However, he doesn't begin serving that sentence until the year 2001! That's because he was out 'on licence' when he was arrested: that is, he had been arrested in 1976, was sentenced to twenty-four years, of which he served twelve (got half-remission), and has got to serve the other twelve before his recent sentence begins! He was married only about six months before he was arrested this time around.

Leslie is in Toronto visiting her parents but is due back in two weeks' time. She is keeping well, is working away and has bought – or at least signed the papers for – a new house off the Glen Road.

You say you missed my story on the twelfth of March on the radio. You weren't the only one. Would you believe it, a fucking love story which doesn't mention Ireland or politics is banned! I haven't publicised the fact and Pam Brighton at the BBC is fairly embarrassed at the whole affair. I have asked for a formal explanation but nothing has been forthcoming and my solicitor is badgering them to pay me the fee.

I stopped writing for *AP/RN* and am presently up to my eyes in an OU arts course. It's just about okay but it's not really what I want to do. It finishes in mid-October and I hope then to get back to the blank page! I wonder did you get away to the USA to do that radio programme on young American writers? If it's in the pipeline don't forget to let me know when it will be broadcast.

I love listening to classical music and I love songs by Schubert and Mahler, such as 'Die Winterreise' and 'Kindertotenlieder', which are based on works by the German poets Wilhelm Muller and Friedrich Ruckert. So, wanting to learn more about these Germans and their works, I asked the prison library, which has access to the main branch, to order me a book. When it arrived I held it like a baby and locked myself in my cell. The entire book was in German! You should have heard me scream to be let out!

Monday 3 August
Hello, honey, and welcome back

I'm not exactly sure when you will be reading this because, although you said in your first letter that you would be phoning the airline to see if you could stay another week, I've heard no more on the subject. That was in a letter I received exactly a week ago and was followed by another the following day, last Tuesday. I am assuming you will be back on Friday and I'll drop Kevin a line so that the fire is lit and there's milk in the fridge.

I don't think I have any bright or good news to enthuse you upon your return except my love for you – which will have little impact if you are in the mood you were in when you were writing from Toronto!

I keep looking through the property market in the *Andersonstown News* and there is no doubt that you have got a bargain in that house in Norfolk. The irony, of course, is that had you been outbid you would still be fuming and felt cheated but now that it is within your grasp the enthusiasm has gone out of you!

The drizzle is sticking to my window like zapped midges. It is not as stormy now as it was just after teatime, when nobody was out in the yard and we were all cursing and were given an early reminder of the six months, beginning in October, when the yards are shut from four and most people become intensely bored. At least I have my books and music. I've almost finished the first of two volumes of the autobiography of the German poet Goethe, *Dichtung und Wahrheit (Poetry and Truth)*. Schubert set several of his poems to music. 'What youth desires', wrote Goethe, 'old age brings it in abundance'.

I met Kevin McMahon the other day when both of us were returning from our visits. He was dressed in the height of fashion and had a huge grin on his face and smelt of deodorant *and* perfume! Well, it had been twenty months since he'd kissed a woman, apart from his sister and mother! Another prisoner's cousin from Armagh was the lucky woman.

Well, honey, let's hope there's some post tomorrow so that I have some idea of what is happening. But I'm keeping my fingers crossed that you are well and can settle back into a routine. Have a good night's sleep and I'll see you on Saturday afternoon with Kleenex and smelling salts on standby. Loves you.

Friday 14 August
To Danny
Sweetheart – what can I say except I love you and I'm very, very sorry. I was in no state to see you last week, and I've been putting off writing you because I just don't know what to say! I regret leaving it to Kevin to tell you of my decision. It was a cowardly and selfish way to handle this. The decision itself was not taken lightly and stems from all the many things we've discussed over the past year. There's not much to add. The house has been sold – subject to a contract – and should be finalised within three months. That's the time scale. I will ask Joelle to store all your things and other household goods. I love you very much – I miss you – I'm worried about you and think of you always. Obviously it would be a mistake to deal with this face to face. Remember the trauma of last year? It is better this way – I hope you'll see that in time – for both of us. As difficult as this is, I know in my heart it's the right decision. When the anger and the pain fade away I hope you will think of me with tenderness. Again, for what it's worth, I love you!
    – L. xxxxx

Saturday 15 August
Dear Leslie
    I deeply regret your decision to end our relationship. I was also hurt by the way you did it given that I had said that I would always support and help you in any difficult decision you made concerning us. However, it is all water under the bridge now. There is no ill feeling, only sadness.
    Last Saturday, at your behest, Kevin brought up a number

of matters, although he had spoken of you leaving within a month and your letter said it might not be for three months. But I want to deal with everything now so that I can begin settling myself. There's no need for any loose ends. Regarding leaving me certain contents of the house, I am quite easy on the subject. It might not be convenient for friends to store (or use) furniture for three years but if some can then that will be fine. Otherwise, simply do what you find is the easiest, whether selling it separately or with the house or giving it away. Regarding my clothes: give them to Springfield Charitable Association, apart from my overcoat, my good tweed jacket, the brown chinos and the cardigan Judette Burt knitted. Kevin can take these clothes over to my da's, along with my books, tapes and personal papers.

Regarding my letters: you should destroy them but please make sure you do it thoroughly! (Don't trust anyone else with this task.) Let the order for the *Independent* lapse, and I'll make my own arrangements concerning my parcel from next week. I shall return to you your photographs, which Kevin can collect next Saturday. I think photographs are different from letters: they are neutral and are part of your history, especially the ones of you as a baby and with family and friends.

Finally, in saying goodbye, I want to thank you for all the true love and tenderness and joy you brought me. I know you squeezed yourself to your very core for me. Thank you again. From the bottom of my heart I wish you a future of love, peace, contentment and great happiness.

Love, Danny.

Thursday 3 September
To Danny
Honey, I deeply regret not going up to see you to talk this out. You know what I'm like though when I get back here – I'm a

total lunatic and not capable of rational thought. I know you would have understood my decision and helped and supported me. I didn't go because of me. I can't control my tears and I just couldn't handle it. How ironic that is, because I know now how badly I've mishandled things. I love you very much. I just want to spend more time with my family. They can look after me for a while till your first parole. Then I can get a new job, a new house and we can start a new life together. That's the plan: not an end but a new beginning. I can't imagine life without you, but if I stay here the situation will weigh me down and I feel I may as well take advantage of this time and get a break. When you were out I couldn't wait to get back here – to you. It will be like that again. By the way, I'm only taking my clothes and the cat. The rest will stay here to be reclaimed. I would like a visit before I go but of course that's up to you.

    L.xxxxxxxxxxxxxx.

Saturday 5 September
Leslie, I got your letter today and I just don't know what you are playing at. Your first letter was not written when you were a 'total lunatic' suffering jet lag but when you were back a week. You often used to complain that I was behaving like a prisoner, yet you certainly made me feel like one who had no say in anything, not even the option of understanding the immediate cause of your decision or of helping you. Now you are saying the real 'plan' is that you are only going home until my first parole. Leslie, don't be coming back for me because I will have moved on. I love you like no one else but it's got to the stage where your statements only tantalise me and cause me anguish. For months I have tried to talk to you about all the issues which you claimed in your first letter we had discussed. You talk about starting a new life together, but what about the next time I

possibly go into jail? Life together for people in love includes the bad times as well as the good times. I know how important your family is to you but I am just full of resentment. The reason you didn't come up on a visit was because you feared that your intention to go home would have collapsed, so you flew in the face of your love for me and took irreversible decisions (house, job) to prop up your intention. This damaged my trust. I hated you, I felt sorry for you and I loved you. It's not true that I've got over it but I will. A visit would be a disaster. You'd say that you were full of regrets at leaving (and you'd mean it) and would threaten to come back to Belfast almost right away. Then you'd be away. And when away this is how it will go: planned (for all I know) or unplanned, you will see someone, possibly fall in love, and get pregnant and find it very difficult to return. Despite all my progressiveness I wouldn't, in the meantime, be able to sleep at night with suspicion and jealousy, with reading between the lines of your letters and with eventually being proved right. It sounds funny (me being the one in jail) but I am not prepared to wait for you, to wait for the time when the letters with the Toronto postmark become a trickle or I become an embarrassment to you. You took a rational decision – I don't know exactly when, but it wasn't on the spur of the moment – to return to Toronto and seek a different type of life (though now you claim something else). I support that decision because although I am disappointed with you and will miss you, it is probably the true you and you'll fit like a jigsaw into Toronto and its culture once you overcome the doubts and second thoughts you are presently experiencing.

 – Danny

EPILOGUE

Wednesday 26 May 1993
To Tim O'Grady
Dear Tim

   Thank you for your letter and the book, which arrived safely a few weeks ago. I began it just last night and was fascinated by the introduction: 'How "Bigger" was born.'

   About my own book: I had written about 30,000 words when, about two weeks ago, I decided upon a pruning exercise and already I've ditched about 8,000 words, panicked, lost faith, found confidence and crashed again; I am now once again picking up the pieces. I would like to have the first draft completed by Christmas. My release date is the twenty-ninth of May 1995 but I am entitled to my first parole in twelve months' time exactly, although I will probably wait until the West Belfast Festival in August 1994 and then take four days. Hopefully, my book will be out at that stage and on the back of its 'prestige' I'll have a concupiscent 'four days and nights' (Leslie having gone back to Canada for good)!

   You mentioned that you were reading up on physics for a story that you have in mind. It's just a pity that you were not more specific. I might have been able to help or point you in the right direction as I enjoy the subject and have read quite a few books on physics and quantum mechanics, etc. (Fuck, I sound insufferable, but I assure you I am only trying to help!)

   Remember I was telling you about being initially turned down by the education officer here on the grounds that I had 'no proven aptitude for studying'? Well, I passed the exam with a distinction. Okay, that's enough of vanity (and how paradoxical that it consolidates as well as corrupts one's character!). Right, I'll go now and get back into Richard Wright's *Native Son*. Have your next pint on me!

P.S. My girlfriend has left me. My wife remarries in two weeks' time. My son tells me I'm to be a granda in August. I've a fucking cyst on my left ball. And when I get out I'll be assassinated. But life is great!

Monday 13 December
To Tim O'Grady
Dear Tim

I hope this finds you well. There's a bloody storm blowing outside as I write. It was so cold last night that I even had to wear pyjamas! About a month ago the administration gave out duvets and withdrew the blankets. ('I did four years on the duvet' wouldn't get you as many free pints as having been a 'blanket man'!) I found the duvet too warm and kept my blankets, but I've no regrets. I don't mind that early-morning shiver when your blood runs thin: it helps you remember your dreams.

I've just finished reading *G* by John Berger. Not an easy read. Next question: what was it about?! I enjoyed his style of writing but not the story. I also recently read *The Hive* by Camilo Jose Cela: a short book but with more characters than *War and Peace* and *Anna Karenina* put together! Furthermore, the story just stops! Totally inconclusive.

How's work with you? Made your first million yet?! I was wondering what I was going to get the kids for Christmas given that I was completely skint, when out of the sky fell a cheque from my publisher! Since we last wrote my son Kevin's girlfriend, Donna, gave birth to a girl. So I now have a grandchild called Paula! They've brought her up about three times since September. She's very cute. Can't wait until she's a toddler. But if she shouts 'granda' after me in the street I'll ignore her! She can call me daddy or Danny!

Well, I finished the book I was telling you about. It's called *On the Back of the Swallow*. After all the cutting and editing it was pruned to 82,000 words. I am quite pleased with it. It was with the censors for a few days and was collected on Saturday. So I'll have an opinion and decision from Mercier some time in the New Year. It is about friendship and the miraculous power of love – and the hero is gay! It is set in an unnamed city (with the geography of Belfast) and the assumption is that the Troubles were settled back in the sixties, forties or twenties – whenever. So, there's no armed conflict, no sectarianism. It's about the individual and society. I hope it is published by the time of my first parole next August. Not that I'll be sober enough to talk about it. I'll be busy rediscovering Bacardi and women!

That's about it for now, Tim. *Native Son* is still doing the rounds here but I shall look after it for you.

Wednesday 10 May 1994

Hi Danny

Hope you're well. I know you said you never wanted to hear from me again but I've wanted to write for a very long time and thought I'd take a chance. I can't believe it's almost two years since we last saw each other, but I've thought of you every day and there have been many days when I've felt as if my heart was just going to stop from the tension. I'm sure you would say it was all self-imposed, and of course you'd be right, and a small note is totally inadequate in which to explain myself fully. I know I've hurt you dreadfully, but I did what I felt I had to do for my own sake. I felt time – my life – slipping by and felt as if I was missing out on too much. I thought that being home with my family would make me happy, but it didn't. I thought another relationship would make me happy, but it didn't. What was at the source of my unhappiness was missing you and loving you. I realise that now. Unfortunately for both of us – but especially you – it was something I had to find out this way. I don't know how else I could have handled events. To be honest I was never able to handle you being in jail but I suppose that's obvious, isn't it? Anyway, as I said, there's a lot to say and not enough space to say it so I would appreciate a visit sometime before July. I know I risk certain humiliation by asking. What a cheek!

Penelope xxxxxxxxxx